THE ATHENIAN REVOLUTION

ESSAYS ON ANCIENT GREEK DEMOCRACY AND POLITICAL THEORY

JOSIAH OBER

Where did "democracy" come from, and what was its original form and meaning? Here Josiah Ober shows that this "power of the people" crystallized in a revolutionary uprising by the ordinary citizens of Athens in 508–507 B.C. He then examines the consequences of the development of direct democracy for upper- and lower-class citizens, for dissident Athenian intellectuals, and for those who were denied citizenship under the new regime (women, slaves, resident foreigners), as well as for the general development of Greek history.

When the citizens suddenly took power into their own hands, they changed the cultural and social landscape of Greece, thereby helping to inaugurate the Classical Era. Democracy led to fundamental adjustments in the basic structures of Athenian society, altered the forms and direction of political thinking, and sparked a series of dramatic reorientations in international relations. It quickly made Athens into the most powerful Greek city-state, but it also fatally undermined the traditional Greek rules of warfare. It stimulated the development of the Western tradition of political theorizing and encouraged a new conception of justice that has striking parallels to contemporary theories of rights. But Athenians never embraced the notions of inherency and inalienability that have placed the

The Athenian Revolution

The Athenian Revolution

ESSAYS ON ANCIENT GREEK
DEMOCRACY AND POLITICAL THEORY

Josiah Ober

PRINCETON UNIVERSITY PRESS

PRINCETON, NEW JERSEY

Library of Congress Cataloging-in-Publication Data

Ober, Josiah.
The Athenian revolution : essays on ancient Greek democracy and political theory /
Josiah Ober.
p.   cm.
Includes bibliographical references and index.
ISBN 0-691-01095-1 (cl : alk. paper)
1. Democracy—Greece—Athens—History. I. Title.
JC75.D36024   1996
321.8′0938′5—dc20   96-19341

This book has been composed in Baskerville

Princeton University Press books are printed on acid-free paper
and meet the guidelines for permanence and durability of the
Committee on Production Guidelines for Book Longevity of the
Council on Library Resources

Printed in the United States of America by Princeton Academic Press

1   3   5   7   9   10   8   6   4   2

For Thomas Kelly and Chester G. Starr,
who taught me Greek history
And in memory of Colin Edmonson and Eugene Vanderpool,
who led me to see Athens

———————————

CONTENTS

ACKNOWLEDGMENTS

THESE ESSAYS were written between 1983 and 1993; during that time I taught at and received research support from three universities: Montana State, Michigan (as a visitor in 1986–87), and Princeton. I also held fellowships at the National Humanities Center, the Center for Hellenic Studies, and the University of New England (Armidale), and grants from the American Council of Learned Societies and the National Endowment for the Humanities. In addition to my academic duties, I served as co-director of the "Democracy 2500 Project" of the American School of Classical Studies at Athens. Each of these institutions has helped to make possible the essays presented here. I had the opportunity to try out preliminary versions of these essays on a number of individuals and at lectures and seminars in a variety of settings. One of my students, Ryan Balot, provided editorial assistance and made substantive improvements in several key arguments. I owe special thanks to Victor Hanson, Charles Hedrick, Brook Manville, Ian Morris, and Barry Strauss—colleagues and friends who have helped to shape my views of classical Athens and with whom I have shared many happy hours in conversation (about Greek history and democracy, among other things) over the years. The four men to whom this volume is dedicated were my teachers and mentors. My best reader and critic is, as ever, Adrienne Mayor.

I am grateful to the following for permission to reprint essays: *Ancient History Bulletin* (Chapter 2), *PS: Political Science and Politics* (September 1993) (Chapter 3), Cambridge University Press, reprinted with the permission of Cambridge University Press (Chapter 4), Yale University Press (Chapter 5), University Press of America (Chapter 6), Routledge (Chapter 7), *Classical Philology* © 1989 by The University of Chicago. All rights reserved (Chapter 8), *Echos du monde classique / Classical Views* (Chapter 9), Cornell University Press, reprinted from *Athenian Political Thought and the Reconstitution of American Democracy*, ed. J. Peter Euben, John R. Wallach, and Josiah Ober, pp. 149–71. Copyright © 1994 by Cornell University. Used by the permission of the publisher, Cornell University Press (Chapter 10), and the Royal Danish Academy of Sciences and Letters (Chapter 11).

The Athenian Revolution

Chapter 1

INTRODUCTION: ATHENIAN DEMOCRACY AND THE HISTORY OF IDEOLOGIES

IT SEEMS only fair to state at the outset that this book, like most of the academic work I have undertaken in the last decade, has its part in a triple agenda: It is intended first to define an approach to understanding the past that might be called a "history of ideologies." It is next meant to help establish the study of classical Greek democracy (and the ideological apparatus that sustained it) as a significant and active subfield within both Greek history and political theory. Finally, it is written in the hope of making ancient historians and political theorists more aware of one another's work.[1] With regard to the third of these ambitions, I believe that the study of classical democracy could serve as a bridge between two disciplines that have much to gain by closer interaction. The potential payoff is considerable: Historical studies grounded in contextual specificity can gain purchase in contemporary debates when informed by the concerns of normative theory. And theory will be both tempered and strengthened by a confrontation with the pragmatic consequences of political thought and practice in a society that developed norms strikingly similar to those of modern liberalism, but predicated those familiar norms on radically unfamiliar grounds. Likewise, in terms of my own intellectual history, these essays stand between the fields of practice and theory. Some (Chapters 3, 4, and 7) are intended to develop and clarify concepts introduced in my 1989 study of democratic practices, *Mass and Elite in Democratic Athens*. Others respond to alternative scholarly treatments of classical democracy (Chapters 8 and 9). Two assess the relationship between democracy and foreign policy (Chapters 5 and 6). Several chapters look forward to and lay some of the groundwork for a book in progress on the origins of critical political theory (Chapters 2, 10, and 11).[2]

These essays on ancient Greek political ideology and democratic theory, written (with the exception of Chapter 6) in the late 1980s and early 1990s, originally appeared in a miscellany of collections and journals aimed at equally diverse audiences (classical historians, political scientists, specialists in interna-

---

[1] Cf. Ober and Hedrick 1993 and 1996.

[2] Extended critical treatments of Ober 1989b include D. Cohen 1991; Morris 1993; Shaw 1991; Yunis 1991; Hansen 1990a; Patterson 1992. I delivered a preliminary version of the book in progress as the Martin Classical Lectures at Oberlin College in February 1994; Ober 1993 and 1994 represent some of the first fruits of the project.

tional relations and military policy). Yet they are all informed by a consistent
and simple idea: Something historically and politically remarkable took place
in the *polis* of Athens between 508 and 322 B.C.[3] This era, which can reasonably be called the "classical period" of Athenian social and political history,
begins with the popular uprising that I argue (Chapter 4) should be regarded
as the inaugural moment of the "Athenian Revolution." It ends with the suppression of popular government by the militarily superior Macedonians. The
sociopolitical phenomenon with which this book is primarily concerned is
dēmokratia—a term coined in late sixth- or fifth-century Athens to denote the
rule of the *dēmos*, the mass of ordinary adult male natives. Athenian democracy
is remarkable because it was the real thing—in classical Athens the demos was
the true political authority. Though political leadership was a key element in
the workings of Athenian government (Chapters 4, 6, and 7), there was no
behind-the-scenes oligarchy of bureaucrats, dealmakers, landlords, warlords,
or aristocrats.[4] The Athenian Revolution in its wider sense (regarded as an era
rather than as a moment) featured a radical and decisive shift in the structures
of political authority and of social relations, and (a matter of special concern to
me) in the concepts and vocabulary with which people thought and talked
about social and political relations. The key element in this revolutionary
change in patterns of thought, speech, and action was a matter of political
sociology: the replacement of a relatively small ruling elite as the motor that
drove history by a relatively broad citizenship of ordinary (non-elite) men. The
consequences of accepting this basic premise are profound in terms of ancient
Greek history and modern political theory. I have argued for the premise in
detail elsewhere.[5] These essays explore some of its consequences.

If democracy is real, then Athenian political history is, imprimis, the story of
(1) the origins and development of a coherent ideology and an articulated
institutional structure that facilitated the process of decision-making by the
demos, especially (although not uniquely) in the Assembly and in the people's
courts, (2) the decisions actually made by the demos, and (3) the results of those
decisions in terms of policy, ideology, and social structure. The essays collected
here consider the role of demotic authority in each of these three historical
aspects of *dēmokratia*, along with a fourth issue: the relationship between democratic political practice and the development of a self-consciously critical literary tradition of abstract theorizing about politics and society. Athenian political theory was written by educated elites for consumption by elite audiences of
readers or listeners. But again, my contention is that the primary impetus for
the phenomenon in question comes "from below," from the demos. Athenian

---

[3] I acknowledge that this claim leaves me open to charges of "Athenocentrism"—see Morris
1993 and the introduction to Chapter 4.

[4] This claim is, of course, controversial: see the introduction to Chapter 3.

[5] Ober 1989b.

political theory is, in my reading, an imaginative and creative (if not always particularly fair, accurate, or attractive) response by Athenian intellectuals to the perceived problems and contradictions that arose as a result of the rule of the people.

The phenomenon of democracy that was "true"—in the sense of being a relatively stable and long-lasting system of government "by the people" that operated without an overt or cryptic ruling elite—is noteworthy given its historical rarity, at least among so-called complex societies. Even in the classical period there were probably never a great many democracies in existence.[6] Through most of Western history, democracy in the sense that I am using the term was either unconceived (i.e., not part of the existing conceptual universe) or merely a memory. But Greek democracy is not only interesting as a historical rarity. The inherent interest of a well-documented example of a real democracy is especially great in the twentieth century, because very influential thinkers, notably Robert Michels and other "elitist" theorists, have denied that a true democracy could exist.[7] Though Michels and the other theorists of elitism are perhaps not much read today, at least by classicists and ancient historians, their ideas have become generalized both in the scholarly culture of classical history and in Western political culture. If we are today, in the late twentieth century, all democrats in principle, most of us nonetheless seem to regard the authority of an entrenched elite as inevitable. The debates among historians and among citizens are, in my experience, not so much about whether a ruling elite exists now or existed in past cultures. Rather, they are about, first, the identity of an aprioristically postulated ruling elite and, next, the question of whether the rule of a given elite is a good or a bad thing. Twentieth-century conceptions of ruling elites are both plentiful and colorful: the socialist vanguard, the military-industrial complex, the Trilateral Commission, the shadow government, the information elite, the best and the brightest—the list could be extended indefinitely. What seems to have been lost in these debates is the notion that a social and economic elite could effectively be controlled by the political authority of the citizenry at large. "We the People" have lost faith in our own powers.[8]

The conceptual situation in which we find ourselves, with true democracy regarded not only as rare but as impossible, would, I believe, be difficult for a classical Athenian to comprehend. A consistent theme in this book is that the Athenians themselves, both ordinary and elite, assumed the reality of democ-

---

[6] Relatively little is known of democracies outside Athens, and none seems to have been as durable or as fully developed: Sinclair 1988, 218–19.

[7] See Michels [1915] 1962 with the comments of Finley 1985b, 3–37; Ober 1989b, 15–17.

[8] This sense of loss provides a primary impetus to various and more or less influential attempts to rethink the role of democracy in modern political and social life, e.g., Bowles and Gintis 1986; Putnam 1993; Bell 1993; Lasch 1995.

racy in their own time. This does not mean that they supposed that democracy was their inevitable lot—both nervous Athenian democrats and disgruntled Athenian aristocrats could and did imagine an Athenian government dominated by the elite (Chapters 7 and 10). But they supposed that in order for an elite to rule, the current ideological and institutional regime (*politeia*) of the Athenians would have to be destroyed—the standard locution for the destruction of democracy was "to overthrow the people" (*kataluein ton dēmon*). Moreover, asserting that Athenians believed in the reality of their democracy is not a matter of a subtle reading of sources "against the grain": the actuality of democracy is frequently and unambiguously asserted in our ancient sources both by those writers who celebrate it and by those who disparage it.[9] Thus the conservative interpretive approach of supposing that our primary sources have something to do with the realities experienced by their authors can lead to a radical conclusion that is potentially disturbing to complacent modern interpreters. This, it seems to me, is all to the good.

My attempt to pay close and critical attention to the sources is the product of my training as an undergraduate under the direction of Thomas Kelly and as a graduate student under Chester G. Starr, and I suppose that whatever merit these essays may possess derives in large part from that ingrained habit of attention. I have, however, tried to avoid allowing my respect for the sources to lead to the formation of banal assumptions about the correspondence between literature and historical reality. Much of the polemical energy of this volume is directed against a naive version of historical positivism whose advocates suppose that it is possible to discover the "objective truth" about the ancient past by "letting the sources speak for themselves." I am at pains to demonstrate why the naive positivist's approach to history is intellectually indefensible and positively dangerous to the historian's enterprise of attempting a fuller and more accurate understanding of the past.

Writing a history of Athenian political ideologies entails an effort to unpack the ideological positions and the associated (though nonidentical) social realities that underpin the rhetorical statements and claims of complex texts. Those texts were typically written to persuade sophisticated audiences (jurors, Assemblymen, elite readers) to think and to act in ways that might not seem, prima facie, to be intuitively obvious or even in their own interests (e.g., to vote for a litigant whose factual case was weak). But it is, I believe, possible to become over-subtle in the process of "unpacking"—to the point at which the source-suitcase is forced to divulge an item that was never packed into it but that the modern interpreter "knew" all along must be in there—such as a

---

[9] Two well-known passages prove the general rule: Thucydides 2.65.9 (in the time of Pericles, Athens was in name a democracy but in fact the rule of one man) and Plato *Menexenus* 238c–d (Socrates' comment, in the mock Funeral Oration he claims to have heard from Aspasia, that Athens' government is called a democracy but is actually an aristocracy in that the best rule with the approval of the many).

ruling elite and its dominant ideology. Most of these chapters deal explicitly with methodological issues of historical interpretion (especially Chapters 2 and 3), but I know of no sure way of navigating between the Scylla of an interpretive naivete that takes the source too much on its own terms and the Charybdis of an overly subtle approach that permits the source to say anything its reader wishes and thereby forbids it to reveal anything that the reader did not know beforehand. Despite our best efforts at methodological explanation, interpretive navigation remains more of an art than a science. I am convinced that the answers to the historical and theoretical questions that haunt me can only be discovered by repeatedly attempting this narrow and difficult passage between free-floating relativism and obdurate positivism. But I leave it to readers and critics to decide whether or not my interpretive ship has made it through intact.

The primary sources are quite plentiful for certain periods of classical Athenian history, most especially for the fourth century B.C. (i.e., the period between the end of the Peloponnesian and Lamian wars: 404–322 B.C.), and sources can, at times, serve as checks on one another. Fourth-century sources include a very rich epigraphic tradition that has recently been analyzed in terms of ideological authority by David Whitehead.[10] My focus in this collection (as elsewhere) is primarily on literary sources: rhetoric (preserved orations delivered in the Athenian Assembly and people's courts) on the one hand, works of historiography and political philosophy on the other. A secondary theme of these essays is that the fourth century is a vital and exciting period in Athenian history, one in which the democracy was at once vibrant and stable. This point of view is increasingly widely accepted among professional Greek historians, but the image of the era after the Peloponnesian War as one of decay, decline, and fall is still pervasive outside the classical profession.[11] This misconception is particularly troublesome when it is propounded by political theorists, and especially by those who are sincerely interested in the example of Athenian democracy and who are otherwise sophisticated in their treatment of classical texts. Part of the burden of this volume is the recuperation of fourth-century Athens as a source of nonphilosophical material useful for political theorizing (especially Chapter 3).

Each of these essays represents an attempt to connect historical reality with ideology, practice with theory. In brief, I suppose that in classical Athens, ideology (a term whose definition I will discuss in the following chapters) is not

[10] Whitehead 1993.

[11] For the emerging scholarly consensus that the fourth century (especially in Athens and in terms of democratic politics) was actually a vibrant era, see Hansen 1991; the essays collected in Eder 1995; and Mossé (1995, 228–30), who was formerly much more inclined to speak in terms of decline. And yet, outside the company of Greek historians, the concept of the golden "Age of Pericles" seems virtually unchallenged: witness the popularity of university courses in classical Greek civilization that focus more or less exclusively on the fifth century.

merely a mask for an underlying reality (e.g., "market-based relationships," "the mode of production," or "people's genuine needs and interests") but rather is among those elements that constitute historical reality: People act in certain ways because they take certain postulates to be true, because they believe things. The connection between ideology and reality is manifested and carried forward by discourse (things people say) and by practice (things people do). Thus we have in play the three apparently discrete categories of believing, saying, and doing. But in writing a history of ideologies, these categories cannot remain fully distinct from one another. A central tenet of these essays is that discourse is an aspect of social practice and, as such, not only reflects beliefs, but brings into being social and political realities. Thus, in the terminology developed by Michel Foucault, power in society is not simply repressive or juridical, it is discursive and productive of the "truths" by which people organize the categories of analysis and the hierarchies of value that constitute the ordinarily unquestioned (and almost unquestionable) order of things. Or, to put it another way (following the fundamental work of J. L. Austin), it is possible to "do things with words" because speech is not merely descriptive but also performative, and because, in the appropriate rule-structured social setting, words will not only refer to a prior reality, they will change that reality. This being the case, it is the historian's job to understand the rules and associated social structures that permit certain forms of speech, by certain speakers and in certain circumstances, to "do things" that similar forms of speech, by different speakers or in other circumstances, cannot do; to trace how the rules change over time and according to what logic and impetus; and to explain the effects of "speech acts"—successful or (in Austin's terms) "felicitous" speech performances—on the society in question (or subgroup within a society) and on its relationships with other societies and subgroups.[12]

The relationship between ideology, discourse, and practice—and how this is mediated within works of literature—remains a hot topic among historians, literary critics, anthropologists, and other scholars. Studying that relationship can yield a variety of interpretive stances. Some of these approaches, as I suggested above when discussing sources, seem to me to be useless or worse (at least from the point of view of the historian or political theorist) because they fall into one of two camps. On the one hand, an interpreter may pretend to have achieved an impossible level of objectivity, a historical "view from nowhere." This stance allows the writer to attack all historiography that proceeds forthrightly from a theoretical standpoint while simultaneously obscuring (often by reference to a "common sense" that is in fact common only to a small population of like-minded interpreters) the author's actual premises and viewpoint. On the other hand, some examples of reader-response criticism seem to demonstrate only the obvious: that the modern interpreter could conjure out

---

[12] On speech-act theory I have found especially useful Austin 1975; Petrey 1988 and 1990.

of a given text that which he/she knew that he/she must find before he/she started reading (e.g., the ontological instability associated with the act of writing that proves that meaning is ultimately indecipherable, which in turn yields the "fact" that the same elites are always/already calling the same shots according to the same rules of power). Both approaches are at once ahistorical and antitheoretical in that they end in evacuating the truly unsettling and educational experience of confronting a way of thinking/speaking/doing that is *not* just like every other.[13]

The error of extreme forms of these two interpretive poles (at least for the historian of ideologies) lies in their shared obsession with ontology, with fundamental, foundational, decontextualized truth claims. The first, positivist, approach supposes that historical truth is unitary, stable, and fully accessible to the objective investigator: once it has been found, the job of interpretation ends. The assumption of the second, reader-response, approach seems to be that it is worthwhile to demonstrate, over and over again, that each truth claim made in a given text is compromised by its situation in a preexisting ideological universe that is informed by the play of power. This endlessly repeated demonstration is, however, only interesting or challenging from the perspective of an interpretive strategy that takes the independent status of foundational truth claims as essential to thought, scholarship, morality, or whatever. From the position of the philosophical (or, with Cornel West, the antiphilosophical) pragmatism associated with John Dewey, the attempt to demonstrate the ontological impossibility of stable, decontextualized truth claims is just as meaningless as the attempt to establish the secure ontological status of such claims: both parties to the debate—the defenders and deconstructors of decontextualized truth—are doing nothing more interesting or useful than quibbling over demographic problems involving angels and pinpoints.[14]

The sort of antifoundationalist intellectual pragmatism I am advocating here (and attempt to put into practice in the following chapters) is concerned with the construction of social and political reality. And thus we come back to speech acts and the movement from belief to discourse to practice as a historical problem, as a problem of context rather than of the ontological status of language or truth. The distribution of social and political power has much to do with how the rules that permit new social facts to be proclaimed are formulated, with who is allowed to be a player in the game, and with who benefits and in what sense (materially or psychologically) from playing the game. This is not, in the 1990s, unfamiliar terrain. The greater part of the groundwork for

---

[13] I do not mean to castigate all, or even most, history or theory written in either a positivist or a reader-response mode—I have learned a great deal from practitioners of both approaches. My argument, rather, is with the extreme and polemical versions of each: with the positivist who is adamantly opposed to the use of theory and the theorist who denies the existence of brute facts.

[14] On philosophical pragmatism, I have found particularly useful Rorty 1982; Barber 1984 and 1988; West 1989; Westbrook 1991; and Gunn 1992.

undertaking the history of ideologies that I am advocating here has been done by Michel Foucault's studies of discourse and social power and by Quentin Skinner's contextualized analyses of the performative dimension of intellectual history.[15] What may be regarded as unusual is the attempt to harness Foucault's and Skinner's insights into a unified approach to the past and its meanings.

My approach does not suggest that it is possible (for the historian or for the subject of his/her investigation) to think, speak, or act in a way that is completely free from influence, including the influence of social/political power—nor, for that matter, that it would necessarily be desirable to do so. Yet I do not take power to be an abstract or reified force that homogenizes all thought, speech, and action.[16] Rather, I suppose that much of the classical literature that I find interesting is informed by the self-conscious struggle of writers who were highly conscious of both intellectual traditions (e.g., Homer) and political power (e.g., democracy) to identify or to construct a space outside the traditional and existing structures and rules of power and discourse. It may be that the struggle is never entirely successful. But the fact that a text demonstrably fails to achieve a hypothetical goal of pure freedom from power and tradition hardly exhausts its interest. Rather, the historian of ideologies will hope to analyze how specific texts simultaneously accept, manipulate, and resist the rules. Societies have power-generated rules as forests have trees, and perfect freedom from power is as elusive as the unicorn. Studying the existing and evolving ecosystem of a forest seems to me very interesting. Demonstrating that this forest, like every other, is in fact characterized by the presence of trees but devoid of unicorns—and necessarily so given the ontological status of "forest" and "unicorn"—seems to me a waste of time.[17]

I like to imagine that the last several paragraphs, suitably translated, would make sense to a classical Athenian. A pragmatic, discursive, speech-act-oriented analysis seems to me inherently useful for studying Athenian politics and society, not only because of its general heuristic force, but because classical Athenian politics operated quite overtly according to pragmatic, discursive, speech-act principles. By making proclamations in the Assembly and in the

---

[15] See Skinner et al. 1988.

[16] I have found especially useful Foucault 1979, 1980a, 1980b; cf. also the work of his critics, e.g., Taylor (1986), Hoy (1988), and Wolin (1988).

[17] This analogy does not lead me to claim that unicorn-hunting is a waste of time for those who sincerely suppose that the beast might exist. But that project requires a degree of optimism and idealism that seems quite absent from the sort of writing to which I am drawing attention here. It is only fair to point out that my work has benefited enormously from various strands of critical theory and postmodern criticism (e.g., Fish 1980; Derrida 1988). The problem is, I think, that the postmodern epigonoi have often tended to repeat ad nauseam thought experiments satisfactorily demonstrated by earlier scholars and/or to apply the analytical results of those studies to increasingly banal objects. This can be very self-indulgent and devalues the genuinely hard work and erudition of some of the pioneers of critical theory and cultural studies.

lawcourts, the Athenian demos self-consciously established and reiterated social and political realities, and it did so without much worrying about the
ontological status of the realities so created. This reading of Athenian political
life takes two distinct, if closely related, directions in this collection. First, the
historical consequences of a politics that is strongly democratic and nonfoun-
dationalist are quite striking: the Athenians, for example, developed the pragmatic analogues of modern rights (i.e., guarantees of liberty, political equality,
and personal security) without elaborating or relying upon a theory of rights
predicated on doctrines of fundamental inherency or inalienability (Chapter
7). The existence of these "quasi-rights" and their distribution within the population of those territories controlled by Athens are important factors in weighing Athens against other societies (actual and hypothetical) on scales calibrated
according to various theories of justice (Chapter 11). On the other hand, the
powerfully pragmatic and relatively free-wheeling process of social construction employed by the Athenians led to the making of policies that contributed
in a significant way to the breakdown of various Panhellenic codes of international behavior—notably to the collapse of established rules of war. Those
old inter-polis rules of military decorum tended to privilege certain classes
(especially the heavy-armed warriors) within Greek society, but they also limited the carnage of battle (Chapters 5 and 6). Democracy is thus implicated in
the processes often called "the crisis of the polis"—not because democratic
values fell into decline, but because democratic practice was so performatively
efficacious.[18]

The second consequence of the forthrightness of Athenian pragmatic con-
structionism was, I would argue, the development (if not the origin) of the
Greek (and eventually of the Western) tradition of political theory and its problematically close association with metaphysics, ontology, and epistemology
(Chapter 10). Various elite writers of the late fifth and fourth centuries expended considerable effort in exposing what they now discovered to be a
shocking lack of secure foundations for Athens' speech-act-based democratic
politics. They wrote texts explaining the social and psychological consequences
of Athenian-style political pragmatism and suggesting theoretical alternatives
to it. In Athens, then, democratic practice is proleptic to political theorizing.
And so on my reading, democracy stands in an oddly isomorphic relationship
to the man who claimed to be Athens' most loyal citizen and was the most
notorious victim of its decision-making apparatus. Like Socrates himself, democratic ideology demanded that citizens conform to a stern ethical code of
behavior predicated on duty to self and community. Like Socrates, the democracy did not claim to know any final answers to moral or epistemological
questions. Yet, like Socrates, the democracy developed some impressively

---

[18] For discussions of the concept of the fourth-century "crisis"—i.e., whether the fourth century saw the decline or fulfillment of the Greek polis—see Eder 1995.

powerful provisional arguments, and those arguments served as a gadfly to the often complacent modes of thought prevalent among certain Athenians, notably among elite intellectuals. Taking the analogy a final step further, the dialogue between democratic practice and elite critical discourse can be imagined as the Socratic maieusis that resulted in the birth of the texts that inaugurate the Western tradition of political philosophy.[19]

Each of the following chapters is introduced by a brief note discussing the essay's origins, ambitions, and situation relative to ongoing debates in classical history and theory. These introductory notes also summarize for each chapter what I regard as its most important arguments and explain the relationship of its arguments to those of the other chapters and to the general goals of the book. The introductory notes should not be necessary to understanding any given essay. But for those readers interested in the broader themes sketched above, the notes may serve as a guide to what the author supposes he was driving at when he wrote this series of meditations on various aspects of democratic Athenian ideology, politics, and society. They also list works of special relevance for each essay that have come to my attention since the essay was written, along with particularly significant critical assessments. With the exception of Chapter 3, the essays have not been heavily revised since their original publication, except in matters of style. Abbreviations follow those found in the *Oxford Classical Dictionary*, second edition.

---

[19] I say this without necessarily accepting Socratic or Platonic theories of the origins of knowledge. And I recognize that Socrates' positions on knowledge, Athens, the state as an abstraction, and his own role are all hotly contested by philosophers.

Chapter 2

MODELS AND PARADIGMS IN ANCIENT HISTORY

In 1988 Charles W. Hedrick, Jr. and I organized a panel on new approaches to Greek political history for a meeting of the American Philological Association. We planned to address the use of theories derived from the social sciences, theory of language, and literary criticism in ancient history. The relevance of employing models and paradigms for writing ancient history had by then become a subject of heated debate among classical historians. Some historians of classical antiquity were then (and remain) adamantly opposed to the self-conscious employment of theories derived from social science or literary criticism to reconstruct the ancient past. This recalcitrance—predicated on allegiance to historical positivism, the "disinterested" search for the objective truth about the past, and the virtue of "common sense"—seems to me at best ill informed and unnecessary, at worst obstructionist and dangerous to the long-term prospects of the enterprise of writing ancient history—or at least to the prospects of writing history that will be read by anyone outside a small (and probably dwindling) group of specialists (see Chapter 1). On the other hand, some of the claims made by advocates of a theory-based history seem to me extravagant, self-indulgent, and sadly ignorant of the long history of the debate among historians over historical objectivity and the role of theoretical constructs in historiography (see Novick 1988).

The panel generated considerable formal and informal discussion, some of it heated, much of it enlightening. This essay, adapted (in light of that discussion) from my panel paper, attempts to demonstrate that the employment by historians of theory in its broadest sense is both inevitable and desirable, that theory cannot be separated from ideologies (ancient and modern), and that self-consciousness about the process will result in history superior to that produced by attempts to cling to fantasies of achieving the view-from-nowhere ideal of perfect objectivity. The central arguments concern the definitions of "usefulness" and "meaningfulness" as they relate to historical context and judgment. These concepts become important points of reference for several subsequent chapters.

JUST AS one cannot create a geometry without preliminary postulates, so it is impossible to write history without employing a priori assumptions and analogies. Thinking about history, like all other cognitive processes, requires one to

This essay was first published in *Ancient History Bulletin* 3 (1989), 134–37.

move from the simpler to the more complex, from the better known to the less well known. Consequently, all historians use models, whether or not they are conscious of the process. Those historians who are willing to state the premises of the models they employ expose the theoretical basis of their work to testing by critics. This, it seems to me, is a good thing.

A historical model is derived from the experience and thought of an individual or a group, and no model is value-free. The use of the model entails importing into the past aspects of ideology that are not native to that past. Ideology, according to my definition, includes assumptions about human nature and behavior, opinions on morality and ethics, general political principles, and attitudes toward social relations.[1] Thus, in my formulation, the use of models is an inevitable part of the historiographic process, and models invariably involve the importation of ideology. Furthermore, model choice and design is influenced by ideology. Since it is impossible for the employer of any given set of models to understand all of the ideological aspects of the models he uses, true objectivity is impossible. But this conclusion should not be a cause for despair. Self-awareness about the influence of ideology will help historians to understand the main constraints any given model entails. And, as Chester Starr has pointed out, it is the job of critics to point out ideological factors the author himself has missed.[2]

There are, of course, a great many models for the historian to choose from, varying in their origins and the truth claims made on their behalf. Some models claim universal and exclusive validity: traditional Marxist materialism, for example, claims to have discovered the universal engine for social change in the evolution of the relationship of classes to the mode of production; all phenomena not covered by this model are regarded by traditional Marxists as "epiphenomena" or "superstructure," and so as unworthy of serious attention. Other models are derived from the analysis of specific historical circumstances and applied to less well-known historical circumstances. These "circumstantial" models are not typically based on universalist truth claims and do not assume explanatory exclusivity. Instead, they are defended on the basis of suitability. The question one asks of such a model is not "Will this model explain all history?" but "Will it help to explain specific aspects of a society in which I am interested?"

Granted the inability of the historian to achieve an objective, ideology-free, "external" standpoint, should all models and the historiographic products derived from them necessarily be regarded as possessing equal analytic / explanatory value? The intuitive answer is, of course, "No." And I think that this

---

[1] For a fuller definition, see Ober 1989b, 38–40. That book is intended as an example of the approach to models and paradigms I advocate here.

[2] Starr 1983, 32.

intuitive conclusion can be defended, if we replace the goal of "objective truth" with a goal of "meaningfulness and usefulness."

The reality of the historical past can never be reproduced—and therefore can never be completely comprehended. But the past can be *represented* in meaningful and useful ways. By this I mean that no historiographic product can recreate the past in all its richness and complexity, but the historian can hope to model the past in ways that are both reasonable and testable. Consider the analogy of cartography. No map can reproduce the reality of even a small geographic region at any given point in time. No scale model could do justice to all of the complexities of the topography, geology, biology, population distribution, and so on of (say) modern Attica. And yet it is possible to produce maps of Attica that are both meaningful and useful. For example, a road map of Attica that would enable a motorist to drive from Sounion to Marathon without getting lost represents meaningful aspects of Attica in a useful manner. Furthermore, our hypothetical motorist can test the map against her own perceptions. If, as she drives along, she perceives many crossroads and interchanges not depicted on the road map, she will judge the map inaccurate and so useless. On the other hand, she may also perceive buildings, trees, and geological formations not depicted on the road map. But this does not cause her to say that the map is useless, since her primary concern is getting from Sounion to Marathon and the road map claims only to be a road map, not a universal map of all perceptible features. If she is interested in these other aspects of Attica she may turn to other maps that do not show roads at all, but represent geological features, topography, and so on in meaningful ways. Each map will be judged by its users on the basis of its clarity and accuracy in representing what it claims to represent.

A historical model or historiographic product should represent some aspect of the past in a way that is meaningful and useful. By useful, I mean that the model—like a map—should help the user/reader to get from one point to another: diachronically, from one point in past time to another, or synchronically, from one set of phenomena to a contemporary set of phenomena. The reader/user of a model (and here I include historiographic products that themselves "model" or represent aspects of the past) will judge the model by criteria similar to those used by our hypothetical motorist. The reader will ask whether the model accounts for all of the perceptible phenomena—that is, the evidence known to the reader—that the model should account for, given the scope of its claims. If the reader knows of a significant body of relevant evidence that the model does not account for, he will likely judge it useless. This is, I think, the process that has led many historians to reject the claims of universalist/exclusivist models. On the other hand, the reader may find that the model has introduced features that demonstrably did not exist in the past. An example would be A. W. Gomme's demonstration that it is invalid to employ a modern naval operations model to ancient naval warfare, because ancient warships could not stay at sea for longer than a couple of days.[3] The "usefulness" criterion therefore allows for the testing of models, and consequently for deciding that model A is better than model B.

A model or historiographic product is (in my formulation) "meaningful" to the extent that it has heuristic value: that is to say, to the extent that it helps people to act in "the real world" and to assess for themselves the significance and implications of their own and others' actions, by viewing those actions against a broader context. The study of the ancient past is not a closed, self-referential system. Interpretations of the past inevitably find their way into extradisciplinary contexts, and can affect decision making and action by nonhistorians in significant ways—as, for example, the recent "historians' debate" in Germany (on the subject of the Holocaust and its historical uniqueness) makes clear. Most historians, I think, intuitively grasp the heuristic function of interpreting the past and recognize that human actions have moral valence; and this intuitive understanding renders it unlikely that historians will treat all models as if they are of equal value.

For the past to be made accessible as a heuristic device, it must be ordered: each individual must, at a given time, "anoint" certain models by granting them explanatory primacy. Professional historians normally take (or at least attempt to take) control of the ordering/anointing process because (inter alia) they themselves are called upon to explain the past in ways that will seem meaningful to nonprofessionals (e.g., in undergraduate lectures), and they recognize their social obligation to provide a reasoned assessment; because they feel that they have a proprietary disciplinary interest in controlling interpretations of the past; and because they have a rational desire, based at least in part on self-interest, in seeing that interpretations of the past used by (for example) politicians are based on the highest possible standards of honesty and rigor.

An integrated set of explanatory models can be described as a paradigm; a set of anointed models that remains in general use over a long period of time, as a dominant paradigm. The paradigm concept was developed by Thomas Kuhn in his analysis of the sociology of scientific knowledge.[4] Kuhn argued that the history of modern science could be explained by the consequent establishment, challenging, and overthrow of a sequence of paradigms. According to Kuhn, scientists in any given field tend to adhere to a single paradigm until a critical mass of data not explained by the paradigm is amassed. The old paradigm is then discarded and a new one adopted that covers the known data. A dominant historical paradigm, then, will be the primary explanatory tool that most historians of a certain time will be likely to use in analyzing aspect x of past society y.

---

[3] Gomme 1933, 16–24.
[4] Kuhn 1970.

Historical paradigm formulation, by its nature, inevitably entails emphasizing the importance of certain categories of past social activity and cultural products, while obscuring others. The ordering process presumes that the activities and products highlighted by the paradigm are "central" to a heuristically meaningful understanding of the society in question. Categories of activity and cultural products relegated to the sidelines by the dominant paradigm may not disappear from view, but are necessarily made to appear relatively insignificant. This can obviously be problematic, as, for example, in the case of long-dominant paradigms that obscured both the contributions and the oppression of women in Greek and Roman societies. But the inevitable tendency of paradigms to emphasize and to obscure is not an argument against paradigms, but rather an argument for an ongoing process of paradigm reformulation.

The development and deployment of historical paradigms is, I believe, necessary and inevitable given the sociology of historical knowledge. Unlike scientists, however, ancient historians do not have the benefit of a constant accumulation of significant new data by which our paradigms can be tested and challenged. The danger therefore exists that our paradigms will become ossified and their ideological postulates will be hidden through constant usage. We may tend to forget that the paradigms we use rest on ideologically based models, and so we may start regarding our paradigmatic products as "objective truth." Meanwhile, because of developments in other academic disciplines and changes in the value system of the society at large, the ideology that underlies our paradigms may become increasingly foreign to those outside the field. As a result of this process, the heuristic value of "professional" readings of the ancient past for explaining the present is diminished, and our work loses (contemporary) meaning. In the end, ancient historiography may be reduced to intra-disciplinary debates over questions that are of primary significance within our paradigm, but meaningless to anyone outside the field. Meanwhile, given the intrinsic heuristic value of the idea of the ancient past, the function of interpreting it for a wider audience will be taken over by persons who may not have an adequate knowledge of or respect for the evidence. Therefore, I would suggest that not only must ancient historians be willing to test their own and their colleagues' models against the available evidence, but they also must think long and hard about the ideological presuppositions entailed in their dominant paradigms. If we do not challenge ourselves, we will simply become irrelevant. And that, it seems to me, would be a bad thing.

Chapter 3

PUBLIC SPEECH AND THE POWER OF THE PEOPLE
IN DEMOCRATIC ATHENS

As an indirect consequence of our collaboration on the panel that produced the previous essay, Charles Hedrick and I became co-directors of a series of public programs intended to commemorate the 2500th anniversary of Athenian democracy. The series included a conference, "Democracy Ancient and Modern," sponsored by the National Endowment for the Humanities and held in Washington, D.C., in April 1993. The conference featured papers and commentary by classical historians and political theorists (see Ober and Hedrick 1996). In the aftermath of the conference, Bernard Grofman proposed publishing a group of papers inspired by the conference proceedings as a forum in *PS: Political Science and Politics*. In the essay that I contributed to that forum, which has been substantially reworked and expanded here, I took the opportunity to develop points that arose in the course of several conference discussions, most notably in a long conversation with Sheldon Wolin on the subject of democracy, power, rhetoric, and the problem of stable government versus revolutionary energies.

The essay attempts several things: to provide a brief sketch of how the institutional structure of Athenian democracy worked in practice, to outline some of the main arguments originally developed in *Mass and Elite in Democratic Athens*, to defend fourth-century Athenian political culture against the charge of stagnation, and to underline why I suppose the historical Athenian experience with democracy holds significance for students of political theory. This chapter sums up succinctly (and, occasionally, polemically) some of the convictions that have driven my work on Athens in the course of the last decade and that are elaborated and defended in the subsequent chapters: Athenian democracy is no mere façade for elite rule but the real thing (i.e., the rule of the demos); public speech is intimately and inseparably related to political power; criticism of democracy and democratic practice are interdependent. This essay, like much of my work, focuses on ideology, communication, and public practices, but it also demonstrates the fundamental importance of constitutional and institutional studies (cf. Chapter 8).

Among my more polemical claims is that ancient historians have gone astray in predicating their understanding of the wellsprings of power in Athens on a model of politics borrowed from Sir Ronald Syme's influential 1939 study of the collapse of the Roman republican government, *The Roman Revolution*. I attempt to show that the conceptual underpinnings of the neo-Symians rest not on simple "common sense," but on a theory of politics closely akin to (and perhaps borrowed from) Robert Michels' prob-

This essay was first published in *PS: Political Science and Politics* (September 1993), 481–85.

lematic and (in my opinion) unproven "Iron Law of Oligarchy." If the "Iron Law" is not a simple *brute fact* of human nature, but rather a contingent *social fact* pertaining in some societies (e.g., Rome) but not in others (e.g., Athens), then the question of whether real democracy could have pertained at Athens must be discussed on its own merits. This means (per Chapter 2) that the hypothesis that political power at Athens might have belonged to the people must be tested against the relevant ancient evidence, rather than simply dismissed as a conceptual impossibility. Much of the evidence for testing this hypothesis is in the form of the speeches written by fourth-century public orators, and so the study of rhetoric becomes an essential prerequisite to understanding Athenian democracy.

I cannot claim to have persuaded all ancient historians that my position on demotic rule at Athens is correct, but much of the new work now being undertaken does seem to recognize that "the rule of the demos" is a problem that must be addressed seriously. The question of whether the mass audience or the elite speaker/writer actually controlled the formal and informal communications that characterized Athenian public life is currently the subject of serious debates; see, for example, Shaw 1991; Morris 1993; Kallet-Marx 1994; Hunter 1994; D. Cohen 1995; and Yunis 1996.

IN THIS ESSAY I will try to defend three premises that are important for my own work on Athenian democracy and that seem to me to be important for all students of democratic theory. First, if we take democracy to mean what ancient Greeks took it to mean—"political power wielded actively and collectively by the demos" (i.e., all residents of the state who are culturally defined as potential citizens, regardless of their class or status)—then Athens was a true democracy. Second, the democracy of Athens, like all democracies, was threatened (actually and potentially) by the attempts of powerful elites to dominate the political realm. Yet exercise of collective power by the Athenian demos prevented elite political domination—and was intended to do so. Thus, in classical Athens, the "power of the people" was not a cover for elite rule. This successful defense of democracy against the forces of elitism was predicated on the domination by the mass of citizens of the conceptual apparatus essential to decision making—that is, by "the ideological hegemony" of the demos. Third, the democratic political order developed at Athens was at once revolutionary in its energies, dynamic in its practices, and remarkably stable. Therefore, even granted that Athens excluded from regular political participation entire categories of persons that Greeks did not regard as potential citizens (slaves, women, most foreigners, children), the historical example of the Athenian experience with democracy should be taken seriously by democratic theorists interested in expanding their grasp of "the bounds of the possible" (as well as of "the thinkable").

Accepting these three premises does not entail the assumption that Athenian democracy was morally unproblematic. Nor does it mean that the Athenian people's power was in some ontological sense "pure," or "undistorted"—indeed, it was arguably through the tightly coiled and convoluted "distortions" of social and political power that the Athenian democratic order succeeded in counterbalancing elite social power. Athens, with its acceptance of slavery, exclusion of women and foreigners from political participation, and jingoistic "blood and soil" doctrine, can hardly be considered a ready-made model for a just modern political society. It can be argued (incorrectly, I believe) that the practice of democracy in Athens was fundamentally dependent upon slavery, or empire, or the exclusion of women and foreigners.[1] More work is needed on the relationship between the egalitarian, democratic political society of the citizens and the larger, hierarchical "whole society" of polis residents (see Chapter 11). But whether Athens was, overall, a just society or even an attractive society is not what I am arguing here. Rather, the question is whether classical Athens provides a genuine historical example of direct and relatively stable mass (versus elite) political power, and, if so, whether that example should be taken seriously by contemporary thinkers interested in democracy.

In writing what would become a foundation-text for historians and political theorists alike, Thucydides the Athenian (as he pointedly describes himself: 1.1.1) had as his central concern the relationship between public speech (*logos*), brute facts (*erga*), and power (*kratos, dunamis*). Thucydides was particularly concerned with how this triad operated within and was affected by the democratic society of Athens.[2] Although Thucydides put his own very original spin on the problem of speech, action, and power, his interest in the speech/fact/power triad was far from idiosyncratic: his younger contemporary, Plato, examined similar issues (notably in *Apology, Crito, Gorgias,* and *Republic*), as did Plato's student Aristotle (in *Politics, Rhetoric,* and *Constitution of Athens*—leaving aside the issue of the authorship of the last). Each of these writers lived most of his adult life in Athens; each was, from his own distinct perspective, profoundly critical of the relationship between speech, fact, and power in the Athenian democracy.[3] The substance of that criticism is interesting to any student of Athenian democracy, but for my present purposes the key point is that each of these thoughtful contemporary witnesses assumed that democracy—the political power (*kratos*) of the mass of ordinary citizens (demos)—was real and that the people of Athens maintained their rule through control of public speech.

If we move from late classical Athens to the late twentieth century of our era, we discover an odd reversal. The classical theorists supposed that the democracy they experienced in Athens was real, but undesirable; many mod-

---

[1] See Ober 1989b, 20–35.

[2] Ober 1993, 1994.

[3] Or, in Aristotle's case, in "extreme" democracies of the Athenian sort: Strauss 1991.

ern democratic theorists assume that a strong, vibrant, participatory, directly democratic political culture is desirable in principle, but that no such culture has ever existed for long—and certainly not in the Athens of Thucydides, Plato, and Aristotle. This reversal is ironic given the foundational status that the three great theorists of classical Athens enjoy in the modern politics curriculum. They are taken very seriously as abstract thinkers, but a central premise from which their abstractions proceeded—that democracy, as "the power of the people," really existed—is ignored. The followers of Leo Strauss are a possible exception to the general rule of dismissing the reality of classical democracy; yet Straussians seem to feel that the empowerment of ordinary people was as disastrous then as it is undesirable today.

Why are liberal theorists of democracy unwilling to countenance the possibility that the ordinary citizens really did rule in Athens? One possible reason is that when theorists turn to the scholarly work of classical historians, they discover that the *communis opinio* (at least until quite recently) has been that Athens was not genuinely democratic: classical historians have commonly claimed that the real political business of Athens was done behind the scenes, by a few wealthy aristocrats who formed themselves into parties, factions, *hetaireiai*, etc. And thus, since the name "democracy" concealed a crypto-oligarchy, the serious student of Athenian political life must learn to ignore the façade of popular rule and focus on relationships (political alliances, marriage connections, extended family ties, inherited clan enmity, etc.) between the power-brokers. Many Greek historians, especially those writing since the Second World War, have tended to be (for the most part unwittingly) staunch adherents of Robert Michels' "Iron Law of Oligarchy."[4]

Though it would be reductive to claim that this allegiance among classical historians to Michels' dictum has a single source, the work of Ronald Syme, especially his vastly influential *The Roman Revolution* (first published in 1939), must bear much of the credit (or blame). Whether or not he himself actually had read Michels (or other early-twentieth-century elitist theorists), Syme was convinced that "in all ages, whatever the form and name of government, be it monarchy, republic, or democracy, an oligarchy lurks behind the façade; and Roman history, Republican or Imperial, is the history of the governing class."[5] Since Syme felt called upon to spell out this conviction, he presumably recognized it as something not universally agreed upon and thus potentially disputable—in short, as a theory (although one he regarded as well established) rather than an unquestionable brute fact of nature. Syme's many students (direct and indirect), however, have tended to take his theory about politics as a given, a commonsense fact of human nature that need be neither

---

[4] "Iron Law": Michels [1915] 1962. For the focus on intra-elite activities by Greek historians, see, for example, Fornara and Samons 1991.

[5] Syme 1939, 7.

asserted nor defended. Thus the "Iron Law of Oligarchy" has come to be the unspoken, unacknowledged, even unrecognized theoretical underpinning for a great deal of historical scholarship that is thought and proclaimed by its authors to be staunchly "antitheoretical."[6]

The political theorist who delves into the specialist literature on Athenian politics is unlikely to know the history of the establishment of Michels' theory into the foundational assumptions used by ancient historians (indeed, this is a history that is still to be written). Thus, when informed by well-regarded specialists that Athens was a crypto-oligarchy, the theorist may be willing to take this conclusion as an objective historical fact. And so, convinced by a specialist literature, founded (as I suppose) on a theory derived from a study of modern political parties, that politics in the ancient world works pretty much like politics in the modern world, the theorist's suspicion that true democracy is impossible is confirmed. The circularity of the argument gets lost in the deference paid by the explorer across disciplinary borders to the body of established opinion he or she feels (rightly or wrongly) inadequately prepared to challenge. And because of this circular argument, the disruptive potential of classical democracy to challenge the assumptions of modern democratic theory is lost. That potential might, however, be recuperated if classical historians were able to show that the "neo-Symian" view of Athenian politics is in error and that Athens was considerably more democratic than a strict interpretation of the "Iron Law of Oligarchy" would allow.

If contemporary access to classical Athenian democracy were exclusively through the literary output of intellectual critics, we might suppose that the assumption by Thucydides et al. that democracy was real was simply a theoretical premise, a straw man that allowed the development of interesting arguments about hypothetical alternatives to politics-as-usual. But in fact there is a very substantial body of primary evidence that supports the view that the ordinary citizens ruled in classical Athens: around 150 speeches, mostly composed by skilled orators for delivery in Athenian lawcourts and the citizen Assembly.[7] This body of material is extraordinarily important for students of Athenian politics because it gives relatively direct access to the language used by elite speakers in Athenian courts and Assemblies. According to the ancient critics, the Athenian demos ruled through its control of public speech. Because we have a large sample of the sorts of speeches made in public forums, it is possible to analyze the ideological underpinnings of the language used by elites when communicating with mass audiences. We can therefore attempt to assess the balance of power implied by the content of that communication and decide whether the oratorical corpus confirms or contradicts the ancient conviction that, in Athens, the people ruled.

---

[6] See, for example, Fornara and Samons 1991, Introduction.

[7] Number of speeches: Ober 1989b: 341–49.

It may be helpful at this point to sketch out the conditions under which the speeches in question were delivered. By the later fourth century, the citizen Assembly (*ekklēsia*) met forty times each year. Meetings, which were usually announced several days in advance, ordinarily lasted about half a day, and were open to all citizens (adult, free, native-born males: a body of perhaps 30,000 persons). Some 6,000–8,000 men typically attended; those who arrived early enough were paid (about an average day's wage) by the state. The agenda of each meeting was established in advance by a council (*boulē*) of 500 citizens selected by lot for an annual term of service; the council also made recommendations on some agenda items. There is no reason to suppose that any class of Athenian citizens was systematically underrepresented at the Assembly, and—given the voluntary nature of attendance—there was no way for a speaker to know in advance the social configuration of any given Assembly. Though it represented only a fraction (perhaps a fifth or a fourth) of the citizen body, each Assembly was taken by the Athenians as synecdochy for the whole of the citizenry. The meeting was called to order by a lotteried "president-for-a-day," who announced (through a herald) the first item on the agenda. After reading the council's recommendation (if any), the president asked, "Who of the Athenians has advice to give?" At this point any citizen in attendance could get up to speak to the issue—advocating a negative vote, revisions to the council's proposal, or a completely new proposal—for as long as his fellow citizens were willing to listen to him. When the Assemblymen tired of listening to a speaker, they would shout him down. After everyone willing to undergo this gauntlet had had his say, the president conducted a vote, usually by show of hands. A simple majority determined the issue, and the president turned to the next item. In this manner, the Athenians conducted all important business, including foreign policy and taxation. The language of many preserved decrees demonstrates that the debate in the Assembly had substantial effect; frequently the actual decree had been proposed at the Assembly by a voluntary speaker.[8]

The people's courts (*dikastēria*) met most days of the year. Most cases, both private suits (*dikai*) and public suits (*graphai, eisangeliai,* etc.), were brought by a private citizen (*ho boulomenos*), on his own initiative, against another citizen. The prosecutor brought his charges before a lotteried magistrate, who then assigned the case to a court (in some instances after mandatory arbitration—every citizen who reached age sixty was required to serve for a year as public arbitrator). The litigants faced a jury of (usually) 200 or 500 citizens over age thirty, who had been assigned to the court through a random drawing and who were paid for their service. There was no presiding judge—or rather, each of the several hundred citizens on the jury was a judge (*dikastēs*). With the exception of the exclusion of citizens under age thirty from the lawcourts, there was little differ-

---

[8] Hansen 1987; with Chapter 8.

ence between the sociological profile of a typical Assembly and that of a typical jury. The prosecutor and the defendant were each given a fixed period (measured by water clock) to present his case (extra time was allowed for the reading of laws, witnesses, etc.). Within his allotted time, each speaker could say pretty much what he wished, and he often digressed to attack the character and past life of his opponent and to defend his own reputation. The Athenian standard of relevance seems very broad by American standards, but it was not infinitely flexible; as in the case of the Assembly, a litigant who irritated his listeners could expect to be shouted down by them.[9] Moreover, many Athenian laws were remarkably vague (e.g., the law that forbade the commission of *hubris* but failed to define it), leaving the judges with considerable leeway in determining whether a wrong had been inflicted. Immediately after the two speeches, the *dikastai* voted, without formal consultation, by secret ballot. A simple majority determined innocence or guilt. In some instances the punishment of a guilty man was mandated by law; in other cases the jury voted again on rival punishments advocated in a second set of speeches by the prosecutor and defendant. The whole affair was done in a day.[10]

In both the Assembly and court the public speaker faced a mass audience of "judges" ready and willing to shout him down if they did not like what they heard. Both the Assemblyman who hoped to get his decree passed and the litigant who hoped to win his case were constrained to construct their speeches very carefully, since a single rhetorical misstep could be fatal to their causes. The public speaker in Athens was often (although certainly not invariably) a member of a relatively small elite by virtue of his wealth and education. Although in principle any Athenian could address the Assembly, in practice much of the debate was carried out by a cadre of skilled "politicians" who were well known to their audiences and were referred to variously as rhetors, demagogues, or the "accustomed speakers." These same men took up a good deal of court time by prosecuting one another for misdeeds ranging from dirty talk in the presence of female relatives, to *hubris*, to sacrilege, to financial misconduct, to high treason. The classical Athenian democracy thus featured a politically active and litigious elite.[11] Was this a dominating elite?

The answer, I think, is no. But, granted the presence in Athens of a group of elite men who were highly active in politics, and granted the tendency of elites to try to dominate the political regime, it well worth asking why the Athenian elite failed to become a dominating elite and under what conditions their political activity *could* be said to constitute dominance.

Classical Athens was a large (by polis standards: total population of around 150,000–250,000) and complex (not "face-to-face") society that confronted

9 Bers 1985.
10 Hansen 1991, 178–224.
11 Ober 1989b, 104–27.

serious external threats. The Athenian democracy could not have functioned effectively without intelligent, thoughtful, and articulate persons who had the leisure to devote themselves to the complexities of foreign policy and finance. That indispensable elite of competence might accurately be defined as a politically dominant elite within a nominal democracy *if* the men in question furthered their own interests by cooperating among themselves to manipulate public institutions. Manipulation might take various forms: (1) Elites might dominate the Assembly and/or courts numerically; (2) elites might manipulate ostensibly open voting by exerting patronal authority over the votes of dependent citizen-clients; (3) elites might control the political agenda and so prevent certain issues from being debated; (4) the mass-dominated institutions of the Assembly and courts might be covers for a decision-making bureaucracy dominated by the elite; or (5) elite discourse and values might define the ideological underpinnings of "democratic" culture itself and thus exercise a hegemonic prior restraint upon the evolution of a genuinely democratic politics.

Most of these possibilities can be readily discounted. (1) Recent research has refuted the notion that the Assembly and courts were dominated by the upper social strata of Athens.[12] Numerical elite domination is inherently unlikely, given the relatively huge numbers involved, and ordinary citizens were encouraged to take part by the practice of pay-for-participation. (2) Though clientage is widely recognized as a vital component of Roman political life, recent research has pointed out the absence of a matrix of similar structures (institutional or social) in classical Athens.[13] (3) The agenda for the Assembly was set by the Council of 500, whose (paid) members were chosen by lot and who were forbidden to serve more than two annual terms. The council's large and rotating membership created an environment inhospitable to the development of an institutional identity conducive to domination by an elite. An attempt to show that the council was the "senior partner" in the government has not gained many adherents among historians.[14] Furthermore, although the "accustomed speakers" were no doubt frequently heard in the Assembly, there is considerable evidence for more casual and occasional participation by a much wider group of speakers.[15] (4) Although annually elected (rather than lotteried) generals (in the fifth century) and elected financial magistrates (in the fourth century) were indeed important players in the government, they had limited decision-making power. Magistrates were forced to undergo rigorous public scrutiny before entering office and a public audit upon leaving office. Magistrates suspected of conspiring against the people could always be (and frequently were) indicted and punished in the people's courts. There is no evi-

---

[12] Markle 1985; Todd 1990.
[13] Millett 1989.
[14] Senior-partner thesis: de Laix 1973.
[15] Hansen 1991, 145–46.

dence to suggest that boards of magistrates ever constituted anything like a hidden government. Until the Macedonian overthrow of the democracy in 322 B.C., the most important political work of the polis was done in the open, in the Assembly and the courts.[16]

It is issue (5)—the presumed ideological hegemony of the elite—that particularly concerns me here, especially because it has been asserted recently by classical scholars whose work is theoretically well informed and is not particularly influenced by Syme.[17] With ideological hegemony, we move from the "gravitational field" of Robert Michels to that of Antonio Gramsci and Louis Althusser, revisionist Marxists who each attempted to explain in cultural terms the problematically stubborn "false consciousness" and lack of revolutionary energy of exploited masses. It is this ideological argument for elite domination that the oratorical corpus is particularly useful in answering. Athenian mass audiences responded vigorously and readily to any comment with which they took issue. Their decisions (votes) had profound consequences for the speaker. Thus the themes and topoi that appear frequently in the oratorical corpus should point quite accurately to what skilled speakers took to be the operative political and social values and opinions (collectively, the "ideology") of the Athenian citizenry. For ideological analysis, the *captatio benevolentiae* is more important than the substantial case that the orator is attempting to make: the latter may contradict what the audience believes; the former must necessarily conform as closely as possible to that same set of beliefs.

My studies of rhetorical topoi (Chapter 7) suggest that, far from being subverted or preempted by elite values, the ideology of the Athenian demos was highly democratic. The Athenians had considerable faith in the potential and actual wisdom of mass audiences. Rather than deferring to elite expertise when it came time to make important decisions, the citizenry believed itself to be collectively the best possible judge of important matters. Moreover, the Athenians did not suppose that any special education was necessary for a citizen to participate fruitfully in collective decision-making since growing up in the democratic polis was itself a sufficient education. According to popular thinking, citizens were educated by the decisions of the Assembly and courts through being reminded of the ultimate source of political power in Athens and through the inherent wisdom of the particular decisions. The people were, by contrast, very suspicious of individual claims to special political knowledge or education; public speakers often attacked their opponents specifically on these grounds, characterizing themselves as ordinary citizens, their opponents as over-clever, highly trained speakers whose rhetorical facility threatened to pervert collective decision making.[18]

[16] Ober 1989b, 327–36.
[17] E.g., Loraux 1986; Wilson 1991.
[18] Ober 1989b, 156–91.

Similarly, the Athenians believed themselves to be a collective nobility. All Athenians could trace their ancestry back to the earliest "earth-born" inhabitants of Attica, and so all Athenians were "autochthonous" and shared a connection to the soil of their homeland. In Athenian ideology, autochthony ensured a firm loyalty to the good of the polis and to the political regime that sustained it. As a result, it was difficult for an individual Athenian to lay claim to special status on the basis of his "high birth." A logical corollary to the autochthony ideology was a tendency for litigants to attack the legitimacy of one another's birth—"foreign blood" was grounds for suspicion regarding one's loyalty to Athens and its democracy.[19]

Popular ideology also dealt with wealth and the power brought by its possession. Athenian society was certainly stratified along the lines of economic class. Moreover, despite the fears of certain members of Athens' wealth elite, no serious attempt was ever made to redistribute property systematically among the citizens—the power of the people was not used to equalize access to the goods that wealth could and did provide its possessors. Yet, on the other hand, democratic ideology both encouraged voluntary redistribution of wealth and limited the political effects of wealth inequality. The ordinary Athenian juror harbored a deep suspicion of the wealthy as a class; he tended to view rich men as arrogant, willful, and at least potentially hostile to the democratic political regime that prevented them from translating their economic position directly into power over others. The rich Athenian litigant, well aware that his fate hung on the opinions of resentful jurymen, was at pains to dispel their distrust by demonstrating himself to be a man of the people. Sometimes a well-to-do speaker sought the sympathy of jurors by assuming the role of a poor man, beset by richer, more powerful opponents. Other speakers pointed out that their private wealth had frequently been put to public uses, in the form of liturgies, special taxes, and voluntary contributions to the state and to impoverished neighbors. By contrast, one's opponents could be characterized as notoriously ungenerous. Historically generous litigants felt entitled to ask jurors to give them the benefit of the doubt when they contended with selfish opponents. Since every rich Athenian had a good chance of finding himself in court, this "market" relationship encouraged private generosity. Yet since the individual litigant was put in the position of the suppliant, the terms of the bargain were controlled by the ordinary citizens—it was they who decided if an elite man's past behavior and current self-representation were adequate compensation for the favor he now requested.[20]

The frequency and importance of formal mass judgment of individual speech acts also tended to inhibit the tendency of elites to act cohesively in their own class interest. The procedures of Athenian Assembly debate and

[19] Ibid., 248–92.
[20] Ibid., 192–247.

litigation placed elite speakers in contention with one another for scarce resources: in the Assembly there could be only one decree passed on a given
measure, and in court only one successful litigant. Moreover, Athenian jurors
were well aware of the dangers that could attend intra-elite cooperation and
were highly suspicious of any aspiring politician who did not engage in fierce
and public litigation with other politicians.[21] Some legal processes seem designed to encourage inter-elite competition and litigation, notably the *antidosis*
(exchange) procedure: Rich citizen A, who found himself saddled with a non-
voluntary liturgy and who thought rich man B's estate had paid less than its
share of liturgies, could formally challenge B to assume the liturgy. If B refused, A could then sue B in court for a mandatory exchange of property so
that A could pay off the liturgy from B's (former) estate. The *antidosis* procedure
encouraged rich Athenians to spy out one another's hidden financial resources
and pitted fellow members of the wealthy elite against one other in courtroom
contests for the sympathy of the masses.[22]

   The Athenian democracy channeled the activity of an aristocratic elite characterized by a highly competitive, agonal ethos into public competitions that
benefited the demos and were judged exclusively by mass audiences. Elite
attributes were not eliminated; indeed, they might be flaunted to good effect in
certain circumstances. But it was the ever-fickle "mob" (*ochlos*) of non-elite
citizens that determined whether the particular circumstances had justified a
particular elite display. The elite Athenian lived and operated under conditions of institutionalized instability. If he wanted what Greek aristocrats tended
to want—political influence, public honors, wide acclaim, and the respect of
society—he was forced to play a game with rules that shifted constantly and
subtly, a game judged by a collectivity that worked according to deep-set demotic ideals. The judges prescribed severe penalties for losers and those caught
breaking the rules: huge fines, banishment, even execution. Yet as losers were
sent off, new players were always waiting in the wings. Paradoxically, the enduring strength of the competitive aristocratic ideology among the Athenian
elite supported the democratic order by providing a constant supply of compe-
tent advisors, each dedicated to explaining to the demos, in word and deed,
the depth of his allegiance to democratic ideals and practice, and eager to
expose his fellow elites' failures of allegiance.

   The game of Athenian political life was hard and often unkind; this is one of
the reasons for the development of antidemocratic positions by Thucydides,
Plato, Aristotle, and other contemporary critics of Athenian democracy. But it
was also entirely voluntary: the elite Athenian who could not stand the game
could pay his taxes and liturgies like a good fellow and keep out of politics.
When he found himself in court, he could point to a record of financial gener-

[21] Ibid., 328.
[22] Cf. Christ 1990.

osity and expect relative leniency in return. He was free to criticize the democracy, in writing and conversation, to his heart's content, so long as he did not (as Socrates did) take his case into the public space or lead others to engage in bloody coups against the democracy.

One final issue demands our attention. Both classicists and theorists have traditionally regarded the fifth century as the really exciting period of Athenian history. The democratic period after the Peloponnesian War (403–322) has sometimes been characterized as an age of decadence and decline—or at least of bureaucratization, institutionalization, selfish individualism, civic flaccidity, and sadder-but-wiser moderation of radical political ideals.[23] And yet virtually all of the texts to which I have referred in this essay were written in the fourth century. Thucydides wrote at the very end of the fifth century and composed at least part of his history after the Peloponnesian War. Plato's and Aristotle's active careers were entirely fourth century. All but seventeen of the speeches I used in my study of Athenian rhetoric were postwar. The period after the war opened with the remarkable (and successful) democratic resistance to the Spartan-imposed regime of the Thirty Tyrants and ended with an equally brave (although ultimately unsuccessful) resistance to Macedonian imperialism. Meanwhile, the Athenian demos radically expanded the scope of payment-for-participation by extending pay to Assemblymen, and did so in the face of financial stringency. Aristotle certainly considered the democracy of his own day (*Politics* 1274a6, 10) as the full realization, the *telos*, of democracy, and regarded fourth-century Athens as an example of the most extreme form of democracy.[24]

How can we account for the "golden-age syndrome" of viewing fifth-century Athenian culture as a glorious, ephemeral moment of radicalism, followed by a rapid and catastrophic decline into dullness and mediocrity? This question is not simply answered, but I will suggest several contributing factors: (1) The period is bracketed by defeats: first in the Peloponnesian War and then at Chaeronea (338 B.C.) and in the Lamian War (322). These military failures contrast with the great Athenian victories over Sparta and its allies in 506 B.C. and over the Persians in 490 and 480–479, and with the imperial wars of the mid-fifth century. This contrast has, I think, encouraged the development of an Erroneous Implied Argument (EIA): Strong, vibrant democracies are universally successful in their foreign-policy initiatives; losing wars is a sign of civic decline. (2) The implicit position that underlies Thucydides' account of the Peloponnesian War is that Athens was likely to fail due to its dysfunctional post-Periclean democratic political culture.[25] Thucydides' reader is led to conclude that even though Thucydides' narrative account breaks off in 411 B.C.,

---

[23] E.g., Mossé 1962, 1973. But see Chapter 1, note 11.

[24] Strauss 1991, 214–17.

[25] See, further, Ober 1994.

Athens must have been utterly demolished by the defeat. EIA: History is bunk.
Thucydides, as a good theorist, was right, and the subsequent history of democracy at Athens is irrelevant. (3) Those who do bother to read fourth-
century oratory (a rather small group compared to Thucydides' readers) find
that the orator Demosthenes, especially, frequently describes his own age as
inferior to the glorious days of the democratic past. EIA: Demosthenes was
describing an objective reality. (4) In the very late fifth and early fourth century, the Athenians codified their laws and introduced a new method for law
making by large, lotteried boards of "lawmakers." Laws (*nomoi*) were now distinct from decrees (*psēphismata*) passed in the Assembly, and no decree could
overrule an existing law. EIA: The cutting edge of radical democracy gave way
to conservatism, or at least "moderation," when Athens moved from "the sovereignty of the people" to the "sovereignty of law."

Arguments 1 and 2, at least as I have characterized them, need little reply; I
trust that few historians or theorists today would be willing to argue in support
of correlating democratic culture directly with military success or would explain military failure in terms of a decayed political culture. Athens' defeat by
Macedon is historically interesting, but the explanation for that defeat must be
sought in Macedonian development and in faulty but democratic decisions
regarding Athens' defenses.[26] Thucydides' analysis of decline and fall simply
cannot account for the democratic restoration of 403 or for the strength and
stability of the democracy thereafter. Argument 3 fails to account for the enduring fascination of the golden-age syndrome in Greek culture generally: already in the *Iliad*, Nestor complains that warriors "these days" are not up to
the old standard, and Hesiod in the *Works and Days* famously describes his own
age as a degenerate "age of iron." Demosthenes' audience did not take his
comments about ancestral excellence and contemporary decline as strictly ref-
erential, but rather as a hortatory speech act: not as an unproblematic description of a widely acknowledged reality, but as a challenge to the citizens to live
up the achievements and democratic principles of previous generations. Argument 4 is more complex; it has recently been made explicitly and in great
detail.[27] Some of the problems involved in applying the terminology of sovereignty to Athenian history are discussed in Chapter 8. Suffice it to say here that
the concept of sovereignty, elaborated in the Western tradition in the context
of legitimating unitary monarchy and then the "balance of powers" doctrine,
can be highly misleading when applied to the historical experience of the democratic polis, which did not evolve from a centralized, monarchical state.

The disdain felt by some political theorists for Athens of the fourth century
seems to be the product of a deep-set distaste for political stability in any form
and an equally strong attachment to "radical democratic moments" of the sort

[26] See Ober 1985a.
[27] Ostwald 1986.

characterized by American political activism of around 1963–74.[28] I certainly do not wish to denigrate work that focuses on insights gained from fleeting revolutionary moments.[29] But I think that the enterprise of democratic theory as a whole will be weakened if we reject, a priori, the possibility that a vibrant democratic culture that originated in a revolutionary moment might subsequently exist for a relatively long period of time and serve as the underpinning for the government of a complex state. Characterizing stability negatively as an entropic decline in revolutionary energy is to ignore the possibility that democratic stability can be achieved through dynamic tensions. Indeed, in Athens, the never-resolved tensions between aristocratic values and demotic ideology, and between apparently contradictory but deeply held political values (e.g., freedom of speech and communal consensus), lay at the heart of the democratic system. The unresolved status of these tensions and contradictions sparked critical political thought and contributed to the ongoing institutional and (to a more limited degree) ideological adjustments that characterized democratic Athenian culture—and that have never ceased to dismay its conservative critics. Those dynamic tensions were negotiated and maintained through the ongoing, public activity of a citizenry willing to maintain, defend, and continually revise a living democratic culture, and willing to tolerate the "company of critics"—like Thucydides, Plato, and Aristotle—of that selfsame culture (see Chapter 10).

Fifth- and fourth-century Athens provides a particularly well-documented historical example of a dynamically stable democratic culture in which a large and socially diverse citizenry directly ruled a complex society that was much too big for a politics of "face-to-face" personal interaction. Those who would reject the reality of democracy in classical Athens need to explain a body of contemporary evidence that consistently asserts that reality. At least until a better historical example of a directly democratic complex society can be found, the Athenian example deserves to be taken very seriously by political thinkers who remain suspicious of "Iron Laws" of politics and by those interested in the possible as well as the conceivable, in history as well as in normative ideals.

[28] E.g., Wolin 1994 and 1996.
[29] See Chapter 4, and Ober 1996.

THE ATHENIAN REVOLUTION OF 508/7 B.C.: VIOLENCE, AUTHORITY, AND THE ORIGINS OF DEMOCRACY

The first draft of this essay was written for a conference on cultural poetics in archaic Greece, held at Wellesley College in October 1990; it was substantially revised in the summer of 1991, when I was Visiting Fellow at the University of New England in Armidale, New South Wales. I owe thanks for help in the process of revision to the conference's organizers (Carol Dougherty and Leslie Kurke), and to many colleagues at UNE, especially to Minor M. Markle, and to G. R. Stanton, whose erudite and insightful comments much improved a paper with whose fundamental tenets he disagreed.

Methodologically, this chapter attempts to put into practice the premises developed in Chapter 2 and thereby to advance the larger project and defend some of the main ideas sketched out in Chapter 3. By reading the scanty sources for a particular event closely and sympathetically—that is, without assuming a priori that Greek writers were misled by their ignorance of sociological "Iron Laws"—I try to break away from two increasingly ossified "Great Man" models, employed by Greek historians since the early 1960s to explain the behavior of Cleisthenes the Alcmaeonid, the figure often credited with "founding" Athenian democracy in 510–506 B.C. In terms of the politics of historiography, the essay cuts two ways: it rejects the Great Man as the motor driving Athenian history, but it also urges the genuine importance of certain historical events as turning points, as moments of rupture that can result in fundamental changes in both ideologies and institutions. The relative importance of discrete events vis-à-vis the *longue durée* of established social structure and the potential of human societies to change rapidly have been much debated by twentieth-century historians. Although there is an increasing interest among some historians in events and narrative, within the area of Greek democracy studies the superiority of the *longue durée* approach is vigorously defended, notably by Ian Morris (1996 and forthcoming).

Among other key questions at issue here are: How important to the history of democracy were the various events of 510–506 B.C., relative to prior and subsequent events and relative to one another? What are the proximate causes and the eventual results of the events at issue? And who (individual or collectivity) is to be assigned credit or blame for the several developments? Arguing that the sources raise serious problems for the

This essay was first published in Carol Dougherty and Leslie Kurke, eds., *Cultural Poetics in Archaic Greece: Cult, Performance, Politics* (Cambridge: Cambridge University Press, 1993), 215–32. Reprinted with the permission of Cambridge University Press.

two most commonly applied explanatory models, I offer an alternative that seems to fit the evidence better. I suggest that the signal event in the history of democracy was the Athenian uprising against the Spartans in 508/7, that this event defined the nature of Athens' subsequent democratic reforms, and that the primary historical agent was the Athenian demos, acting on its own initiative and without aristocratic leadership. This reading demotes Cleisthenes from his accustomed central position as "leader" of the progressive movement and new government, although it allows him to play an innovative and indeed essential role as an interpreter of mass action and designer of institutions capable of framing and stabilizing a new ideology.

My explanation for the Athenian Revolution requires not only (as with Chapter 3) exposing and assessing the theoretical underpinnings of other scholars' arguments, but also (as Chapter 2 suggests will be necessary) importing concepts and ideas from outside archaic Greek history. In this case, the primary external "supplement" to the sources is the example of the French Revolution. Rather than attempting to argue that the Athenian and French revolutions offer a full set of historical parallels, however, I take a detour through the history of revolutionary France in order to demonstrate that focused and effective revolutionary activities can be carried out by masses of citizens in the absence of established leaders or traditional structures of leadership. The goal is not to show that sixth-century B.C. Athens was fundamentally similar to eighteenth-century France, but rather to show that the argument "a leaderless uprising could not have occurred because such things do not happen" is misinformed.

My reading of the French and Athenian revolutions is, in part, predicated on the speech-act theory developed by J. L. Austin; and speech-act theory remains a key methodological tool in several of the subsequent essays. Where I part company with some other recent work influenced by Austin is in my insistence that speech acts must be read together with other sorts of action: the proof of the revolutionary speech act must be sought in the rebellion. The analysis of revolutionary action and its radical implications for subsequent democratic regimes develop directly from the premises sketched in Chapter 3. Comparisons could be extended; it would be interesting to look, for example, at the American Revolution (especially in light of G. Wood 1992) or the Russian revolutions of 1917 and 1989–91.

From the time of its first, oral, presentation, my Athenian Revolution thesis has generated controversy. I retain oddly fond memories of a distinguished classicist eloquently admonishing the Wellesley audience not to believe a word of it on the grounds that (sources be damned!) Cleisthenes simply must have been in Athens directing affairs throughout the revolution. My focus on the demos and my decentering of Cleisthenes as the key historical actor is discussed in critical detail by David Ames Curtis in the translator's foreword to a new English translation of the classic work on Cleisthenes by Lévêque and Vidal-Naquet (1996, xiii–xvii). Meanwhile, Vidal-Naquet, in his new author's introduction to the same work (xxiv–xxv), acknowledges that "our principal error [in the French original of 1964] seems to me to have given in to the temptation to gather everything under the name of Cleisthenes." In several new essays Kurt Raaflaub (1995, and 1996a, b, and c) attempts to demonstrate that my argument for the primary importance of the events of 510–506 is in error and that the true origin of Athenian democracy (should one desire a single date) is 462 B.C., with the constitutional reforms associated by later authors with the name Ephialtes. I offer a reply to Raaflaub in "Revolution Matters" (Ober 1996). In that essay (to be published along with Raaflaub 1996b and c), I restate, and attempt to buttress and extend, some of the main arguments presented here.

THE PERIODIZATION of history is, of course, a product of hindsight, and most historians realize that any past era can accurately be described as an "age of transition." Fixing the end of the archaic period and the transition to the classical is thus a historiographic problem, one that reflects contemporary scholarly inclinations more than it does ancient realities. Nevertheless, since historians cannot work without periodization, and since English-language historiography seems to be entering a post-Annales phase characterized by a renewed interest in the significance—especially the symbolic and cultural significance—of events,[1] it may be worthwhile to look at a series of events that can be taken as the beginning of a new phase of Greek history. The events we choose to mark the transition will be different for any given region or polis, but for those interested in Athenian political history, the end of the archaic and the beginning of something new may reasonably be said to have come about in the period around 510 to 506 B.C., with the revolutionary events that established the form of government that would soon come to be called *dēmokratia*.[2]

If the "Athenian Revolution" is a historically important event (or series of events), it is often described in what seem to me to be misleading terms. Historians typically discuss the revolution in the antiseptic terminology of "constitutional development," and their narrative accounts tend to be narrowly centered on the person and intentions of Cleisthenes himself. Putting Cleisthenes at the center of the revolution as a whole entails slighting a significant part of the source tradition. And that tradition, which consists almost entirely of brief discussions in Herodotus (5.66, 69–78) and the *Athēnaiōn Politeia* (20–21), is scanty enough as it is. The reconstruction of the events of 508/7 offered here is simultaneously quite conservative in its approach and quite radical in its implications. I hope to show that by sticking very closely to the primary sources, it is possible to derive a plausible and internally coherent narrative that revolves around the Athenian people rather than their leaders. A close reading of the

---

[1] See the introduction to Hunt 1989.

[2] This is a traditional breaking point: Burn (1960, 324), for example, ends his narrative of archaic Athenian history with the expulsion of Hippias. Hansen (1986) argues that *dēmokratia* was the name Cleisthenes used from the beginning. The relevant ancient sources are conveniently collected, translated, and annotated in Stanton 1990, 130–67.

sources shows that the dominant role ascribed to elite leaders in modern accounts of a key point in the revolution is supplementary to the ancient evidence. All historians supplement their narratives with assumptions, models, and theories; supplementation of the source material, in order to fill in apparent gaps and silences, is an inevitable part of the process of even the most self-consciously narrative (rather than analytical) forms of historical writing. But such supplements (especially those that are widely accepted) must be challenged from time to time, lest they become so deeply entrenched as to block the development of alternative readings that may explain the source tradition as well or better.

Both of our two main sources state that during a key period of the revolution, Cleisthenes and his closest supporters were in exile. They imply that the main Athenian players in the revolt were corporate entities: the *boulē* and the demos. The ascription of authoritative leadership in all phases of the revolution to Cleisthenes may, I think, be attributed to the uncritical (and indeed unconscious) acceptance of a view of history that supposes that all advance in human affairs comes through the consciously willed actions of individual members of an elite.[3] In the case of other historical figures, for example Solon, proponents of this elite-centered Great Man approach to history can at least claim support in the primary sources. But although he *is* regarded by the sources as the driving force behind important political reforms, Cleisthenes is not described in our sources as a Solon-style lawgiver (*nomothetēs*). The *Athēnaiōn Politeia* (20.4) calls him *tou dēmou prostatēs* (the leader who stands up before the people) and, though the label is anachronistic for the late sixth century, it seems to me a pretty reasonable description of Cleisthenes' historical role: like later Athenian politicians, Cleisthenes' leadership was not dependent on constitutional authority, but rather upon his ability to persuade the Athenian people to adopt and to act on the proposals he advocated. In sum, I will attempt to show that though Cleisthenes is indeed a very important player in Athens' revolutionary drama, the key role was played by the demos. And thus, *dēmokratia* was not a gift from a benevolent elite to a passive demos, but was the product of collective decision, action, and self-definition on the part of the demos itself.

---

[3] For representative statements of the centrality of Cleisthenes' role, see Zimmern 1961, 143–44: "Cleisthenes the Alcmaeonid, the leader of the popular party, . . . made a bid for power. [After the Spartan intervention and the occupation of the Acropolis,] *Cleisthenes and the councillors* [my emphasis] called the people to arms and blockaded the rock . . . [upon the surrender of the Spartans] Cleisthenes was now master of the situation." Murray 1980, 254: "Kleisthenes 'took the people into his party' . . . proposed major reforms, *expelled Isagoras* [my emphasis], and in the next few years held off the attempts of the Spartans and their allies to intervene." Forrest 1966, 194: "Finally, with the *demos'* firm support, *he was able to rout Isagoras* [my emphasis] together with a Spartan force." Other textbooks do point out that Cleisthenes was in exile, e.g., Sealey 1976, 147; Bury and Meiggs 1975, 36; and especially M. Ostwald in *The Cambridge Ancient History*, 2d ed. (1988), 4:305–7. The modern account of the revolution closest in spirit to the one I offer here is perhaps Meier 1990, 64–66.

Having advocated the study of historical events, and having simultaneously rejected the individual intentions of the elite leader as the motor that necessarily drives events, I shall go one step further out on the limb by suggesting that *the* moment of the revolution, the end of the archaic phase of Athenian political history, the point at which Athenian democracy was born, was a violent, leaderless event: a three-day riot in 508/7 that resulted in the removal of King Cleomenes I and his Spartan troops from the soil of Attica.

In order to explain the events of 508/7, we need to review the revolutionary period that began in 510 B.C.—a fascinating few years characterized by a remarkable series of expulsions from the territory of Attica and returns to it. The series opened with the ouster of Hippias, son of Peisistratos. In 510 the Spartans, urged on by multiple oracles from Delphic Apollo, decided to liberate Athens from the rule of the Peisistratid tyrant. A preliminary seaborne invasion of Attica was repulsed by the tyrant's forces. King Cleomenes I then raised a second army, which he marched across the Isthmus into Athenian territory. This time Hippias' forces failed to stop the invasion. With the Spartans in control of Attica, the tyrant and his family were forced to retreat to their stronghold on the Acropolis. The Acropolis was a formidable obstacle, the defenders were well supplied with food and drink, and the Spartan besiegers were initially stymied. Indeed, it looked as if they might abandon the attempt after a few days (Hdt. 5.64–65). But then Hippias made the mistake of trying to smuggle his sons past the besiegers and out of Athens. They were caught by the Spartans and held hostage. Hippias then surrendered on terms, and was allowed to leave Athens with his family. Thus ended the tyranny.[4]

But the liberation raised more questions than it answered. Who would now rule Athens? One might suppose that the spoils of political authority would end up going to the victors. But as Thucydides (6.53.3; cf. Aristophanes *Lysistrata* 1150–56) pointed out, few Athenians had played much part in the expulsion. The victorious Spartans, for their part, had no interest in progressive political innovation. They surely intended Athens to become a client-state, with a status similar to that of their allies in the Peloponnesian League. This would presumably mean that Athens would be governed by a rather narrow oligarchy, the form of government that (at least in the mid-fifth century: Thuc. 1.19) Sparta mandated as standard for all members of the league.[5] The Spartans did not permanently garrison Athens (this was not their style), but after withdrawing their forces they remained very interested in Athenian politics. In the aftermath of the "liberation," King Cleomenes, the dominant figure in late-sixth-century Sparta, encouraged attempts by Isagoras and other Athe-

[4] For the tyranny and its end, see D. M. Lewis in *The Cambridge Ancient History*, 2d ed. (1988), 4:287–302, with sources cited.

[5] The government would not have been called an oligarchy because the word had not yet been invented; for the history of the term, see Raaflaub 1983.

nian aristocrats to establish a government that would exclude most Athenians from active political participation.

In the period 510–507 the political battlefield of Athens was disputed not between men who called themselves or thought of themselves as oligarchs and democrats, but rather between rival aristocrats. We cannot say exactly what sort of government Isagoras envisioned, but in light of subsequent developments it seems safe to assume that he intended to place effective control of affairs into the hands of a small, pro-Spartan elite. Isagoras' main opponent was Cleisthenes the Alcmaeonid. Despite the fact that Cleisthenes himself had been willing to accept the high office of archon under the Tyranny, some elements of the Alcmaeonid family had probably been active in resistance to the Tyrants.[6] Cleisthenes, obviously a leading figure among the Alcmaeonids by 508/7, may have felt that his family's antityrannical activity had earned him a prominent position in the political order that would replace the Tyranny. But that position did not come automatically. Indeed, Isagoras, with his Spartan connections, was gaining in influence and was elected archon for 508/7 B.C.[7] Thus, as Herodotus (5.66.2) tells us, Cleisthenes was getting the worst of it. In response, Cleisthenes did a remarkable thing: *ton dēmon prosetairizetai.* I will leave this phrase untranslated for the time being, for reasons that will become clear later. At any rate, because he had in some way allied himself with the demos, Cleisthenes now began to overshadow his opponents in the contest for political influence in Athens (Hdt. 5.69.2).

It is worth pausing at this point in the narrative to ask what the social and institutional context of the struggle between Isagoras and Cleisthenes would have been. Herodotus and the author of the *Athēnaiōn Politeia* employ the political vocabularies of the mid-fifth and late fourth centuries, respectively. But we must not apply the model of politics in Periclean or Demosthenic Athens to the late sixth century. Isagoras and Cleisthenes had recourse to few if any of the weapons familiar to us from the political struggles of those later periods—

---

[6] Accommodation and resistance of Alcmaeonids to the tyranny: Lewis in *The Cambridge Ancient History*, 2d ed. (1988), 4:288, 299–301. But cf. the skepticism of Thomas (1989, 263–64), who argues that the Alcmaeonids may have made up the tradition of their antityrannical activity and the story of their exile under the Peisistratids from whole cloth.

[7] Isagoras as archon: *Ath. Pol.* 21.1. The attempt by McCargar (1974) to separate Isagoras, opponent-of-Cleisthenes, from the archon of 508/7 on the grounds that *some* archons in this period were evidently relatively young (perhaps not much over thirty) and Isagoras *may* have been relatively mature seems to me chimerical, especially in light of the extreme rarity of the name. *Ath. Pol.* 22.5 claims that after the institution of the tyranny, and until 487/6, all archons were elected (*hairetoi*). The Tyrants had manipulated the elections to ensure that their own supporters were in office (see Rhodes 1981, 272–73); exactly how the elections would have been carried out in 509/8 (and thus what Isagoras' support consisted of) is unclear. We need not, anyway, suppose that Isagoras' election was indicative of a broad base of popular support; more likely his support was centered in the (non-Alcmaeonid) nobility. On the power of the archaic archon, see *Ath. Pol.* 3.3, 13.2 with the comments of Rhodes 1981, ad locc.

ideologically motivated *hetaireiai* (aristocratic clubs), ostracism, the *graphē para-nomōn* (a legal procedure for use against those proposing illegal decrees) and other public actions in people's courts, finely honed orations by orators trained in the art of rhetoric. What shall we imagine in their place?

Late-archaic Athens was surely more dominated by the great families than was Athens of the fifth and fourth centuries. On the other hand, it would be a serious mistake to suppose that the scion-of-a-great-family/ordinary-citizen relationship can be seen in fully developed patron/client terms—for late-archaic Athens, the model of Roman republican politics is as anachronistic as is that of democratic politics. The reforms of Solon had undercut the traditional authority associated with birth. The policies of the Tyrants themselves had gone a long way in breaking down the traditional ties of dependence and obedience between upper- and lower-class Athenians. Moreover, Solon's creation of the formal status of citizen—a result of prohibiting debt slavery and of legal reforms that made Athenians potentially responsible for one another's welfare—had initiated a process whereby the demos became conscious of itself in forthrightly political terms. The Tyrants had encouraged political self-consciousness on the part of the masses of ordinary citizens by the sponsorship of festivals and building programs. The upshot was that by 510–508 B.C. the ordinary Athenian male had come a long way from the status of politically passive client of a great house. He saw himself as a citizen rather than as a subject, and at least some part of his loyalty was owed to the abstraction "Athens."[8]

And yet, the political institutions in which an Athenian man could express his developing sense of citizenship were, in early 508, still quite rudimentary and were still dominated by the elite. We may suppose that the traditional "constitution," as revised by Solon, still pertained. Thus there were occasional meetings of a political Assembly that all citizens had the right to attend. But it is unlikely that those outside the elite had the right or power to speak in that Assembly; nor could they hope to serve on the probouleutic council of 400, as a magistrate, or on the Areopagus council.[9] Cleisthenes, as a leading member of a prominent family and as an Areopagite, surely did have both the right and the power to address the Assembly. It seems a reasonable guess that it was in the Assembly (although not necessarily uniquely here) that he allied himself to the demos, by proposing (and perhaps actually passing) constitutional reforms. The masses saw that these reforms would provide them with the institutional means to express more fully their growing sense of themselves as citizens. By these propositions and/or enactments Cleisthenes gained political influence, and so Isagoras began to get the worst of it (Hdt. 5.69.2–70.1).[10]

---

[8] See Ober 1989b, 60–68; Manville 1990, 124–209; Meier 1990, 53–81. On the lack of formal patronage structures in classical Athens, see Millett 1989.

[9] Solonian constitution: Ober 1989b, 60–65, with references cited. For the Areopagus from the time of Solon to Cleisthenes, see Wallace 1989, 48–76.

[10] Cleisthenes' connection with the demos is underlined by Hdt. 5.69.2: ὡς γὰρ δὴ τὸν

But if Cleisthenes now had the people on his side, Isagoras was still archon, and moreover he could call in outside forces. No matter what measures Cleisthenes had managed to propose or pass in the Assembly, a new constitutional order could become a practical political reality only if the Assembly's will were allowed to decide the course of events. Isagoras, determined that this would not be allowed, sent word of the unsettling developments to Cleomenes in Sparta. Cleomenes responded by sending a herald to the Athenians, informing them that, ostensibly because of the old Cylonian curse, they were to expel (*exeballe*) Cleisthenes and many others from the city (Hdt. 5.70.2). Cleisthenes himself duly left (*autos upexesche*: Hdt. 5.72.1).

Even after Cleisthenes' departure, Isagoras and/or Cleomenes must still have felt uneasy about the Athenian situation. A smallish (*ou . . . megalēi cheiri*) mixed-nationality military force, featuring a core of Spartans and led by Cleomenes, soon arrived in the city (*parēn es tas Athēnas*: Hdt. 5.72.1). Cleomenes now, on Isagoras' recommendation, ordered further expulsions; Herodotus (5.72.1) claims that a total of 700 families were driven out (*agēlateei*). The archon Isagoras and his Spartan allies were clearly in control of Athens. That could have been the end of what we might call the progressive movement in Athenian politics. Athens might well have become another Argos—an occasionally restive but ultimately impotent client-state of Sparta. After all, the Spartans were the dominant military power in late-sixth-century Greece, whereas Cleisthenes and the other leading Athenians who opposed Isagoras were now powerless exiles.

But, of course, that was not the end of it. What happened next is the moment of revolution I alluded to earlier. According to Herodotus, Isagoras and Cleomenes next (*deutera*)

> attempted to abolish the *boulē* (*tēn boulēn kataluein epeirato*),[11] and to transfer political authority to a body of 300 supporters of Isagoras. But when the *boulē* resisted and refused to obey (*antistatheisēs de tēs boulēs kai ou boulomenēs peithesthai*), Cleomenes, together with Isagoras and his supporters, occupied the Acropolis (*katalambanousi tēn akropolin*). However, the rest of the Athenians (*Athēnaiōn de hoi loipoi*), who were of one mind (*ta auta phronēsantes*) [regarding these affairs], besieged them [on the Acropolis] for two days. But on the third day a truce was struck and the Lac-

---

Ἀθηναίων δῆμον πρότερον ἀπωσμένον τότε πάντως πρὸς τὴν ἑωυτοῦ μοῖραν προσεθήκατο, and by *Ath. Pol.* 20.1: ὁ Κλεισθένης προσηγάγετο τὸν δῆμον, ἀποδιδοὺς τῷ πλήθει τὴν πολιτείαν. Since Wade-Gery's seminal article (1933, 19–25), it has been widely accepted that the Assembly was the arena in which Cleisthenes won the favor of the people; cf. discussion by Ostwald 1969, 149–60.

[11] The implied subject of the verb *epeirato* is either Cleomenes or Isagoras. The grammar seems to point to Cleomenes, although presumably it was Isagoras (as archon) who gave the official order to the *boulē*. The point is in any case merely procedural: Herodotus' narrative demonstrates that Cleomenes and Isagoras were working hand in glove throughout.

edaemonians among them were allowed to leave the territory [of Attica]. (Hdt. 5.72.1–2)

In the aftermath of the expulsion of the Spartans, at least some of the non-Spartan members of Cleomenes' army (perhaps including Athenian supporters of Isagoras, although not Isagoras himself), who had been detained in Athens, were summarily executed (Hdt. 5.72.4–73.1). After these events (*meta tauta*) the Athenians recalled (*metapempsamenoi*) Cleisthenes and the 700 families (Hdt. 5.73.1). A new constitutional order (presumably resembling the order proposed by Cleisthenes or enacted on his motion before he was expelled) was soon put into place.[12]

Meanwhile, Cleomenes felt that the Athenians had "outraged" him "with both words and deeds" (*periubristhai epesi kai ergoisi*: Hdt. 5.74.1). I would gloss Herodotus' statement as follows: Cleomenes had been outraged by "the words" (of the *bouleutai* when they refused the dissolution order) and "the deeds" (of the demos in its uprising against the Spartans and the Athenian quislings). The Spartan king wanted revenge. He still planned to put Isagoras into power in Athens, but his counterattack of 506 fizzled due to a lack of solidarity in the Peloponnesian ranks on the one side and Athenian unity and military discipline on the other (Hdt. 5.74–77). Within just a few years, Athens had moved from the position of Spartan client-to-be to that of a powerful, independent polis. Athens twice had been occupied by an outside power, and the Athenians had rejected the rule of a narrow elite in favor of a radical program of political reforms, risen up successfully against their occupiers when the reform program was threatened, institutionalized the reforms, defended the new political order against external aggression, and begun on the road that would soon lead to democracy. It is an amazing story, and Herodotus (5.78) points out to his readers just how remarkable was the Athenian achievement. This, then, was the Athenian Revolution.

Herodotus' account is quite closely followed, and perhaps in a few places amplified, by the account of the Aristotelian *Athēnaiōn Politeia*. I will focus on three aspects of the story that seem to me particularly notable. Two are familiar topoi of Cleisthenes scholarship; the third is not.

The first peculiarity is that Cleisthenes, an Areopagite and a leading member of a fine old family, was willing in the first place to turn to the demos—the ordinary people, who, as Herodotus points out, "formerly had been held in

---

[12] Herodotus (5.66.2) implies that at least some of the reforms were put into place before Cleomenes' arrival; *Ath. Pol.* (20–21) discusses the reforms after giving the history of the revolution proper. I think it is most likely that some reforms were proposed and perhaps actually enacted by the Assembly before Cleomenes' arrival, but presumably there would not have been time for all the details of the new constitution to have been put into place. See below for the question of when the Council of 500 was established. For a review of the chronological issue, see Hignett 1952, 331–36; Rhodes 1981, 244–45, 249; Chambers 1990, 221–22.

contempt" (*proteron apōsmenon*: Hdt. 5.69.2). The second striking thing is that after his recall from exile, Cleisthenes *fulfilled* the promises he had made to the demos (in the form of proposals or enactments of the Assembly). He fully earned the trust they placed in him by establishing a form of government that, at least in the long run, doomed aristocratic political dominance in Athens. Much ink has been spilled over Cleisthenes' apparently peculiar behavior. Since Cleisthenes' actions seem to fly in the face of the aristocratic ethos ("Thou shalt not mix with the lower sort") and to contradict a common assumption about human nature itself ("Thou shalt always act in self-interest"), sophisticated explanations have been devised to explain what he was up to. Among views of Cleisthenes in the scholarly literature, two dominate the field, at least in the English-speaking world. One, well represented by David M. Lewis' influential article in *Historia*, is what we might call the "cynical realist" view, which holds that Cleisthenes was no true friend of the Athenian demos, but instead he benefited (or at least intended to benefit) the Alcmaeonids by extraordinarily clever gerrymandering in his establishment of the demes.[13] Lewis' "realist" view was advanced to counter the other dominant view: the "idealist" view of an altruistic Cleisthenes. This second viewpoint is perhaps best exemplified by the work of Victor Ehrenberg, who saw Cleisthenes as a selfless democratic visionary.[14]

I would not want to deny that Cleisthenes embraced a vision of a new society (see below) or that he hoped for a privileged place for his own family in that society. Yet neither the "realist" view of Cleisthenes the diabolically clever factional politician, nor the "idealist" view of Cleisthenes the self-consciously altruistic Father of Democracy, adequately accounts for the third peculiarity in Herodotus' story—the uprising that doomed Isagoras and his partisans by forcing the surrender and withdrawal from Attica of the Spartans. Although the sparing accounts of Herodotus and the *Athēnaiōn Politeia* do not give us a great deal to work with, it appears that a spontaneous insurrection against Isagoras and the Spartans followed in the wake of Cleomenes' attempt to abolish the *boulē* and his occupation of the Acropolis. Without the uprising, the Cleisthenic reforms would have remained empty words: proposals or enactments voided by the efficient use of force by an outside power.

We will probably never know the details of what actually happened between Cleomenes' attempt to dissolve the *boulē* and his surrender on terms, but we can at least say what did *not* happen, and this may be useful in itself. First, and

---

[13] Lewis 1963.

[14] Ehrenberg 1973, 89–103: In 510 Cleisthenes was "a man of new and radical ideas" (89); in 508 he gained support "by revealing plans of a new democratic order" (90); "his reforms were . . . the first examples of democratic methods" (91). Cleisthenes was not primarily interested in personal power, rather "power was to him a means of creating the constitutional framework for a society on the verge of becoming democratic" (91). For Ehrenberg, then, Cleisthenes is both selfless and a strong leader whose place is "at the helm" (102). Cf. Ehrenberg 1950.

perhaps foremost, we should not imagine the siege of the Spartans on the Acropolis as an organized military campaign. Whatever may have been the form of the pre-Cleisthenic Athenian military forces, there is no mention in Herodotus or the *Athēnaiōn Politeia* at the siege of military leaders, or of any other sort of formal leadership—no reference to a polemarch or to *stratēgoi*, no *naukraroi* calling in their clients from the fields. Now, the silence of our sources is a notoriously slippery ground for argument, but (as demonstrated by their accounts of, e.g., Cylon and the *naukraroi*, Solon and the Eupatrids, and Peisistratos and the Alcmaeonids) both Herodotus and the author of the *Athēnaiōn Politeia* were very interested in aristocratic leadership—whether it was individual or collective and institutional. I find it hard to believe that the presence of aristocratic leaders at the insurrection could have been forgotten or their identity fully suppressed in the sixty years or so between the revolution and Herodotus' arrival in Athens. Surely this brave resistance to the Spartan occupiers of the Acropolis is just the sort of thing that aristocratic families would remember for several generations. And it was just this sort of family tradition that formed the basis of much of Herodotus' Athenian narrative. One cannot, of course, exclude the possibility that Herodotus intentionally covered up the role played by leaders. But why would he want to do so? To further glorify the Alcmaeonid Cleisthenes? Yet even if Herodotus did favor the Alcmaeonids (which is far from certain), the hypothetical leaders would have been Alcmaeonid allies, since Cleisthenes was immediately recalled and his constitutional reforms enacted.[15] In the end, positing aristocratic leadership for the action that expelled the Spartans is an *ignotus per ignotum* argument, a modern supplement that relies for its credibility entirely on the unprovable (and elitist) assumption that aristocratic leadership in such matters would have been *sine qua non*. It is preferable in this case to trust our only sources and suppose that Herodotus and the *Athēnaiōn Politeia* mention no leaders because Athenian tradition recorded none, and that Athenian tradition recorded none because there were none—or at least none from the ranks of the leading aristocratic families.

Moreover, there is no mention in Herodotus or the *Athēnaiōn Politeia* of Athenian hoplites at the siege of the Acropolis: according to Herodotus, it is *Athēnaiōn hoi loipoi* (the rest of the Athenians) who, united in their view of the situation, do the besieging. *Athēnaiōn Politeia* (20.3) mentions *to plēthos* and *ho dēmos*. This does not, of course, mean that no men wearing hoplite armor took part in the siege—but it is noteworthy that there is no suggestion in either source that anything resembling a "regular" army formation was called up. This might best be explained by the hypothesis that no "national" army ex-

---

[15] For a detailed discussion of the role of oral traditions (of family and polis) in Herodotus' construction of his account of the revolution, and a vigorous attack on the hypothesis that Herodotus was an Alcmaeonid apologist, see Thomas 1989, 144–54, 238–82.

isted in the era before the carrying out of Cleisthenes' constitutional reforms. If there was no national army properly speaking, then archaic Athenian military actions were ordinarily carried out by aristocratic leaders (presumably often acting in cooperation with one another): men who were able to muster bodies of armed followers.[16] If this is right, the mass expulsion recommended by Isagoras and carried out by Cleomenes (which no doubt focused on aristocratic houses) would have completely disrupted the traditional means of mustering the Athenian army—and this may well have been among their motives for the expulsion. It is not modern scholars alone who doubt the ability of masses to act without orders from their superiors.

The action that forced the surrender of the Spartans was evidently carried out in the absence of traditional military leaders and without a regular army. How then are we to visualize this action? The Athenian siege of the Acropolis in 508/7 is best understood as a riot—a violent and more or less spontaneous uprising by a large number of Athenian citizens. In order to explain Cleomenes' actions, we must assume that the riot broke out very suddenly and was of relatively great size, intensity, and duration.[17]

After their occupation of the Acropolis, Cleomenes and his warriors were barricaded on a natural fortress, one that had frustrated the regular Spartan army during the siege of Hippias only a couple of years earlier. Yet on the third day of the siege the royal Spartan commander agreed to a humiliating conditional surrender—a surrender that left his erstwhile non-Lacedaemonian comrades to the untender mercies of the rioters. Cleomenes' precipitous agreement to these harsh terms must mean that he regarded the forces arrayed against him as too numerous (throughout the period of the siege) to contemplate a sortie. Why could the Spartans not simply have waited out the siege, as Hippias had been prepared to do? Given the undeveloped state of archaic Greek siegecraft, it is unlikely that the Spartans feared a successful assault on the stronghold. It is much more likely that (unlike Hippias) they had not had time to lay in adequate supplies. This suggests that Cleomenes had occupied the Acropolis very quickly, which in turn probably means that he was caught off guard by the uprising. This inferential sequence supports a presumption that the uprising occurred quite suddenly. What, then, was the precipitating factor?

[16] Frost 1984.

[17] I am assuming throughout that Cleomenes was an experienced and sane military commander, and that his decisions were made accordingly. On the dubious tradition of the madness of Cleomenes, see Griffiths 1989. It is interesting to note how the demos' action simply disappears in some respectable scholarly accounts, e.g., Ehrenberg 1973, 90: "Cleomenes and Isagoras met, however, with the resistance of the council . . . which they had tried to disband and which was most likely the Areopagus. . . . The Spartans withdrew, Isagoras was powerless, and many of his followers were executed."

Herodotus' account, cited above, describes the action in the following stages:

1. Isagoras/Cleomenes attempts to dissolve the *boulē*.
2. The *boulē* resists.
3. Cleomenes and Isagoras occupy the Acropolis.
4. The rest of the Athenians are united in their views.
5. They besiege the Spartan force.
6. Cleomenes surrenders on the third day of the siege.

If we are to follow Herodotus, we must suppose that steps 1, 2, 3, 5, and 6 are chronologically discrete and sequential events. Step 4 cannot, on the other hand, be regarded as a chronological moment; word of events 1–3 would have spread around Athens through the piecemeal word-of-mouth operations typical of an oral society. Presumably those living in the city would have learned what was going on first, and the news would have spread (probably very quickly, but not instantaneously) to the rural citizenry.[18] Herodotus' language (*ta auta phronēsantes*—"all of one mind") supports the idea of a generalized and quite highly developed civic consciousness among the Athenian masses—an ability to form and act on strong and communal views on political affairs.

If we take our lead from Herodotus' account, two precipitating factors can be adduced to explain the crystallization of opinion and the outbreak of violent anti-Spartan action on the part of the Athenian demos. First, the riot may have been sparked by the Spartan attempt to dissolve the *boulē* and the *boulē*'s resistance (thus the demos' action would commence as a consequence of steps 1 and 2, but before step 3). According to this scenario, Cleomenes and Isagoras will have been frightened by the sudden uprising into a precipitous defensive retreat to the nearby stronghold of the Acropolis. Alternatively, the riot might have broken out only after the Spartan occupation of the Acropolis (thus after step 3). On this reading of the evidence, the riot would be precipitated by the Spartan's offensive (in both senses of the term) takeover of the sacred Acropolis. This second hypothesis would certainly fit in with Herodotus' (5.72.3–4, cf. 5.90.2) story of Cleomenes' sacrilegious behavior and disrespect to the priestess of Athena. Yet this scenario is not, to my mind, fully satisfactory. It does not explain why Cleomenes felt it necessary to bring his entire force up to the Acropolis. Why did Isagoras and his partisans (*ho te Kleomenēs kai ho Isagorēs kai hoi stasiōtai autou*: Hdt. 5.72.2) go up to the Acropolis with Cleomenes? And if the occupation of the Acropolis by Spartan forces was a deliberate and unhurried act of aggression, how are we to explain the failure to bring up enough supplies to last even three days?[19]

---

[18] On how information was disseminated in Athens, see Hunter 1990.

[19] Herodotus' statement that Cleomenes seized the Acropolis and was subsequently thrown out along with the Lacedaemonians (ἐπεχείρησέ τε καὶ τότε πάλιν ἐξέπιπτε μετὰ τῶν Λακε-

It is certain that *Athēnaiōn Politeia* (20.3) saw Cleomenes' move to the Acropolis as a defensive response to a riot: when "the *boulē* resisted (*tēs de boulēs antistasēs*) and the mob gathered itself together (*kai sunathroisthentos tou plēthous*), the supporters of Cleomenes and Isagoras fled for refuge (*katephugon*) to the Acropolis."[20] Here the move to the Acropolis is specifically described as a defensive reaction to the council's resistance and the gathering of the people. *Athēnaiōn Politeia*'s statement has independent evidentiary value only if its author had access to evidence (whether in the form of written or oral traditions) other than Herodotus' account—on which he obviously leaned heavily. This issue of Quellenforschung cannot be resolved in any definitive way here, but it is not de facto unlikely that the author of *Athēnaiōn Politeia*, who certainly had independent information on Cleisthenes' actual reforms, could have read or heard that Cleomenes and Isagoras fled to the Acropolis when a mob formed subsequent to the unsuccessful attempt to dissolve the *boulē*. At the very least, we must suppose that *Athēnaiōn Politeia* interpreted Herodotus' account of the move to the Acropolis as describing a flight rather than a planned act of aggression.[21]

Finally, let us consider the only other classical source for these events: Aristophanes' *Lysistrata* (lines 273–82). Here the chorus of Old Athenian Men, girding themselves for an assault on the Acropolis (held by a mixed-nationality force of women), urge each other on "since when Cleomenes seized it previously, he did not get away unpunished, for despite his Laconian spirit he departed giving over to me his arms, wearing only a little cloak, hungry, dirty, hairy-faced . . . that's how ferociously I besieged that man, keeping constant guard, drawn up seventeen ranks deep at the gates." This is not, of course, history, but a poetic and comic description. Cleomenes' surrender of arms and his hunger are plausible enough, but the overly precise reference to "seventeen

---

δαιμονίων: 5.72.4) makes it appear likely that the whole force had gone up to the Acropolis together, had been besieged together, and had surrendered together. It is unlikely that a significant part of Cleomenes' forces joined him on the hill after the commencement of the siege, and Herodotus says nothing about any of his men being captured in the lower city before the surrender. It is worth noting that Cylon (Hdt. 5.71; Thuc. 1.126.5–11) and Peisistratos (twice: Hdt. 1.59.6, 60.5) had earlier seized the Acropolis, each time as the first stage in an attempt to establish a tyranny. Cleomenes' case is different in that his move came *after* he had established control of the city.

[20] Stanton (1990, 142, 144 n. 6) translates *sunathroisthentos tou plēthous* as "the common people had been assembled," on the grounds that "the verb 'had been assembled' is definitely passive." But I take the (morphologically) passive participle *sunathroisthentos* as having a reflexive rather than a passive meaning; on the distinction, see Rijksbaron 1984, 126–48. For a reflexive meaning for the passive participle of *sunathroizō*: Xen. *Anabasis* 6.5.30; of *athroizō*: Thuc. 1.50.4, 6.70.4; and especially Aristotle *Pol.* 1304b33.

[21] For a discussion of the relationship between Herodotus' narrative and *Ath. Pol.* 20–21, see Wade-Gery 1933, 17–19; and Rhodes (1981, 240–41, 244), who argues that Herodotus was *Ath. Pol.*'s sole authority for 20.1–3. For general discussions of *Ath. Pol.*'s use of sources, see Chambers 1990, 84–91.

ranks" is unlikely to reflect historical reality. Nevertheless, as Rosalind Thomas points out, the Aristophanes passage probably does represent a living popular tradition about the siege.[22] And that tradition evidently focused on the military action of the people rather than on any doings of their leaders.

Although certainty cannot be achieved in the face of our limited sources, I think it is easiest to suppose that a spontaneous riot broke out when the *boulē* resisted. Caught off guard, Cleomenes and Isagoras retreated with their forces to the Acropolis stronghold to regroup. Rapidly spreading news of the occupation of the Acropolis further inflamed the Athenians, and so the ranks of the rioters were continually augmented as rural residents took up arms and streamed into the city. From Cleomenes' perspective, the bad situation, which had begun with the resistance of the *boulē*, only got worse as time went on. Stranded on the barren hill without adequate food or water, and with the ranks of his opponents increasing hourly, Cleomenes saw that his position was hopeless and negotiated a surrender. This scenario has the virtue of incorporating all major elements of Herodotus' account and the two other classical sources for the events, explaining Cleomenes' behavior in rational terms, and accommodating the means of news transmittal in an oral society.

If, as I have argued above, the Athenian military action that led to the liberation of Athens from Spartan control was a riot, precipitated by the refusal of the *bouleutai* to obey Isagoras' or Cleomenes' direct order that the *boulē* dissolve itself in favor of the 300 Isagoreans, how are we to explain the relationship between the *boulē*'s act of defiance and the uprising itself? In the absence of direct textual evidence for either the motives of the *bouleutai* or their relationship to the demos, I offer, for comparative purposes, the example of another famous revolutionary refusal by a political body to dissolve when confronted with authority backed by force. Although such comparisons are supplementary, and not evidentiary in a formal sense, they are useful if they expand common assumptions about the limits of the possible, in this case by showing that an act of disobedience could indeed precipitate a revolution.

On June 17, 1789, the representatives of the Third Estate of the Kingdom of France, a body originally called together by the king, declared themselves to be the National Assembly of France. This act of self-redefinition was not accepted as valid by the existing, and heretofore sovereign, authority of the kingdom. Six days later, on June 23, King Louis XVI surrounded the assembly hall with some 4,000 troops and read a royal proclamation to the self-proclaimed Assemblymen in which he stated that the Third Estate's act in taking the name "The National Assembly" was voided; all enactments of the so-called National Assembly were nullified. Louis concluded his speech with

22 Thomas 1989, 245–47.

the words, "I order you, gentlemen, to disperse at once." But the National Assembly refused either to disperse or to renounce its act of self-naming.[23]

According to the brilliant interpretation of these events by Sandy Petrey, the Third Estate's renaming of itself, and Louis' declaration that the renaming was void, set up a confrontation between speech acts—both the Third Estate and Louis made statements that were intended to have material effects in the real world of French society; both sides were attempting to *enact* a political reality through the speech act of naming (or, in Louis' case, "unnaming"). In the normal environment of prerevolutionary France, the king's statement would have been (in the terminology of J. L. Austin's speech-act theory, on which Petrey's interpretation is based) "felicitous" or efficacious—the Assembly would *be* dissolved because a sovereign authority had stated that it was dissolved. Yet, as Petrey points out, in a revolutionary situation, speech acts are not, at the moment of their enunciation, either felicitous or infelicitous *ipso facto*. Rather, their felicity or efficacy is demonstrated only in retrospect. In this case, the National Assembly did not dissolve when so ordered. By refusing to acknowledge the power of the king's speech to create real effects in the world, the Assembly contested the legitimacy of the king's authority.[24]

The confrontation of speech acts was not the end of the story. Louis subsequently attempted to enforce his will through the deployment of military force. This attempt was frustrated by the outbreak of riots in the streets of Paris. In the words of W. Doyle, in the weeks after the confrontation of June 23, "nobody doubted that the King was still prepared to use force to bring the Revolution to an end. The only thing that could prevent him was counterforce, and as yet the Assembly had none at its disposal. It was saved only by the people of Paris."[25] And thus the French Revolution was launched. Because the revolution succeeded, it turned out that the Third Estate's act of renaming had been felicitous and Louis' proclamation of nullification infelicitous; if the proof of the pudding is in the eating, the proof of the revolutionary speech act is in the rebellion.

Although the efficacy of its speech acts were as yet undemonstrated, the self-redefinition of the Third Estate as the National Assembly on June 17 and the refusal of the Assemblymen of France to acknowledge the force of the king's proclamation of dissolution on June 23 helped to precipitate a revolution because they contested the "inevitability" or "naturalness" of the power of the

---

[23] "Je vous ordonne, Messieurs, de vous séparer toute de suite." For the resolution of the Abbé de Sieyès renaming the Assembly, and the response of Louis at the "Royal Session" of June 23, see Wickham Legg 1905, 18–20, 22–33. For a narrative account of this stage of the revolution, see Doyle 1980, 172–77.

[24] Petrey 1988, esp. 17–51. Petrey's work is based on the ground-breaking linguistic theory of Austin 1975.

[25] Doyle 1980, 177.

king's speech to create political realities. Once the king's official proclamations were no longer regarded as expressions of sovereign authority, political discourse ceased to be a realm of orderly enactment and became a realm of contested interpretations. The success of any given interpretation was no longer based on its grounding in eternal and universally accepted truths about power and legitimacy; rather, success in interpretation was now contingent upon the subsequent actions of the French people acting en masse—in this case, by rioting and besieging the Bastille.

The parallels between the early stages of the French and the Athenian revolutions are certainly not exact, but both similarities and differences may be instructive. First, it is much less clear in the Athenian case where, at any point in the story, sovereign authority lay—or indeed, if we should be talking about sovereignty at all. Isagoras was archon in 508/7, and so the dissolution order issued to the *boulē* could be seen as carrying the weight of legitimately sanctioned authority. But the archon of Athens did not (I suppose) command the absolute sovereignty claimed by Louis XVI, and the perceived legitimacy of Isagoras' authority was probably not enhanced by his employment of foreign military support. What of the comparison of the Athenian *boulē* to the National Assembly? This will depend on what body Herodotus meant by the word *boulē*. There are three choices (and all have had supporters among modern scholars)—the Areopagus Council, the Solonian Council of 400, or a newly established Council of 500. The parallel to the National Assembly is closest if we follow the hypothesis, recently revived by Mortimer Chambers, that the *boulē* in question was (perhaps a pro tem version of) the Council of 500, set up according to Cleisthenes' proposals and the Assembly's enactment before the arrival of the Spartans. This hypothesis would go far in explaining both Cleomenes' interest in eliminating the council and the brave determination of the councilmen to resist. But Chambers' argument, based in part on his rejection of the existence of a Solonian Council of 400, must remain for the time being an attractive speculation.[26] In any event, we cannot be sure exactly what powers the *boulē* claimed or its constitutional relationship to the archon.

Yet despite these caveats and uncertainties, several relevant factors in the French and Athenian cases seem quite similar. Herodotus' revealing comment that a king was "outraged by both words and deeds" (5.74.1) fits the French Revolution as well as the Athenian. In both cases, because of a verbal act of defiance by a political body, "official" political discourse—previously regarded by all concerned as authoritative and stable, as productive of acts of establishment, as a *thesmos*—became a battleground contested by two mutually exclusive interpretations regarding the source of legitimate public authority. Isagoras (or Cleomenes) said the *boulē* was dissolved. The *bouleutai* denied, by their resistance, the validity of this statement. As in the case of the French Revolu-

---

[26] Chambers 1990, 222–23.

tion, it would be the actions of the ordinary people in the streets that would determine which of the opposed interpretations was felicitous and efficacious—rapidly evolving realities would decide whether the statement of Isagoras or of the *bouleutai* conformed to reality. In both revolutions, the official authority's recourse to military force was stymied by superior unofficial force in the form of mass riots. Both revolutions featured short but decisive sieges (the Acropolis and the Bastille) by leaderless crowds of citizens; both sieges ended in a negotiated surrender by the besieged leaders of organized military forces.[27] Furthermore, both uprisings featured summary (and, I would add, morally reprehensible) killings of individuals identified as enemies of the revolution. The Athenian Revolution, no less than the French, was baptized in the blood of "counter-revolutionaries."[28] Yet the difference between Athens and France in this regard is also salient: the decade after 507 saw no equivalent to either Jacobinite Terror or Thermidorian reaction.

In terms of assigning credit (or blame) for the uprising and its aftermath, it is important to note that though the brave action of the bourgeois gentlemen of the Third Estate in naming themselves the National Assembly helped to foment the French Revolution, those gentlemen did not take the lead in storming the Bastille,[29] and they were not able subsequently to control the direction of the revolution. Nor were the *bouleutai* in control of the Athenian Revolution. Neither Herodotus nor *Athēnaiōn Politeia* assigns the *boulē* a leadership role in the insurrection after its refusal to disperse: according to Herodotus, after the *boulē* refused to obey the dissolution order, Cleomenes and Isagoras occupied the Acropolis, and *ta auta phronēsantes, Athēnaiōn hoi loipoi* besieged the Acropolis—taken literally, this comment would seem to exclude the *bouleutai* from any role at all. For *Athēnaiōn Politeia* (20.3), it was when "the *boulē* resisted and the mob gathered itself together" that "the supporters of Cleomenes and Isagoras fled to the Acropolis," and subsequently it was *ho dēmos* that besieged them. Both

[27] For the siege of the Bastille, see Godechot 1970, 218–46. The Bastille was a formidable, if dilapidated, fortress, guarded by a small force of eighty-four pensioners and thirty-two Swiss mercenaries. For the week before the assault of July 14, its commander, Governor de Launey, had refurbished the defenses to withstand an assault. Yet "he had only one day's supply of meat and two days' supply of bread, and moreover there was no drinking water inside the fortress . . . de Launey may . . . have thought that if he were attacked by an unarmed or ill-armed crowd the assault would not last longer than one day and that at nightfall the rioters would disperse" (219). It is tempting to suppose that Cleomenes thought along similar lines.

[28] On the killing of Governor de Launey and seven other defenders of the Bastille on July 14, and of other agents of the Old Regime in the days thereafter, see Godechot 1970, 243–46. The Athenian killings have been questioned on the grounds of the wording of *Ath. Pol.* 20.3 (Κλεομένην μὲν καὶ τοὺς μετ' αὐτοῦ πάντας ἀφεῖσαν ὑποσπόνδους), but as Ostwald (1969, 144 with n. 6) points out, this need only refer to the Lacedaemonian troops; cf. Rhodes 1981, 246–47.

[29] For the composition of the crowd (mostly artisans from Paris) that stormed the Bastille, and the absence of Assemblymen or any other formal leaders, see Godechot 1970, 211, 221–26, 230, 237–39.

authors seem to agree on the importance of the *boulē*'s act of defiance, but both also agree in seeing the key event as the uprising of the Athenian masses.[30]

Finally, how are we to interpret the political implications of this riotous uprising and its relationship to the subsequent Athenian political order—to the "constitution of Cleisthenes"? Once again, a comparative approach may offer some clues. The highly influential work of E. P. Thompson on food riots in eighteenth-century England, and that of Natalie Z. Davis on religious riots in sixteenth-century France, has led to the development of a useful approach to the historical assessment of rioting. This model is discussed in some detail in a recent article by Suzanne Desan, who points out that, according to Thompson and Davis, violent collective actions in early-modern England and France were not merely random outbreaks indicative of generalized popular dissatisfaction. Rather, these riots are best read as acts of collective self-definition, or redefinition. The English peasants were, for example, rioting in support of the reenactment of what Thompson described as a "moral economy"—a view of the world that was actually quite conservative in that it assumed the legitimacy of paternalistic (or at least clientistic) relations between peasantry and local aristocracy.[31]

The riot of 508/7 can thus be read as a collective act of political self-definition in which the demos rejected the archon Isagoras as the legitimate public authority. As Herodotus' account suggests, the riot was the physical, active manifestation of the Athenians having come to be "of one mind" about civic affairs. This reading clarifies the general role of Cleisthenes in the Athenian Revolution and the scope of his accomplishments. More specifically, it helps to explain the relationship between Cleisthenes and the demos in the months before and after the definitive moment of the riot.

Let us return to the problems of the context and meaning of Herodotus' famous and problematic comment (5.66.2) that *Kleisthenēs ton dēmon prosetairizetai*. This phrase is often taken to be a description of a straightforward

---

[30] Cf., for example, Hammond 1959, 185–86: "The Council resisted. It raised the people against Cleomenes and Isagoras, who seized the Acropolis and found themselves besieged"; Ostwald 1969, 144: "The Council refused to be intimidated and, with the support of the common people, besieged the acropolis"; Stanton 1990, 144 n. 6: the council in question must have been the Areopagus, since unlike the councils of 400 or 500, it "would have been sufficiently permanent and would have contained a sufficient accumulation of politically experienced men to organize resistance to a military force. A major thrust was the assembling of the common people . . . and this could have been achieved by the influence which ex-arkhon clan leaders in the Areopagos held over their retainers." The Areopagus leadership theory would need to explain how Cleomenes' force could be strong and decisive enough to "drive out" 700 families dispersed through Attica (cf. Stanton [1990, 141 n. 14], who questions the number 700), but too weak to stop at most 100–200 men (numbers of Areopagites: Wallace 1989, 97 with n. 23; Hansen 1990b—from which we must deduct those expelled with the 700), who were presumably gathered in one place to hear the dissolution order, from organizing a resistance.

[31] Desan 1989.

event with a straightforward subject and object. A. de Sélincourt's Penguin translation is typical: "Cleisthenes . . . took the people into his party." But we need not give the middle form *prosetairizetai* quite such a clearly active force, nor need we imagine it as describing an event that occured in a single moment. I would suggest as an alternate (if inelegant) translation: "Cleisthenes embarked on the process of becoming the demos' trusted comrade."[32] Herodotus' account certainly implies that Cleisthenes had developed a special relationship with the demos *before* his expulsion from Athens. That relationship, which I have suggested above was characterized by proposals or enactments in the Assembly, was evidently the proximate cause of Isagoras' calling in of Cleomenes. But there is no reason to suppose that the process referred to by the verb *prosetairizetai* was completed before Cleisthenes was expelled. In short, I would suggest that Cleisthenes did not so much absorb the demos into his *hetaireia*, as he *himself* was absorbed into an evolving, and no doubt somewhat inchoate, demotic vision of a new society, a society in which distinctions between social statuses would remain but in which there would be no narrow clique of rulers.

The sea change in Athenian political practice implied by Cleisthenes' new relationship with the demos was not signaled by an act of noblesse oblige—opening the doors of the exclusive, aristocratic *hetaireia* to the masses. Rather, it was a revolution in the demos' perception of itself and in an aristocrat's perceptions regarding his own relationship, and that of all men of his class, to the demos. Cleisthenes acknowledged the citizens of Athens as equal sharers in regard to the *nomoi* (laws), and under the banner of *isonomia* the men of the demos became, in effect if not in contemporary nomenclature, Cleisthenes' *hetairoi*.[33] We must remember that Herodotus' terminology is that of the mid-fifth rather than the late sixth century. But in the fifth century, when Herodotus was writing his *Histories*, Athenian *hetairoi* were expected to help one another, and to seek to harm their common enemies. The demos looked out for Cleisthenes' interests by attacking the Spartans and by recalling him immediately upon their departure. Political friendship is a two-way street, and Cleisthenes had no real option other than to look after the interests of the demos by devising and working to implement (through enactments of the Assembly) an institutional framework that would consolidate and stabilize the new demotic vision of politics. That vision had grown up among the Athenian citizen masses in the course of the sixth century and had found an active, physical manifestation in the riot that occurred during Cleisthenes' enforced absence from the scene. The "constitution of Cleisthenes" channeled the en-

---

[32] It is important to keep in mind that the terminology is in any event Herodotus', not Cleisthenes'. It was probably not in use in Cleisthenes' day, and reflects rather the political vocabulary of the mid-fifth century: Chambers 1990, 221.

[33] On *isonomia* and its meaning, see Ober 1989b, 74–75, with literature cited.

ergy of the demos' self-defining riot into a stable and workable form of government.

In sum, Cleisthenes was not so much the authoritative leader of the revolution as he was a highly skilled interpreter of statements made in a revolutionary context and of revolutionary action itself. This is not to deny any of his brilliance, or even his genius. But it is to see his genius *not* in an ability to formulate a prescient vision of a future democratic utopia, *nor* in an ability to hide a selfish dynastic scheme behind a constitutional façade, but rather in his ability to "read"—in a sensitive and perceptive way—the text of Athenian discourse in a revolutionary age, and to recognize that Athenian mass action had created new political facts. Cleisthenes saw that the revolutionary action of the Athenian demos had permanently changed the environment of politics and political discourse. After the revolution there could be no secure recourse to extra-demotic authority. If Athens were to survive as a polis, there would have to be a new basis for politically authoritative speech, but that basis must find its ground in the will of the demos itself. Having read and understood his complex text, Cleisthenes knew that there could be no turning back to rule by aristocratic faction—or at least he saw that any attempt to turn back the clock would bring on a bloodbath and make effective resistance to Sparta impossible. And so, acting as a good *hetairos*, well deserving of the *pistis* (good faith) placed in him (*Athēnaiōn Politeia* 21.1) by his mass *hetaireia*, Cleisthenes came up with a constitutional order that both framed and built upon the revolution that had started without him.

Chapter 5

THE RULES OF WAR IN CLASSICAL GREECE

In 1991 I was invited by Yale University's International Security Program to present a paper as part of a series on the laws of war in historical perspective. I cheated on the assignment, by focusing on Greece rather than on all of classical history. This decision was not (merely) a product of laziness or ignorance of the Roman material; it was driven by a conviction that Greek and Roman cultures operate by very different sets of social rules. The tendency of ancient historians to explain phenomena by reference to a pot-pourri of Greek and Roman material, on the basis of the assumption that both were "classical" (or "traditional Mediterranean") cultures, has caused a good deal of histo-riographical mischief. It is no doubt a fine and pedagogically necessary thing for ancient historians to be fully conversant with both Greek and Roman cultures (among others). But looking at the two classical cultures together is a better source of contrasts than of close comparisons. The insidious effect of translating Michels' "Iron Law" from repub-lican Rome to democratic Athens (Chapter 3) is only one example of the pernicious difficulties that unexamined comparativism can throw up.

I cheated on my assignment a second time by spending very little time on "laws" and devoting most of my attention to less formal "rules" or even "traditional practices" of Greek warfare. Although it would be possible to discuss "internationally recognized" laws dating from the Hellenistic period intended to regulate inter-state violence of var-ious kinds, these agreements seem marginal to the wider project of providing an intro-duction to the Western tradition of inter-state military agreements. Moreover, as is apparent throughout this book, I am less interested in formal laws than I am in informal but socially mandated protocols and rules of behavior. Any study of Greek history that remains exclusively focused on written laws and formal institutions seems to me to miss the heart of matter: the silken web, at once delicate and adamant, of practices, dis-course, and ideology that sustains and (in different contexts) forces rapid and funda-mental changes in culture, state, and society.

The central argument of this chapter is that international rules limiting the practice of warfare are social artifacts produced by a particular social order and a particular structure of social and political power. The rules may, in a sense, benefit society as a whole. More to the point, however, they benefit that particular segment of society capable of mustering the political and social clout adequate to arranging matters in the best interests of its members. In the archaic and early classical periods, the primary

This essay was first published in Michael Howard, George J. Andreopoulos, and Mark R. Shulman, eds., *The Laws of War: Constraints on Warfare in the Western World* (New Haven, Conn.: Yale University Press, 1994), 12–26, 227–30.

beneficiaries of the rules of war were the heavy-armed infantrymen, the hoplites, who did the bulk of the fighting. The rules, for the centuries during which they pertained, limited casualties among the hoplites and ensured that the "middling" hoplite class remained the gravitational center of Greek society. The form of political organization associated with the domination of the hoplite class is oligarchical, that is to say, citizenship was defined by a property qualification—albeit a given oligarchy may be quite open and the property qualifications for citizenship low enough to assure a large percentage of the adult, free, male population will enjoy the privileges of citizenship. But this system depends for its stability on a significant degree of exclusivity, on the systematic exclusion of some native free males from the ranks of the hoplite-citizens. Thus a hoplite society cannot be a democratic society in Greek terms.

The second part of the essay suggests that the development of true democracy in Athens was eventually fatal to the regime of "war by the rules." And so, once again, we may speak of an Athenian revolution—but in this case the consequences are considerably less appealing than those discussed in the previous chapter. A detailed argument linking the growth of democracy with the collapse of the hoplite regime was recently made by Victor Hanson (1995 and 1996), to whom I am indebted for many discussions, over many years, of the issues under consideration here. Unlike Hanson, however, who argues that democracy subverted the hoplite ethos and was structurally incompatible with a rule-oriented international military order, I focus on the impact of a specific decision of the Athenian democracy: the decision to abandon Attica to invaders in 431 B.C. and thereby to refuse the Peloponnesian challenge to battle in the opening round of the Peloponnesian-Athenian War. The political background to this momentous decision is discussed at greater length in Chapter 6.

My tendency to seek out and analyze a particular event that is associated with a particular historical figure who is arguably less an agent than a conduit of change, and that is made possible by a long series of prior ideological and institutional adjustments, and that precipitates a dramatic shift in sociopolitical order generally, has obvious affinities with the interpretive strategy developed in Chapter 4. There are other contested points of interpretation that arise here: Was the hoplite class a true "middle class"? Did the hoplite ideology of the archaic period remain in any meaningful sense "dominant" in democratic Athens? Were "subhoplites" (*thētes*) at Athens regarded (by themselves or others) as somehow marginal figures, as less than full citizens? Was the development of the Athenian empire and navy the primary and necessary cause of the development of full democracy of the fifth century? My answer in each case is "no" (see, further, Ober 1996); but compare, for example, Raaflaub (1996b and c) and Strauss (1996) for other points of view.

The essay concludes on a rather mixed note: the possibility that the development of democracy, rather than limiting violence (as the Kantian Enlightenment tradition would have it), could actually result in a dramatic increase in the level of military violence is surely a sobering one for any sincere democrat. And yet, once again, the remarkable fact of Athenian fourth-century social and political stability comes into play: unlike fragile oligarchic regimes that proved unable to adapt to the volatile and unforgiving new military environment of the post–Peloponnesian War world, the Athenian democracy proved capable of meeting the challenge—at least until new forms of military organization and technology were developed in Macedon by King Philip II and his corps of engineers.

The relationship of warfare and military organization to classical Greek social structure in general and to Athenian democracy in particular remains a fruitful area for research. It has received a good deal of attention of late; in addition to the studies noted above, see van Wees (1992, 1994) and Cartledge (forthcoming).

WHEN APPROACHING the subject of agreements regulating the conduct of inter-state warfare, it is important to separate the relatively informal, socially mandated and enforced "rules" of war from legally enacted "laws" of war.[1] Here, my emphasis will be on the former, since there is little evidence that the archaic and classical Greeks enacted internationally recognized laws governing the practice of warfare. There are only two real candidates for long-term, formal, sworn agreements intended to control the form taken by armed conflict among the mainland Greek states. First, a tradition reported by the geographer Strabo (10.448) claims that in the course of the War of the Lelantine Plain on the island of Euboea in about 700 B.C., the contending parties (including most of the big states) agreed to ban the use of projectile missiles. A second tradition, mentioned by the orator Aeschines (2.115), suggests that after the so-called First Sacred War (fought over control of the oracle of Delphi) of about 600 B.C., the victorious states swore never again to cut off besieged fellow Greeks from food or water. Upon examination both traditions look very dubious—the supposed covenants are reported only by relatively late sources, and they were certainly not always honored in practice.[2] Moreover, despite the existence of the Amphyctionic League (an "international" organization of Greek peoples that regulated the affairs of Delphi), there is no evidence for the Greek development of what H. L. Hart called "first order" rules regarding military conduct—that is to say, no organized procedure for enacting the laws that might govern inter-state warfare.[3] In the absence of securely attested and formal "second order" laws (actual sworn covenants), and without evidence for first order rules by which such covenants might have been devised, there is not much to say about classical Greek laws regarding general military conduct.

---

[1] Describing rules as informal does not, of course, mean that they were easily ignored, nor does legal enactment guarantee conformity in practice. General treatments of the problem include Ducrey 1968, 288–301; Vernant 1968, 18–22; de Romilly 1968, 207–20; Garlan 1975, 23–77; Karavites 1982; Ducrey 1985, 280–82; Connor 1988, 3–27.

[2] See Wheeler 1987, 157–82.

[3] Hart 1961.

On the other hand, Greek combatants did recognize a number of rules of engagement, and these rules do seem to have been normative in that their breach could occasion indignant comments in our sources. The rules of war, which in the late fifth century were sometimes referred to as "the common customs (*koina nomima*) of the Hellenes" (Thuc. 3.59.1, 6.4.5; cf. Eur. *Heraclidae* 1010), range from what might be called neoformal rules to practices conditioned largely by practicality. There was in antiquity no canonical list of "the rules." But the following, in descending order of formality, seem to me to sum up the most important of the unwritten conventions governing inter-state conflict:[4]

1. The state of war should be officially declared before commencing hostilities against an appropriate foe; sworn treaties and alliances should be regarded as binding.
2. Hostilities are sometimes inappropriate: sacred truces, especially those declared for the celebration of the Olympic games, should be observed.
3. Hostilities against certain persons and in certain places are inappropriate: the inviolability of sacred places and persons under protection of the gods, especially heralds and suppliants, should be respected.
4. Erecting a battlefield trophy indicates victory; such trophies should be respected.
5. After a battle, it is right to return enemy dead when asked; to request the return of one's dead is tantamount to admitting defeat.
6. A battle is properly prefaced by a ritual challenge and acceptance of the challenge.
7. Prisoners of war should be offered for ransom, not summarily executed or mutilated.
8. Punishment of surrendered opponents should be restrained.
9. War is an affair of warriors, thus noncombatants should not be primary targets of attack.
10. Battles should be fought during the usual (summer) campaigning season.
11. Use of nonhoplite arms should be limited.
12. Pursuit of defeated and retreating opponents should be limited in duration.

I will risk asserting, as a broad generalization, that most of these informal rules were followed, most of the time, in intra-Greek warfare of about 700 to 450 B.C. The main problem in proving this assertion is the very lacunary nature of our sources for the practice of intra-Greek warfare in the seventh and sixth centuries. But when the evidence is assembled, as it has been by W. K. Prit-

---

[4] Rule 1: Adcock and Mosley 1975. Rules 2–4: Garlan 1975, 57–64; Ducrey 1968, 295–304; Pritchett 1971–92, 2:246–75; Lonis 1979; Karavites 1982; Goodman and Holladay 1986, 151–71; Ducrey 1985, 271–75. Rule 5: Garlan 1975, 61. Rule 6: Pritchett 1971–92, 2:147–55. Rules 7–8: Ducrey 1968, noting (334–36) that the Peloponnesian War was a watershed. Rules 9–12: Hanson 1989, esp. 15–18, 25–26, 177–84.

chett and Victor Hanson, the impression of a relatively clear set of rules is strong.

There is more evidence to back up my next two assertions: First, rules of war pertained primarily in intra-Hellenic conflicts (rather than in wars between Greeks and non-Hellenes). And second, these rules, especially numbers 5–12, tended to break down in the period 450 to 300 B.C.[5] The bulk of this essay is devoted to investigating the implications of the premise that the three assertions are correct: that the informal rules of war listed above did in fact pertain among Greeks before the mid-fifth century, that they were developed in the context of intra-Greek warfare, and that "war by the rules" was considerably less common after the mid-fifth century B.C.

If we assume that the rules of war listed above did once pertain in mainland Greece, we may ask in whose interest the rules were developed and maintained. Raising the question of interest seems valid, in that any argument that assumes that a universal sense of fair play and decency was an innate part of early Greek military culture is easily falsified. Even a casual reading of Homer's *Iliad* makes it clear that some of the rules of war I have listed were not deeply rooted in Homeric society. The warriors of the *Iliad* do indeed show some respect for sworn truces and for the sacrosanctity of heralds, but otherwise the conventions of Homeric warfare are quite different. Achilles' brutal treatment of his fallen enemy, Hector, may be an extreme, but one can cite, for example, the night raid of Odysseus and Diomedes, culminating in Diomedes' cold-blooded execution of the war prisoner Dolon and slaughter of sleeping men (10.454–97). Use of projectile weapons (spears, arrows, rocks) is key to the action in the *Iliad*; pursuit of retreating enemies is vigorous and savage. There is no campaigning season, and no formal distinction between Hellene and barbarian. Homeric society is at least partly a poetic fiction, but I think that one can safely assume that most of the Hellenic rules of war with which we are concerned crystallized in a historical era after the Homeric epics were written down, that is to say, after the mid- to late eighth century B.C. If this is right, then the Greek rules regarding the proper conduct of warfare were presumably formulated in the course of the seventh century—the age in which Greek warfare came to be dominated by the highly organized formation of massed heavy infantry known as the hoplite phalanx. And thus, it is reasonable to seek an answer to the *cui bono* question among the ranks of the hoplites themselves.[6]

---

[5] Greek versus non-Greek warfare: Lonis (1969), in a thorough review of the evidence, points out that the practice of war between Greeks and "barbarians" need not necessarily have been more brutal than that between Greeks, but offers abundant evidence for breaches in the rules, especially during the Persian Wars of 490–478 and the wars between the western Greeks and the Carthaginians. Cf. Ducrey 1985, 271–83. Breakdown after 450: Ober 1985a, 32–50, and 1985b.

[6] Homeric warfare: Kirk 1968, 93–117; van Wees 1988, 1–24. Date of *Iliad*: Easterling and Knox 1985, 42–51. Although some sort of mass fighting surely antedates the "hoplite reform" of the early seventh century, it seems to me to go too far to claim (as does Pritchett [1974–91, 4:44])

Who were the hoplites? Or, more precisely: Who *could be* a hoplite and how was the class of "the hoplites" defined? The answer varied somewhat over time, and from polis to polis. But the simple answer is that an adult free male could be a hoplite if he could afford the capital investment in the appropriate arms and armor, and could afford to spend a good part of the summer marching about the countryside and fighting when called upon to do so. The typical hoplite was an independent subsistence farmer: a man who owned enough land—perhaps ten or fifteen acres—to support himself and his family without the need for family members to work for wages on a regular basis. At Athens, the polis for which our evidence is best, in 594 B.C. the reformer Solon distributed political privileges hierarchically among four economic classes. Membership in each class was determined on the basis of annual agricultural production. Those in the top class must be able to demonstrate that their farms could generate 500 standard units of produce. Membership in the second class of "cavalrymen" required 300 units. The third class, requiring a minimum of 200 units, was dubbed the *zeugitai*, or yokemen. This third census group is the Athenian equivalent of the hoplite class—its members were probably called yokemen either because they were metaphorically yoked together in the phalanx or because they could afford a yoke of oxen. Both etymologies (whether right or wrong) are appropriate: the hoplites were in essence yoked together when they marched in the phalanx, since each hoplite soldier depended upon the men next to him in the line as surely as an ox depended upon its yokemate. And the minimum size of a moderately successful independent farm was probably about the size of holding at which keeping a yoke of oxen for plowing and other hard labor was economically feasible—roughly ten or eleven acres.[7]

How large was the hoplite class as a percentage of the total free (male) population? The simple answer would usually be "a substantial minority." Basic infantryman's equipment was not outrageously expensive.[8] Given the frequency of conflict in Greece and the dominance of phalanx tactics, every Greek state had a vested interest in maximizing the pool of heavy infantrymen, and hence it was counterproductive to deny those who could afford hoplite armor and weapons the opportunity to use them. In the period of the battles of Marathon and Plataea (490, 479 B.C.) Athens could field some 9,000 hoplites, which represented perhaps a fifth to a third of its free adult males.[9] Assuming

---

that the equipment changes of the seventh century had no significant impact on the techniques of battle or on Greek society. Evolution of hoplite equipment and the phalanx: Hanson 1991, 63–84.

[7] Solonian classes: Whitehead 1981, 282–86. Plot size and draught animals: Ober 1985a, 19–23. The unit of measurement (*medimnos*) is equivalent to about 1.5 bushels. The actual yield of an average hoplite farm would not have been anywhere near 200 bushels of grain, but the figures were meant to refer to total "wet and dry" yield, including olive oil, wine, and perhaps other sorts of produce as well.

[8] Cost of armor: Jackson 1991, 229: at least thirty drachmas in the late sixth century.

[9] In 479 the Athenians fielded 8,000 hoplites at Plataea, at a time when a good number of

that the sociological distribution of Athens' preimperial-era population was not radically atypical of central and southern Greek norms, we may suppose that in the period 700 to 450 B.C. hoplites typically represented roughly 20 to 40 percent of a Greek polis' free adult males. The hoplite class (including here the families of the hoplites themselves) would thus have represented a minority of a Greek city-state's total population: an elite indeed, but not a tiny or particularly exclusive elite. Moreover, when speaking of hoplites, we must use the term "class" with some care: the heavy infantry did not represent an economically homogeneous group, and the relationship of individual hoplites to the economic mode of production will have varied. Although in some poleis (e.g., Athens) the very wealthiest citizens served in the cavalry, in every polis, some hoplites were considerably wealthier than others.[10] Rich hoplites in many poleis undoubtedly employed slaves in working their estates. Others depended on occasional employment of wage laborers. Those at the bottom of the group depended primarily on the labor of draught animals and family members. Only a very few of the richest hoplites will have avoided the necessity of working their land with their own hands.

Phalanx warfare evolved rapidly in the early seventh century B.C.; it was soon fully institutionalized as the dominant mode of violent dispute resolution between the Greek poleis. And it was the hoplites themselves, as a relatively broad-based social elite, who benefited most from the rules of warfare that had evolved in the course of the seventh century. These informal rules ensured that it was the heavy infantrymen who dominated intra-Greek military encounters (rather than the wealthier cavalrymen, poorer light-armed skirmishers, or more specialized archers and slingers). During the archaic and early classical periods, the Greek way of war, which placed the heavy infantry in the center of the action, supported and reinforced the privileged social position of the hoplite class vis-à-vis the very rich and the poor. Because their arms determined the outcome of military encounters, the hoplite class occupied a clearly defined middle ground between the small elite of leisured aristocrats and the majority of males who were unable to afford hoplite equipment. Although it is dangerously anachronistic to speak of a self-conscious Greek "middle class," the hoplites, as a well-defined social group, staked out a broad and central position in polis society, and their social centrality had clear political ramifications.

Athenian hoplites were serving as marines on the Athenian triremes (Hdt. 9.28.6, 8.131). Athenian demography in the period of the Persian Wars: Labarbe 1957, 199–211; in general, Hansen 1985. It is important to remember that slaves were also part of the society, and in some poleis (e.g., Sparta) the nonfree population was a very significant part of the total population. The total size of the Athenian slave population is unknown, but I doubt it was very large before or after the wealthy imperial period of the mid- to late fifth century; see Wood 1988. Sallares (1991, 53–60) has recently argued that the slave population of Attica was only about 20,000, about one-sixth that of the citizen (native-born adult males and their families) population.

[10] Athenian cavalry: Bugh 1988.

If we view the world from the perspective of the hoplite class, we can see how the practice of warfare limited the influence of both the very rich and the poor. The rich men who served in the cavalry gained thereby an opportunity to display their wealth in a conspicuous fashion—but their role in battle was limited to scouting and protecting the flanks of the phalanx. The free poor and the unfree (whether slaves or helots) were relegated to a largely logistical role in times of war: they could carry the gear of the fighters, but were not effective fighters themselves. Because traditional Greek ideology strongly linked social and political status with the ability to fight in defense of family and community, the leisure class often found it difficult to impose a political order exclusively dominated by the very rich. By the same token, the poor and unfree could "legitimately" be excluded from political participation and various social privileges. In short, the practice of hoplite warfare tended to define the limits of, but also to undergird, the social and political hierarchies of the Greek polis.[11]

On the other hand, the experience of the phalanx helped to promote an egalitarian ethos within the ranks of the hoplites themselves. The rich hoplite might have prettier armor, a fancier crest, and a more highly decorated shield than the struggling farmer of ten acres who stood next to him in the line, but the two men used offensive weapons that were virtually identical, and each was utterly dependent upon the other in matters of defense. Steadfastness was the primary virtue of the hoplite warrior. In times of combat, it was equally disruptive to the all-important cohesion of the phalanx to leap out in front of the line or flinch back from it. The goal of the phalanx was complete homogeneity of effort. Men who were economic unequals were thus equalized in combat, and this egalitarian habit translated from battlefield to polis life. Hoplite egalitarianism reached its apogee in classical Sparta, where the educational, sociocultural, economic, and political systems all emphasized the complete homogenization of a hoplite class that was coextensive with the citizenry.[12]

Although few Greek poleis took either hierarchy or egalitarianism to Spartan extremes, hoplite warfare was an important structural element in late archaic and early classical Greek society in that it reified existing lines of social distinction (especially between independent farmers and poor laborers) and at the same time promoted social and political equality within the ranks of the upper third or so of polis society. The socially constructed and socially maintained rules of war buttressed this social system. Each of the rules numbered 5–12 above helped to maintain the long-term practical workability of the hoplite-dominated sociomilitary system: Since to request one's dead was to admit defeat, and that

[11] Role of cavalry in battle: Bugh 1988, 35–38; Spence 1993; see also Chapter 6. In the fifth century at Athens the state supported the rich cavalryman with a financial subsidy for his cavalry mount: Bugh 1988, index s.v. *katastasis*. Link in Greek ideology between fighting for one's land and citizenship: Vidal-Naquet 1986, 94–99.

[12] Methods of fighting: Hanson 1989, passim. Sparta: Cartledge 1977, 11–23.

request could not legitimately be refused by the victors, the outcome of a single battle was generally regarded by both sides as decisive, at least for a season. Thus wars tended to be brief affairs that could be fought effectively by "amateur" farmer-soldiers. The rituals of challenge to battle and acceptance of the challenge, the limitation of combat to a short campaigning season, and the limited use of nonhoplite arms lessened the impact of war on farm lands, and ensured that only appropriate "players" took key roles on the field of battle. Generally lenient treatment of defeated enemies, the ransoming of prisoners of war, and the lack of determined pursuit of retreating soldiers kept casualties within an acceptable range. The ideologically significant ritual of the battle could thus be performed quite frequently (and thus its social impact could be maximized) without risking demographic catastrophe for the participants.[13]

It is perhaps in the relative uninvolvement of noncombatants in late archaic and early classical Greek warfare that the social bases of the rules of hoplite combat are manifested most clearly. Traditional hoplite war is in essence warfare without strategy: the aim of each phalanx was to engage the other phalanx head-on. This ritualized (although genuinely violent and bloody) form of conflict was efficient in that it determined which side was superior quickly and decisively. Although tactical maneuvering, or even trickery, might be employed in the attempt to fight from the most advantageous position, the goal of each side remained simple: to meet the enemy soldiers in an open battle. This was not the only way the Greeks could have chosen to fight. The hierarchical society of the polis offered a seemingly obvious target for a strategy based on sociopolitical subversion. Those who were disadvantaged by the Greek social system (the unfree and subhoplite populations) represented a potential Achilles' heel for many poleis; revolts by Sparta's helot population demonstrated just how willing the oppressed might be to turn against their masters. Invaders who persuaded the poor and unfree to fight their oppressors, or simply to withhold their labor inputs (most obviously by running away), would severely hamper their opponents' war effort. Yet until well into the Peloponnesian War, the strategy of encouraging discontent among the enemy's lower social strata was not employed. It is hardly necessary to point out that Greeks were both inventive and capable of serious analytical thought. But in Greece, as in other human societies, innovation was channeled by social priorities. Until the last third of the fifth century, strategies based on attacking the enemy's social and economic system were effectively "banned" by the informal rules of war—rules that thereby further reinforced the existing social order.[14]

[13] Limited damage to crop land: Hanson 1983. Casualty rates: Krentz 1985a, 13–20. Krentz's figures may be actually be too high since they necessarily derive from well-attested "great battles" in which casualties were probably atypically high.

[14] War without strategy: Hanson 1989, 19–26; Ober 1991d, 173–96. On Sparta's vulnerability to helot insurgency, see the exchange by Talbert 1989, 22–40; and Cartledge 1991, 379–85. Use of social disruption strategies in Peloponnesian War: Ober 1985a, 35–37.

Between about 700 and about 450 B.C., intra-Greek wars were fought by fellow participants in what we might fairly call the hoplite-centered social order. Because of constraints imposed by the rules of war, these conflicts rarely became a matter of a polis' national survival. It was a very different matter when Greeks fought non-Greeks. In the best-documented series of "Greek-barbarian" conflicts, the Persian Wars of 490–478 B.C., the issue for many poleis was national survival, and the Persian invaders were not participants in the sociomilitary system I have sketched out above. Although the Greek defenders at Marathon and Plataea used hoplite formations against the numerically superior Persian forces, they did not employ the ordinary norms of intra-Greek combat. In their conflict with the Persians, the Greeks summarily executed heralds (Hdt. 7.133), and offered no formal challenge to battle or exchange of war dead. Retreating Persian soldiers were pursued relentlessly and slaughtered in their thousands at Marathon, and most of the Persian survivors of the battle of Plataea were massacred after the Athenians successfully stormed their camp. Greek conduct during the Persian Wars demonstrates clearly the essentially voluntary nature of the rules of intra-Greek conflict and points to the possibility of a voluntary defection from those rules.[15]

In the century after about 450 B.C.—and especially during the Peloponnesian War of 431–404 B.C.—the informal Greek rules of war broke down. Thucydides' history of the Peloponnesian War demonstrates how the rules listed above were violated in the course of the long and drawn-out conflict—for example, in executions of enemy ambassadors, seamen, and allied troops (by both Athens and Sparta), and in massacres of captured prisoners of war: Thebans by Plataeans in 431, Plataeans by Thebans and Spartans in 427, Melians by Athenians in 415, Athenians by Syracusans in 413. The last of these atrocities was set up by a sustained strategic pursuit of the Athenian army by Syracusan forces. But perhaps the most striking departure from previous practice was the conscious employment of systematic pressure on the enemy's social system: In 425 the Athenians threatened the internal stability of Sparta by constructing a military base at Pylos in Messenia from which they encouraged helot insurrection. The Spartans eventually responded with a permanent base at Decelea in Attica, precipitating the flight of over 20,000 Athenian slaves. Although hoplite-phalanx battles were still being fought, and some of the old rules still honored in specific circumstances, the general structure of "war by the rules" was shattered in the late fifth century and never effectively reconstructed thereafter.[16]

The question that confronts us, then, is why the socially stabilizing system of war by the rules fell apart. Although prodromic symptoms of the breakdown

---

[15] Marathon: Hdt. 6.113–17; Pausanias 1.15.4, 1.32.6. Plataea: Hdt. 9.70.4–5.

[16] War atrocities: Thuc. 2.67.4, 3.32.1, 2.5.7, 3.68, 5.116.4, 7.86–87; sustained pursuit by Syracusans: Thuc. 7.72–85. Pylos: Thuc. 4.3–41; Decelea: Thuc. 7.19–28.

can be detected well before 431, the great Peloponnesian War fought by the hegemonic alliances led by Sparta and Athens is clearly implicated. As Thucydides points out in the introduction to his history (1.1, 1.23.1–3), this was a war unlike any that had been fought on Greek soil. Thucydides implies that at the outbreak of the war, Sparta (with its agricultural, helot-based economy) was the quintessential hoplite power and Athens was a very nontraditional naval power. The Spartans entered the war expecting a typical conflict that would be decided by phalanx battles fought according to the usual rules. The Athenians had something rather different in mind. Thus it is to Athens that we must turn in attempting to understand why it was that the system of war by the rules failed to survive the fifth century B.C.[17]

In the mid-fifth century, the polis of Athens was exceptional in several ways. Very big by mainland Greek standards at about 1,000 square miles and with an adult male citizen population of at least 40,000 to 50,000, Athens was a preeminent naval power and controlled a great Aegean empire. Moreover, Athens was a democracy. A series of revolutionary political reforms, initiated in the sixth century and largely complete by 450 B.C., had resulted in the evolution of a startlingly original form of direct government "by the people." Key political decisions in Athens—including all matters of state finance and foreign policy—were made in open and frequent Assemblies at which every citizen had an equal vote. Legal matters were decided by people's courts staffed by large juries of ordinary citizens. Most government officials were chosen by lot; a few—including the generals—were elected to renewable annual terms of office. Leaders (including the redoubtable Pericles) maintained their positions by demonstrating ability in handling financial and military affairs and by rhetorical skill in public debates. The existence at Athens of the political system of democracy had important social ramifications. In Athens all citizens, regardless of their property holdings, regardless of whether or not they could afford hoplite armor, were political equals in that each Athenian's vote in the Assembly and lawcourt was of equal weight. Because the relatively poor (those who could not afford hoplite arms) were in the majority and had developed a sophisticated consciousness of their own place in Athenian politics, the political center of gravity at Athens was lower than in nondemocratic poleis. And this low center of political gravity gave Athens remarkable stability.[18]

Athens' democratic political culture meant that the implicit social contract between economic classes of natives—foreign-born slaves and resident aliens were another matter—was based on premises very different from those assumed in the typical "hoplite-centered" polis. Social inequality as a result of

---

[17] Compare de Ste. Croix (1972), who places the blame for the war squarely on Sparta. Whether or not one accepts this verdict, de Ste. Croix's book is a superb collection of the sources and modern scholarship.

[18] Ober 1989b, esp. 53–95.

differential access to economic assets certainly remained, but Athenian society (that is, the society of adult, free males) was much less hierarchical than that of other poleis. The formal equality of citizens, along with the practice of democratic politics in the Assembly and courtroom, served to unify the Athenian citizenry across the boundaries of economic class—in much the same way that the mutual interdependence of the hoplites in the phalanx unified the hoplite class elsewhere. The difference, of course, is that the Athenian citizenry (citizens and their families) was a much larger percentage of the total population.

In part as a direct consequence of democratic ideology, the hoplites were considerably less self-consciously a "class" in Athens than they were in other, nondemocratic poleis, and Athenian society was not dependent for its stability on maintenance of a stable hoplite ideology. This blurring of the lines between the hoplites and the poorer citizens of Athens can be traced in the aftermath of the oligarchic coup of 411 B.C. The Athenian hoplites played a key role in overthrowing the narrow oligarchy of the Four Hundred, and they participated in the establishment of a new government in which full citizenship would be limited to the hoplite class. This so-called Constitution of the Five Thousand earned Thucydides' praise (8.97.2), but it never jelled into a stable government. Within a few months, Athens had evolved back into a full democracy—the Athenian hoplites simply did not have an adequate sense of themselves as a distinct group to sustain a form a government based on hoplite identity. The role of the hoplite class in the maintenance of social stability at Athens was further undercut in the early to mid-fifth century by the burgeoning importance of the Athenian navy. The rise of the navy was contemporary with the flowering of Athenian democracy. The creation of a major naval force in the mid-480s, at the behest of the politician and general Themistocles, allowed Athens to play a central role in the defeat of the Persians at Salamis in 480 B.C., and subsequently led to Athens' hegemony over the Delian League—a coalition of Aegean coastal and island states organized after the defeat of the Persians. With the evolution of the Delian League into an Athenian empire in the second quarter of the fifth century, the navy became the key arm of Athens' military forces. As Aristotle later recognized, the growth of Athenian naval power was linked to the development of democracy because traditional Greek ideology linked the value of the citizen to his role in the defense of the state. The trireme warships of Athens were rowed largely by citizens who could not afford hoplite armor—as the navy's role became increasingly decisive for Athens' position in the Greek world, the poorer citizens took a correspondingly larger role in the governance of the state.[19]

I suggested above that in many Greek poleis the informal rules of warfare aided in the survival of the hoplite class and abetted its social and political

---

[19] The constitution of the Five Thousand: Harris 1990, 243–80, with literature cited. Importance of the navy to democracy: Ober 1989b, 83–84.

dominance. In terms of military conventions, a key result of the conjoined development of democratic political culture and the navy at Athens was the social and political displacement of the Athenian hoplites. The mass of ordinary citizens, rather than the hoplite class, now defined Athens' political and military center of gravity. As a result, Athens' social structure was no longer fundamentally dependent on a continued adherence to the hoplite ideology—nor to the rules of war that sustained that ideology. The interests of the hoplite class no longer determined either the general direction or the specific decisions of Athenian internal and foreign policy. And so by the mid-fifth century the Athenians could afford to break the rules of war. Their unique social system meant that the Athenians need not fear social instability as a result of this breach of convention, and their unique political system meant that men with a primary stake in maintaining the rules were no longer in charge.

Democratic government at Athens led to the formation of an implicit social contract that integrated the interests of middling and poorer citizens and so allowed Athens' extraordinarily large manpower resources to be safely and efficiently deployed in naval operations. This factor proved to be of key importance in the creation and maintenance of Athens' overseas empire. By 450 B.C., Athens was a major imperial power, controlling some 160 subject states— this was the first (and only) really successful empire run by a Greek polis. Whatever the subjects of the empire may have thought about their position, the empire was run for Athens' profit, and the financial resources that accrued to Athens as a result of hegemony were enormous by Greek standards.[20] By the date of the outbreak of the Peloponnesian War, Athens had amassed a large strategic financial reserve—and as Thucydides points out (1.141.2– 1.142.1), that cash reserve had a decided bearing on how Athens chose to fight the war with Sparta. Traditionally, Greek wars were decided quickly, usually by a single battle. No Greek state dominated by the hoplite class would desire (or could afford) a long, indecisive conflict.[21] But democratic, imperial Athens could. Once again, unique circumstances, linked to the existence of the democracy, naval power, and empire, rendered the traditional rules of war irrelevant to the Athenians.

So far, I have laid out the structural factors that made it *possible* for Athens to ignore the rules of war. But I do not suppose that just because this approach had become *possible* it was in any sense *inevitable*. Before the possibility could become an actuality, someone had to see that recent developments had enabled a new approach to war, had to come up with a concrete operational plan, and had to persuade the Athenians to go along with the plan. That someone was Pericles. The two Periclean Assembly speeches in Thucydides'

---

[20] Athenian empire: Meiggs 1972.

[21] The focus of hoplite warfare on decisive battle is the central thesis of Hanson 1989.

history, along with Thucydides' own comments, make it clear that Pericles had in fact devised a strategic plan for fighting the Peloponnesian War.[22]

The conflict Pericles foresaw was that of a land power against a sea power, and on the face of it the land power seemed to hold the advantage. In a traditional war by the rules, Sparta and its allies would march into Athenian territory; the smaller, less highly trained Athenian phalanx would meet the invader's challenge by marching out into the open fields, and would be defeated. The Athenian navy would never become a factor in the conflict, and Athens would have lost the war in the first year. Not liking the implications of this scenario, Pericles determined to change it. His plan was simple and radical: since the Spartans would win a war that was fought according to the traditional Hellenic rules of engagement, Pericles reasoned that Athens might be able to win by opting out of the rules. This was a key moment in the history of Greek warfare in that it was the beginning of truly sophisticated long-term strategic analysis. Rather than worrying about the tactical problem of how to win a particular battle, Pericles thought through the interplay of a variety of forces—military, financial, political, and psychological—over the course of a war that he knew would take several years at least. He had, in essence, invented grand strategy.

The key to success, in Pericles' plan, was for the Athenian land army to avoid engagement with the Peloponnesian army: when Sparta invaded Attica, the Athenian hoplites must refuse the ritual challenge to battle and remain barricaded behind Athens' walls. Without an army of defenders to fight, the Spartan-Peloponnesian phalanx would be rendered impotent. The invaders would not risk assaulting the walls. Nor was Sparta likely to attempt a siege of the city-Piraeus complex: this would require a huge counter-wall, and the Peloponnesians could not spare the manpower to hold it. Finally, the Spartans could not hope to starve the Athenians out; Athens' empire provided the revenues, and its Long Walls and its warships security. Athenian merchantmen would resupply the city-fortress from grain markets in Egypt and south Russia. Given Athens' clear naval superiority, deep financial reserves, and independence from the hoplite ideology, the defensive side of Pericles' strategy was thoroughly rational.[23]

But how was Athens to defeat Sparta? The Spartan center of gravity—in military, social, and political terms alike—was the hoplite-citizenry of the Peloponnese, and Athens' navy could not threaten these men directly. An indirect approach might be more productive. Sparta's hoplite class lived from the surplus generated by the oppressed and potentially restive helots of Laconia and Messenia. With Sparta distracted by helot revolts, the Peloponnesians would

---

[22] Thuc. 1.140–44, 2.60–65.
[23] Pericles' strategy: see Chapter 6.

be stymied. In the event, although a series of naval raids was launched against the Peloponnesian coasts, Athens established no base in Spartan territory during the first six years of the war. It seems likely that despite his radical decision to ignore some of the traditional conventions of engagement, Pericles foresaw no need for a wholesale abandonment of the rules of war. His initial offensive goal was probably a limited one: control of Megara, a small city-state whose territory lay north of the Isthmus of Corinth and west of Attica. Megara was strategically located across the land routes from the Peloponnese into central Greece. The passes through the Megarian mountains were defensible: the Athenians had set up the battle of Tanagra by occupying the Megarian passes in 458 B.C. If Athens could permanently control the Megarian passes, the Spartans would be bottled up in the Peloponnese, and Athens would have a free hand in central and northern Greece. Thus, Pericles aimed at the containment, rather than the overthrow, of Sparta: an extension to the mainland of the operational plan that had worked well in the Aegean against the Persians since 478. And containment of Sparta, he believed, could be achieved by a limited withdrawal from the conventions of hoplite warfare.[24]

When the Peloponnesian army arrived in Attica late in the summer of 431 B.C., Pericles' war plan was put into effect: the Athenians evacuated the country districts, took up residence in the city, and refused battle with the Peloponnesian army. The invaders were stymied and left Attica a few weeks later, having accomplished virtually nothing. Once the Spartans and their allies were safely back in the Peloponnese, Pericles sent the Athenian land army into Megarian territory, where it ravaged Megara's small agricultural plain. If this pattern had kept up for a few years, all might have gone as Pericles had planned. Eventually, the Spartans would have become frustrated with their meaningless incursions; eventually the Megarians, with their access to Aegean trade cut off by the Athenian fleet and their agriculture disrupted annually, would have been forced to submit to Athens.[25]

But of course that was not the way it actually worked out. A devastating plague reduced Athenian manpower, imperial subjects became restless, Athenian generals turned to the strategy of social disruption, and their Spartan counterparts proved equally capable of employing innovative strategies of social subversion and economic coercion. In the end, the Athenians lost because the Spartans realized that the war could be won by expanding the theater of operations and their own resource base. Persian subsidies allowed Spartan admirals to launch attacks on the states of Athens' empire, to threaten the overseas grain routes, and to challenge the navy that guarded the empire and

---

[24] Raids into the Peloponnese: Westlake 1945, 75–84. The Megara strategy: Wick 1979, 1–14.

[25] The first year of the war and its events: Thuc. 2.1–33, with Kagan 1974, 43–69.

the sea lanes. By the end of the war, the Spartans had proved just as willing to ignore the customs of engagement as their opponents were, and the old regime of war "by the rules" was a dead letter.[26]

Cut free from traditional constraints, a new style of warfare developed rapidly in the fourth century B.C. Although hoplite-phalanx battles were still fought (witness, for example, the battles of Nemea, Leuctra, and Mantinea), intra-Greek conflicts were no longer limited in duration, there was no fixed campaigning season, and the combatants were less frequently citizen-hoplites. The employment of mercenaries, often highly specialized light-armed fighters, meant that the pursuit and annihilation of defeated enemies became more common. Noncombatants were increasingly the targets and victims of strategies based on social disruption and destruction of economic resources.[27]

The new style of combat had considerable impact on Greek society. The practice of war now tended to undermine, rather than support, the existing social order of many poleis. With the abandonment of the rules of conflict that had undergirded it, the old hoplite ideology lost its coherence; the center could no longer hold. Without the mediating factor of the political and social dominance of the hoplite class, the underlying conflicts between rich and poor escalated more easily into bloody internecine conflict. Moreover, the strategies of economic coercion employed by fourth-century armies produced serious economic dislocations and widespread impoverishment. And thus the new warfare contributed materially to the wave of civil wars that wracked so many Greek poleis in the late fifth and fourth centuries—the conditions that Thucydides (3.69–85) described as pertaining in Corcyra in 427 B.C. became a recurrent theme in the history of many Greek states.

Paradoxically, Athens, the state whose policies appear to have done most to precipitate the breakdown of the traditional rules of war, exhibited extraordinary social and political stability in the decades after the end of the Peloponnesian War.[28] Once again, the explanation can be sought in Athens' well-developed and resilient democratic political culture. Since Athens did not depend on the hoplite ideology for the maintenance of social order, the collapse of that ideology had few directly adverse effects on the polis. Just as, in the second half of the fifth century, the existence of the democracy had made a break with the traditional rules conceivable, so, too, in the fourth century the democracy allowed Athens to weather the social storms generated by war without rules. And so, despite the traumatic loss of the Peloponnesian War, by the mid-fourth century the Athenians found themselves in much better shape than their victorious rivals, Sparta and Thebes—poleis whose social and politi-

---

[26] Spartan innovations in the Decelean War: Thuc. 1.19–28, 8.5–44; Xen. *Hellenica* 1.1.1–1.6.38, 2.1.1–2.2.23; Plut. *Lysander.* Cf. Kagan 1987.

[27] New warfare of the fourth century: Ober 1985a, 37–50, and 1989a.

[28] Athenian stability: Ober 1989b, 17–20.

cal regimes were intimately bound up in what I have been calling the hoplite ideology.

Finally, what of the relationship of the Greek rules of war and military technology? When compared to modern society, the ancient Greek world was notoriously nontechnological. There is, however, one area in which the Greeks did demonstrate considerable technological inventiveness: siege weaponry and its defensive corollary, military architecture. The link of military technology with the rules of war is quite clear. During the period in which hoplite warfare dominated the Greek scene, there was little advance in siegecraft. Hoplite equipment and training were ill-adapted to the conduct of efficient siege operations, and relatively simple walls were sufficient to deter most assaults. But with the breakdown of hoplite warfare and the rules that had sustained it, siegecraft and defense against siege became more serious issues. Not surprisingly, the period from 400 to 300 B.C. saw rapid advances in both military architecture and siege technique.

Because warfare in the age after the Peloponnesian War tended to be destructive to state economies and civilian populations, Greek poleis expended considerable effort to exclude enemy forces from economic and population centers. City walls were built and rebuilt: at Athens, for example, major work was undertaken on the city circuit in the period around 395–385, and again in 337, 307, and in the third century. Perhaps even more impressive were efforts to exclude enemy troops from economically vital rural areas. The Thebans constructed a stockade around their central agricultural districts in the 370s. And in the middle decades of the fourth century, Athens, Thebes, and probably other poleis as well constructed elaborate systems of border fortifications intended to preclude enemy forces from entering and ravaging the interior.[29]

By the mid-fourth century both besiegers and defenders were typically utilizing catapult artillery. Originally invented as a siege weapon by arms-makers employed by the tyrant Dionysios I of Syracuse in 399 B.C., the nontorsion (crossbow-type) catapult was a frightening antipersonnel weapon. Early catapults were not strong enough to endanger well-built stone walls, however, and so for a time the expenditure of polis assets for perimeter defense seemed the most logical course of action. But not for long: by about 340 B.C. engineers in the employ of Philip II, king of Macedon, had developed the first true torsion (hair- or sinew-spring) catapults. Torsion machines, which threw large stone balls, proved their worth by smashing city walls at Alexander's epic siege of Tyre in 332 B.C.[30]

[29] Athenian work on the city walls: Wycherley 1978, 7–25. Theban stockade: Munn 1987, 106–38. Border defenses: Ober 1985a, passim.

[30] Development of siege artillery and its effect on military architecture: Marsden 1969, 1971; Garlan 1974; Will 1975; Ober 1987, 569–604.

It is hardly an accident that the first version of catapult artillery was developed in the workshops of an imperialist Sicilian tyrant, the second phase in imperial Macedonia. Technological development and rearmament with the new machines required financial assets that much exceeded the means of ordinary Greek poleis. By the late fourth century, few individual poleis could hope to win conflicts against the great dynasts who controlled the money and manpower generated by Macedonian expansionism. As we have seen, border-defense strategies were a primary response of several Greek poleis to the military situation precipitated by the collapse of the traditional conventions governing the conduct of intra-Hellenic warfare. But the new artillery technology developed by Philip's engineers helped to render border-defense strategies obsolete. Rural forts proved unable to hold off Hellenistic generals in the late fourth and third centuries.[31] The dynastic successors of Alexander, with their highly trained mercenary armies and their superior artillery, dominated the military landscape. The upshot was that polis citizens were left with no very effective military response to the threat offered by hostile forces deployed by the several new "great powers." The city-states of Greece, with their limited economic and manpower resources, could not compete in the new military climate, and therefore the age of the truly independent polis drew to a close.

In conclusion, the relationship between the Greek sociopolitical order and the "rules of war" that I have attempted to trace above leads to a paradox—and one that quite frankly gives me pause. Archaic and early classical Greek social mores and political culture supported a form of warfare that was highly, if informally, rule-oriented. The rules of early intra-Greek warfare successfully constrained the horrors of war while supporting an overtly hierarchical social order. In the late sixth and fifth century, the polis of Athens discovered in democratic politics a way to broaden the base of the social order. As a result, Greek culture blossomed as never before. Classical Athens witnessed the apogee of polis culture, marked by bold innovations in many spheres: literature, visual arts, philosophy—and military strategy. Unfettered by the need to maintain a rigid social hierarchy, Athenian leaders were free to experiment with military strategies that ignored some of the constraints imposed by the traditional rules of war. Though it was not their intent to overthrow those rules, this initial period of experimentation precipitated an unprecedented series of innovations in military strategy, personnel, and technology. And these innovations in turn did overthrow the rules of war, and in the process undermined the social and political order on which independent polis culture depended. Athenian democracy was, in this sense, the condition of its own impossibility. This is, I believe, a profoundly disturbing conclusion for any citizen of a democratic state. On the other hand, fourth-century Athenian history— democratic Athens' successes and relative stability compared with the failure

---

[31] Ober 1985a, 220.

of poleis that depended on the hoplite ideology—may suggest that "more democracy" is the most appropriate response to crises precipitated by the new options presented by democracy. It is perhaps in forcing historians of politics, culture, and society to confront paradoxes such as this one that the study of international security finds some part of its justification.

Chapter 6

THUCYDIDES, PERICLES, AND THE STRATEGY OF DEFENSE

This essay was written in 1983–84, as a contribution to a Festschrift for my dissertation advisor, Chester Starr, and while I was a resident fellow of the National Humanities Center. I was at the time engaged in completing the final revisions of *Fortress Attica* and doing the research for a preliminary draft of *Mass and Elite in Democratic Athens*. As the oldest essay in the present collection it bears the traces of earlier intellectual interests (e.g., in the centrality of topographical specificity to the development of the argument). It is included here because its argument develops logically from that of the previous chapter and because it introduces or develops several recurring themes: the dynamic tension between the "rational" policy preferences of the political leader (Pericles) and the interests and concerns of the Athenian demos; the ways in which that tension was played out in Assembly meetings and in the formation and implementation of actual Athenian policy; and the internal conflict manifested in the text of the historian (Thucydides) who is at the same time a reporter and a critical interpreter of events, concerned with both facts (what actually happened) and norms (what should have happened in the past and should happen in the future).

The main goals of the essay are, first, to reconstruct an overlooked chapter in the history of the development and implementation of Athenian defense policy before and during the Peloponnesian War, and next (more ambitiously), to explore the traces in a classical text of what I suppose to be its author's attempts to be at once an honest historian and a penetrating critical theorist. As in Chapter 4, the method involves a close attention to the sources: I argue that Thucydides' narrative of Athenian defensive measures (the employment of cavalry and garrisons to limit the impact of enemy ravaging) cannot be fully squared either with the "city-island" strategy advocated by Pericles in speeches reported by Thucydides or with Thucydides' own assessment of the proper goals of the Athenian strategy during the war. Rather than attempting to square the circle, I suggest that the incompatibility of narrative and analysis is indicative of the problems innate to history as critical theory: Thucydides, as a critic of post-Periclean democracy, encourages his reader to adopt a view of the course of events that remains blind to some of the evidence of his own account. Running against the trend in Thucydides scholarship that sees such contradictions as evidence of bad faith (e.g., Badian 1993, 125–62), however, I see this conflict as an inevitable (and not necessarily undesirable) outcome of serious historiography. As an essentially honest (although

This essay was first published in Eadie and Ober 1985, 171–88.

hardly objective) historian, Thucydides provides his reader with evidence that will support interpretations to which he does not subscribe and which he cannot advocate. Surely modern historians can ask no more, from our sources or ourselves. I returned to the issue of Thucydides as theorist and historian in Ober 1993 and 1994.

Much of the argument turns on how Athenian cavalry figured in Pericles' defensive strategy. A good deal of work on the Athenian cavalry has appeared since this essay was first published. Some of it deals either sympathetically or critically with the two main theses (on Athenian defense and on Thucydides) presented here. G. Bugh (1988) discusses the cavalry as an Athenian public institution; Iain Spence (1990; cf. 1993) recapitulates many of the points made here on the role of cavalry in Athenian defenses, while disagreeing with my interpretation of Thucydides; Worley (1994) discusses the cavalry as a military fighting force.

It is human nature always to rule over those who yield,
but also to guard against those who are about to attack.
—Thuc. 4.61.5: speech of Hermocrates

Take care, Pericles, you are ruling free men, you are
ruling Greeks, citizens of Athens.
—Plut. *Moralia* 813D–E: Pericles to himself

THUCYDIDES' ACCOUNT of Pericles' grand strategy in the Peloponnesian War has long fascinated historians, who have often tried to explain how Athens could have won the war given the essentially defensive strategy Thucydides ascribed to Pericles.[1] I shall not attempt to solve that vexing problem here, but rather pose another, related question: what part did the defense of the Athenian countryside play in Pericles' overall strategy? Few modern historians have bothered with this question, since Thucydides seems to give a simple answer, namely, that the defense of Attica was never an issue because the rural citizens were withdrawn to the city, where they were safe behind the circuit walls. Upon closer scrutiny, however, this apparently straightforward solution appears inadequate, as Thucydides' own narrative demonstrates that Pericles in fact took serious measures to protect rural property. An investigation of Pericles' local defense preparations should reveal some of the underpinnings of his strategy; it may also shed some light on two other important issues. How did the Athenian democracy function during the time of Pericles' political leader-

[1] Modern studies include Westlake 1945; Chambers 1957; de Wet 1969; Knight 1970; Cawkwell 1975; Holladay 1978; Wick 1979. Knight (Pericles' strategy was completely defensive and would have failed) and de Wet (Pericles' strategy was essentially offensive and could have succeeded) define the two poles of the argument.

ship (*prostateia*), and what is the relationship between narrative and analysis in Thucydides' *History*?

Thucydides' summary of Pericles' strategy (2.66.7) is unambiguous. Pericles told the Athenians they would win the war if they (1) remained on the defensive (*hēsuchazontas*), (2) maintained their fleet, (3) resisted the temptation to expand their empire during the war, and (4) did not endanger the city. What Pericles meant by "remain on the defensive" is made clear in two of his speeches to the demos. In 431, at an Assembly called to consider a final Spartan peace proposal, Pericles argued against compromise and laid out his plan for dealing with the Peloponnesian invasion. The Peloponnesian land force, being superior in numbers, would ultimately defeat the Athenian army in battle. Therefore, the Athenians must not fight the Peloponnesians on land. If the Athenians were islanders they would be perfectly secure, therefore they should act as if their city were an island and abandon their land and homes in the countryside. Pericles considered land and country homes liabilities, since their threatened loss might tempt the citizens to meet the Peloponnesians in battle. Indeed, he wished he could persuade the Athenians to sack their own lands to show the Peloponnesians how little they cared for such trivialities (1.143.5). The Athenians were convinced by this speech and refused the Spartan peace proposal (1.145). After the Spartans had mustered their army and were marching toward Attica, another Assembly was called at which Pericles gave the same advice as before: the Athenians must move their property into the city from the rural districts, refuse battle on land, guard the city, equip the fleet, and keep a firm hand on the allies (2.13.2). The Athenians agreed; they brought their families and moveable property within the city walls, disassembled the wooden frameworks of their country houses, and sent their livestock to Euboea and the other islands (2.14.1). Even in 430, after the ravages of the plague, Pericles stuck by his conviction (*gnōmē*) that the Athenians must not meet the invaders in the field (2.55.1–2), and he reiterated his position in the Assembly. Athens' strength, he said, lay in her powerful fleet (2.62.2), and this *dunamis* must not be compared to country houses and land, which are no more important than gardens or fancy ornaments and which only seem significant now because of their unavailability (2.62.3).

Pericles' strategy, as described by Thucydides, was highly original and completely logical.[2] He knew that Athens had insufficient manpower to both man a fleet large enough to maintain the empire and fight the Peloponnesians on land. The Peloponnesians' strength lay in their land army, and Pericles knew they would attempt to provoke battle by invading Attica. If the Athenians fought the Peloponnesians they would eventually lose too many men to be able to keep up the fleet. The Athenians were not constrained to fight in defense of their land, however, because the state had sufficient disposable wealth, gener-

[2] Ober 1985a, 35–36, 51–52.

ated from imperial revenues, to feed the population and maintain the war for several years.[3] If the Athenians did not lose men in battle, they would retain enough manpower to maintain their navy and hence the empire from which the revenues accrued. The Peloponnesians could not match the Athenian navy at sea. Therefore, if the Athenians did not fight in defense of Attica (and avoided wasting their strength on imperial expansion), they could not lose the war. Q.E.D. Thucydides appreciated the logic and states that in his opinion Pericles' strategy would have proved successful had it been followed to the letter (2.65.13).

Pericles, however, not only had to devise a rational war plan, but also had to persuade a sometimes irrational democratic Assembly to agree to it; in this case there were good reasons for him to expect opposition. The strategy of abandoning the state territory (*chōra*) and refusing to meet another Greek army in battle was not only original, it was revolutionary and contravened the unwritten rules of agonal combat. It was one matter for the Athenians to abandon Attica in the face of the barbarian Persian invaders in 480, quite another for hoplites to refuse the formal challenge to battle by fellow hoplites, to stand quietly on the city wall watching homes burned and fields ravaged, all the while imagining the taunts of insolent invaders.[4]

The Peloponnesians, on their part, certainly expected the Athenian army to meet their invasion force in the field. Thucydides (5.14.3) says that at the beginning of the war the Spartans believed they would destroy Athens' *dunamis* by ravaging Athenian land. The ravaging would, they assumed, bring the Athenian army out to fight. Archidamus, in addressing his army before the invasion of 431, suggested that there was "every reason to expect them [the Athenians] to risk a battle . . . when they see us in their territory laying it waste and destroying their property" (2.11.6). Until the capture of the contingent on Sphacteria in 425, many Spartans continued to believe that eventually the Athenian hoplites would come out from behind the walls to fight in defense of their land, as brave men should.[5] How could Pericles persuade the Athenian soldiery to hold back?

---

[3] Kagan (1969, 340; and 1974, 37–40) suggests that for financial reasons Pericles planned for the war to last for no longer than three years. Knight (1970, 153 n. 1) cites Thuc. 1.141.5 (Pericles states that the financial stress of an "unexpectedly" long war will wear down the Peloponnesians) against the contention that Pericles planned for a short war.

[4] On the forms of agonal warfare, see Ober 1985a, 32–35. Cawkwell (1975, 70) notes correctly that the abandonment of Attica was a "radical" step, but I cannot agree with him that the rest of Pericles' strategy was conventional.

[5] The Peloponnesians invaded Attica annually (Thuc. 2.47.2, 3.1.1, 3.26.1–3, 4.2.1), except in 429 (when they concentrated on attacking Plataea instead, 2.71.1) and 426 (when the planned invasion was aborted due to an earthquake, 3.89.1). Even if some Spartans had doubts about traditional methods (Archidamus expressed such doubts in two speeches: Thuc. 1.81.6, 2.11.3–5), we must assume, therefore, that there was a good deal of support for the invasion strategy. On Archidamus and the Archidamus speeches, see de Romilly 1962; Bloedow 1981. On Spartan

And what of the interests of the rural citizens? Thucydides clearly states that at the outbreak of the war the majority (*hoi pleious*: 2.16.1) of Athenians lived in the countryside and were therefore directly affected by Pericles' defense strategy. Thucydides' description of Pericles' plan implies that rural residents stood to lose everything left in the countryside, and they could hardly expect their lives in the city to be pleasant.[6] The rural majority could have voted for an open battle strategy in hopes of protecting their farms. Furthermore, it was not property alone that was at stake. Each household had its sacred hearth and private shrines to think of. In the public sphere there were the olive trees sacred to Athena as well as various rural festivals and fertility cults.[7] The Athenians would be giving up a great deal when they abandoned their land.

Thucydides was well aware of the sacrifice the rural citizens made in choosing to come into the city, and he describes their plight in detail. It was difficult (*chalepōs*), he says, for the Athenians to move, since they were used to living in the country (2.14.2); indeed, autonomous village life was even more characteristic of the Athenians than of other Greeks (2.15.1). The Athenians had only just finished rebuilding farms sacked in the Persian Wars (2.16.1) and were "dejected and aggrieved" at the prospect of leaving homes (*oikias*) and the ancestral sacred things (*hiera*). In sum, says Thucydides, the move to the city was for each rural citizen the equivalent of abandoning his own polis (2.16.2).

Thucydides' vivid description of the rural citizens' despair at leaving their lands leads his reader to expect an explanation of why they were ultimately willing to do so. Thucydides never offers an explicit answer, but his implicit explanation is clear: Pericles was first man of Athens, the most persuasive in speech and most powerful in action, and he controlled the demos (1.39.4, 1.127.2–3, 2.65.7–10). Hence, when Pericles suggested that the Athenians do something, they might grumble, but they did it.[8] But was it really quite so simple? Recent scholarship has shown that Pericles had more in common with

---

strategy in the Archidamian War, see Brunt 1965; Cawkwell 1975, 53–70; Moxon 1978; Kelly 1982.

[6] Thucydides emphasizes the squalid conditions in which the evacuees lived: 2.17, 2.52.1–2.

[7] The sanctity of the central hearth: Farnell 1896–1909, 5:358–65. Many farms had other sacred places; on three cult-related rupestral inscriptions found at a single farm in the Laurion district, see Langdon and Watrous 1977, 162–77; Wickens 1983, 96–99. On the sacred olive trees (which were located on private farms), see Lysias Oration 7. Davies (1981, 75–76) postulates that Thucydides' stress on the rural way of life and cults shows that Athenians had a "comparative detachment" from and a "curious lack of emotional involvement" in their real estates, which I think overstates the case.

[8] Thucydides' assessment of Pericles' position is accepted by, among others, Delbrück (1975–85, 1:137–38), who praises "the power of the mind of Pericles, who was able to persuade the sovereign Athenian Citizenry to adopt a strategy that was so hard to grasp," and Kagan, who speaks of Pericles' "political magic" (1969, 193–94) and suggests that Pericles' "power" to persuade the Athenians to leave their farms was due to his "*auctoritas*" (1974, 54–56).

his demagogic successors than Thucydides would have us believe; like them, Pericles had to manipulate and cajole the demos to accomplish his political and strategic goals.[9] If we cannot wholly accept Thucydides' assessment of Pericles' ability to force his will upon his fellow citizens, we must ask what sorts of argument and inducement he might have offered to persuade them to agree to give up their homes, temples, and sense of agonal honor.

First, Pericles might have played on Athenian hopes that the Peloponnesians would not actually penetrate central Attica. In 446/5 a Peloponnesian invasion of Attica had been aborted before the invaders had advanced farther than the Thriasian plain (1.104.2). Thucydides states (2.21.1) that in 431 the Athenians remembered this event and hoped that the current invasion would also be halted before crossing Mount Aigaleos. But the mass evacuation of 431 would have been unnecessary if the Athenians could be sure the Peloponnesians would stay west of Aigaleos. Clearly those Athenians living east of the Thriasian plain who had evacuated recognized the possibility that the Peloponnesians would advance. But even if the invaders did advance, one might argue, the Athenians need not have expected them to do a great deal of damage. After all, agonal warfare did not require an efficient destruction of enemy property, since the defending hoplites tended to show up for battle before much ravaging had occurred. The fact that the Peloponnesians would not be experienced ravagers may have been some comfort to the Athenians, but the devastation of Attica during the Persian Wars was still in living memory. The Athenians had more reason than most other mainland Greeks to associate enemy occupation of unguarded land with economic ruin.

An explanation might be sought in the composition of the Athenian Assembly. Undoubtedly a relatively higher percentage of city dwellers than of rural citizens attended the Assembly regularly, and the Old Oligarch ([Xen.] *Ath. Pol.* 2.14) claims that the demos (meaning the urban mob) was not eager to make peace since, unlike the "farmers and rich men," the masses who lived in the city had nothing to lose in case of invasion.[10] Yet surely even those rural citizens who seldom exercised their franchise would make a point of attending any meeting that was to decide on a question so germane to their interests. The possibility that Pericles may have packed the Assembly with urban voters is not sufficient explanation in the face of Thucydides' clear statement that the majority of citizens lived in the countryside.

Propaganda provides another possible clue. It seems likely that Pericles' great building program had the effect of fostering the identification of the *astu*

[9] See the seminal article by Finley (1962, esp. 14–16). There were, of course, differences between Pericles and his successors (see Connor 1971), and his personal prestige no doubt helped Pericles persuade the Athenians to vote his way on many issues, but there were limits to what the Athenians would agree to on the basis of prestige alone.

[10] It is often assumed (e.g., by Hansen [1979a, 48]) that the preponderance of voters at normal meetings of the Assembly was townsmen.

(i.e., the walled city) with the polis as a whole. The very building of the Long Walls to Piraeus may have conditioned the Athenians to the idea that they might have to man them, and manning the walls implied abandoning the countryside. Not all citizens would make that connection, but those who did may have been comforted by the iconography of the shield of the great statue of Athena Parthenos in the Parthenon. E. Harrison has demonstrated that the background of the Amazonomachy depicted on the shield was a city wall; the eponymous heroes of the Cleisthenic tribes are shown fighting on the wall against the besiegers.[11] If the ancestral heroes could face invaders at the wall rather than in the field, their descendants would not shame themselves by doing the same.

Along with employing iconography to persuade the Athenians that city defense was noble and brave, Pericles played on the darker side of his audience's emotions by appealing to their passion for revenge. From 431 on the Athenians sent out large fleets to ravage Peloponnesian territory, and the land army marched against Megara twice each year. In his first speech Pericles specifically links the expected Peloponnesian invasions and the planned Athenian raids: "If they march by land against our *chōra*, we will sail against theirs" (1.143.4). Pericles goes on to say that Athenian raids will hurt the Peloponnesians more than the loss of all Attica will hurt the Athenians. Perhaps he believed this: Thucydides suggested that in 424 the Spartans thought they could stop the infuriating Athenian raids by attacking the land of Athens' allies (4.80.1); *mutatis mutandis*, Pericles might have had similar hopes in 431. Whether or not the raids would be effective in winning the war, they would keep the Athenians from feeling themselves helpless victims, unable to strike back at their tormentors.[12]

At least some of these factors no doubt helped to pave the way for Athenian acceptance of Pericles' strategy; even collectively, however, they do not provide a sufficient condition for Athenian willingness to withdraw from the countryside. The rural citizens were being asked to give up a great deal; they must have been given some assurance that the state would make an effort to minimize the extent of their material losses. But how could rural property be protected if the countryside were abandoned?

A solution may be sought by examining the defensive response of a similar Greek state faced with an analogous situation. Thucydides makes a point of comparing Sicilian Syracuse with Athens. Syracuse, like Athens, was a wealthy, populous, democratic state whose citizens, when faced with large-scale invasion in 415, chose initially to withdraw behind city walls.[13]

[11] Harrison 1981.

[12] Grundy (1948, 1:331) suggested that the raids might have been intended to improve Athenian morale. Westlake (1945, 79), commenting on the first edition of 1911, found this "not quite convincing," but Kagan (1974, 29 n. 49) feels that it is a possible explanation.

[13] Comparison of Athens and Syracuse: Thuc. 7.55.2, 8.96.5. According to Nicias (6.20.4),

Thucydides' narrative of the Sicilian expedition includes a detailed description of Syracuse's local defense strategy. The Syracusans, as it turns out, guarded their territory with cavalry and rural garrisons. Despite initial losses in battle suffered by the hoplite force, the Syracusan cavalry and garrisons effectively protected rural assets. The enemy hoplites were forced by cavalry raids to move about in large units in tight formation; any hoplite who left the formation was cut down by mounted skirmishers. The camp followers of the invaders were slaughtered when they attempted to collect water and firewood and could not spread out to scour the countryside for provisions. Since the enemy could never disperse his forces to ravage, damage to rural resources was kept to a minimum. The role of the Syracusan garrisons is less clear, but they seem to have served as bases for the cavalry and as centers of local resistance.[14]

The cavalry/garrison defense strategy employed by Syracuse was a major factor in the failure of Athens' Sicilian expedition, but, according to Thucydides, it should have been anticipated. In a speech to the Syracusan Assembly, the demagogue Athenagoras predicted that if the Athenians did invade Syracusan territory, they would be unable to venture out of their camp due to the cavalry (6.37.2). Nor, apparently, were the Athenians blind to the defensive potential of the cavalry. Nicias, in his second speech against the expedition in 415, stated that the main advantage the Sicilians would have over the Athenians was their numerous cavalry (*hippous . . . pollous*: 6.20.4), and he feared that the Athenians might be shut off from the land by the horsemen (6.21.1, 6.22, 6.23.3). Perhaps Nicias was guessing, or perhaps Thucydides inserted the passage in the speech so this man who "had lived his whole life in accordance with virtue" (7.86.5) would accurately predict the future. There is, however, good reason to suppose that Nicias and his fellow Athenians well understood the defensive use of cavalry and garrisons because, as we shall see, Athenian cavalry and garrisons had been on active duty in Attica since the beginning of the Peloponnesian War.

Could Pericles have believed, or at least have persuaded the Athenians to believe, that Athenian cavalry and garrisons would be able to defend Attic property? Certainly the Athenian cavalry was sufficiently numerous, about equal (1,200 regular and mounted archers in 431: Thuc. 2.13.8) to the "not less than 1,200 horsemen" the Syracusans fielded in 415 (6.67.2). Indeed, one of the similarities between Athens and Syracuse noted by Thucydides was that both states possessed large navies and large cavalry forces (7.55.2). Like the

---

Syracuse depended upon grain grown in its home territory, but Lamachus' (6.49.3) suggestion that a quick attack on Syracuse in 415 would catch the Syracusans in the countryside while still engaged in bringing their property into the city seems to indicate that at least a temporary evacuation was effected.

[14] Syracusan cavalry tactics: Thuc. 6.52.2, 6.70.3, 6.71.2, 6.98.3, 7.4.6, 7.10.4, 7.13.2, 7.42.6, 7.44.8, 7.78.3–7; rural garrisons: 6.45, 6.94.2.

Syracusans, the Athenians enjoyed the support of allied cavalry contingents (unknown numbers of Thessalians in 431: Thuc. 2.22.2) and had hopes of getting more (from Thrace: 2.29.5). Unlike the Syracusans, however, the Athenians could expect a substantial number of horsemen to accompany the enemy invasion force. The Boeotians had about 1,000 available (*Hellenica Oxyrhynchia* 16.3–4), but some of these might be tied down at Plataea or kept behind on home-guard duty. The number of other cavalry available for duty in Attica is unknown, but is unlikely to have been very large.[15] On the whole, the Athenians might reasonably hope to field cavalry at least equal in number to that of the invaders, and the Athenian cavalry would have the support of the garrison posts.[16]

Could the Athenian cavalry have guarded rural property against Peloponnesian hoplites? Xenophon, who had a great deal of experience as a cavalry commander, thought so. In discussing Athenian options in the face of a potential Boeotian invasion in the 360s, he points out that the Boeotian cavalry was about equal in number to Athens' (*Cavalry Commander* 7.1). Xenophon hopes the Athenian hoplites will meet the invaders in the field, but if "the city falls back on the navy and is content to keep her walls intact, as in the days when the Lacedaemonians invaded . . . and if she expects her cavalry alone to protect all that lies outside the walls . . . then we need first the vigorous support of the gods and second, a skillful commander" (7.4). Xenophon states that, although it will not be easy for Athens' cavalry to contain the invading forces, containment is quite possible, and he presents a good deal of practical advice on the conduct of hit-and-run raids and the use of strongholds against the invaders (7.5ff.).

If Xenophon, with the experience of the Peloponnesian War to reflect upon, considered cavalry defense against large invading forces feasible, it is reasonable to suppose that before the war the Athenians may have believed that their cavalry, supported by rural garrisons, would be able to limit the damage the Peloponnesians could inflict upon Attica. A brief review of the activities of the cavalry and garrisons during the Peloponnesian War shows that they were in fact expected to fulfill an important role in the defense of Athenian rural property.

At the outbreak of the war, Athens had 1,200 cavalry of its own, an unknown number of allied Thessalian cavalry, and garrisons in strongholds at

[15] The invaders' cavalry came from the Boeotians, Phocians, and Locrians (Thuc. 2.9.3, 2.12.4), but clearly the Boeotian contingent was the most important. Before the battle of Delium in 424 the general Hippocrates suggested that an Athenian victory would ensure the safety of Attica, since without the support of Boeotian cavalry the Peloponnesians would not invade (Thuc. 4.95.1–2). Knight (1970, 153) states that the Peloponnesians had a "great advantage" in "hoplite, *cavalry* [my italics] and light-armed forces," but cites no evidence for this contention.

[16] Hippocrates left behind 300 Athenian cavalry to guard the fort at Delium during the battle (Thuc. 4.93.1), demonstrating that cavalry could be used in close support of fortified outposts.

Oinoe, Panakton, Eleusis, Oropos, and perhaps elsewhere.[17] Upon crossing into the northwestern Athenian borderland in 431, Archidamus attempted to capture Oinoe, but failed (Thuc. 2.18–19.1). He then proceeded southeast to the Thriasian plain. After ravaging the plain his army apparently attempted to cross the Daphni pass to the Athenian plain; as the Peloponnesians approached the entrance to the pass they were met (at "the Rheiti") by Athenian cavalry. Although the Athenians were driven off, Archidamus decided to avoid the narrow pass and took the longer route north of Aigaleos to the deme of Acharnai (2.19.12).

After the Peloponnesians had established their camp at Acharnai, Pericles "constantly sent out the cavalry" to prevent the Peloponnesians from sending "outriders from their main force" or "ravaging the fields near the city" (2.22.2). At a place called Phrygioi (exact location unknown) the Athenian and Thessalian cavalry engaged a Boeotian cavalry group, but were driven off with light casualties when Peloponnesian hoplites came up in support. The Athenian tactics were similar to those later used by the Syracusan cavalry against the Athenian hoplite army, and seem to have been effective. The Peloponnesian army left Attica through one of the northeastern passes (2.23) without ever having entered the main part of the Athenian plain, much less the fertile Mesogeia or other areas of southern Attica.[18] Despite the shock of the invasion and the near crisis when the numerous Acharnians realized their territory had been selected for the Spartan camp (Thuc. 2.21.2–3; cf. Plut. *Pericles* 33.5–7), Pericles had reason to be proud of his preparations: the no-battle strategy was working according to plan, and the Athenians expressed their approval of his leadership by electing him to deliver the eulogy over the war dead (Thuc. 2.24.6–8).

The next year the Peloponnesian army returned, and this time was able to ravage the Athenian plain and the Mesogeia during the nearly forty days they stayed in Attica (2.47.2, 2.55, 2.57.2). The property-protection scheme had apparently broken down completely. The failure was due in part to the disrupting influence of the plague (which had killed 300 cavalrymen by 427; 3.87.3), but also because of the (unexplained) absence of the Thessalian cavalry, and because Pericles took 300 cavalry with him on a naval raid (2.56.1). Cavalry available for local defense in the summer of 430 must have been less than half that available in 431; the difference in numbers was a key factor in Spartan ability to ravage at will in central and southern Attica.

---

[17] Oinoe: Thuc. 2.18–19.1, 8.98; Panakton: Thuc. 5.3.5, 5.18.7, 5.35.5, 5.36.2, 5.40.1–2, 5.42.1–2, 5.44.3; Eleusis: Plut. *Alcibiades* 34.3–5; Oropos: Thuc. 8.60.1. I discussed the physical remains and function of these and other sites (for which there are no testimonia) in Ober 1985a, 130–80.

[18] Busolt (1893–1904, 3.2:930) suggested that the Athenian cavalry limited Peloponnesian movements in 431. His theory was noted, but rejected, by Kagan (1974, 51, 57 n. 48), on the grounds that "there is no evidence that the cavalry presented a serious problem to the Peloponnesians." Cf. also below, note 21.

The Athenian demos was shocked. A peace mission was hastily dispatched to Sparta (2.59), but the Spartans now saw no reason to make peace on terms favorable to Athens. Despair set in, and with it anger at the originator of the defense plan that had failed. "The demos had lost what little they had, while the upper classes had lost their lovely country estates, both buildings and expensive furnishings" (2.65.2). Although the devastation of their armed forces by the plague (3.87.3) left them little choice but to stick with Pericles' strategy, the Athenians expressed their displeasure with their *prostatēs* by temporarily deposing him from the generalship and by fining him (2.65.3).[19]

After Pericles' death in 429, his no-battle strategy was maintained, but so was the attempt to limit the damage caused by the annual invasions. In 428 the Athenian cavalry rode out "as usual" against the invaders and succeeded in keeping the light-armed retainers of the Spartans from leaving the protection of the hoplites or plundering near the city (3.1.1). Again Athenian cavalry tactics are paralleled by the later successful attempt by the Syracusan horsemen to limit foraging by Athenian camp followers. After the capture of the Spartan force on Sphacteria in 425, the invasions ceased, but when the Peloponnesian garrison was established at Decelea in 413, the Athenian cavalry returned to action on a daily basis (*hosēmerai*). Its mission was much the same as before: to harass the garrison (*pros te tēn Dekeleian katadromas poioumenōn*) and to guard Athenian land (*kai kata tēn chōran phulassontōn*). The cavalrymen saw such constant duty that their horses frequently went lame (7.27.5).[20]

Happily, the cavalry could look to the surviving garrison posts for help. In 411/10 an Athenian raiding force from the Oinoe fort successfully attacked a Corinthian contingent on its way home from Decelea (8.98). In the same year the Decelea garrison, along with reinforcements from the Peloponnese, approached the walls of Athens, hoping to precipitate the surrender of the city. Instead, the cavalry, supported by some hoplites and light-armed men, rode out and drove the enemy away from the walls. The Peloponnesians retreated in disarray, and the reinforcements were sent home (8.71.1–3).

The picture that emerges from Thucydides' narrative is clear and consistent. At the outbreak of the war the Athenians expected their cavalry and outpost garrisons to limit the damage done by the invaders to rural property. The defensive forces succeeded in restricting enemy movements during the first invasion, but failed in the second year, prompting Pericles' dismissal. After-

[19] Thuc. 2.65.3; Plut. *Pericles* 35.4. For a review of modern studies of Pericles' impeachment and the view that it was the outcome of political faction fighting, see Roberts 1982, 21, 30–34, 59–62.

[20] The defendant in Lysias 20.28 mentions that his brother was a cavalryman who killed an enemy soldier based at Decelea. In Lysias 14.20 the defendant notes that Athenian cavalrymen had done much damage to Athens' enemies during the war.

wards, the Athenians continued to use cavalry and garrisons to protect as much of their land as possible.[21]

Whether or not the rural Athenians' faith in the cavalry and garrisons was the primary reason they were willing to abandon their farms, the rural protection scheme must have been a necessary condition of their agreement. Perhaps Pericles really felt it would be a good thing for the Athenians to ravage their own lands, but of course he could not possibly have convinced them to do so. On the contrary, Pericles, like other Athenian politicians, had to present the majority of voting citizens with an attractive "legislative package" if he hoped to retain his influence and hence his ability to implement long-term policy. So he secured the demos' agreement to his no-battle strategy with a promise (which he may or may not have believed he could keep) that their lands would be guarded after they had come into the city.

Thucydides himself mentions the cavalry and garrisons frequently enough to allow the preceding reconstruction, but in his analytic passages and speeches he completely ignores local defense.[22] Perhaps he considered the rural defense plan unimportant, but, assuming my thesis is correct, Pericles could not have implemented his no-battle strategy without it. Thucydides' narrative shows that the cavalry was constantly fighting the invaders and that garrisons were left in the borderlands for the duration of the war; one might reasonably expect him to explain what they were supposed to accomplish. Why does he not?

Thucydides was convinced that Athens' real strength lay in its empire. The Mytileneans informed the Peloponnesians in a speech that the war will not be waged in Attica as some may think, but over the places from which Attica derives wealth—the allied states (3.13.5–6, cf. 1.122.1). The empire was held by sea power, against which the Spartan land army was helpless no matter how often it might invade Attica, as Alcibiades pointed out in his speech of 415 (6.17.8).[23] Besides the fleet, only city walls were necessary to defend the state.[24]

---

[21] Brunt (1965, 266) mentions in passing that Athenian forts and cavalry must have limited the damage done to Attica in the Archidamian War. Hanson (1983, 77–78, 105–6) notes the role of garrisons and cavalry in Athens' defense and argues (109–43) that damage to Athenian agriculture was fairly limited even during the Decelean War.

[22] Pericles suggests (1.142.3) that the Peloponnesians will find it difficult to establish a fort in Attica: "We should have raised fortifications against them" (*ekeinois hēmōn anteteichismenōn*), which could be construed as a reference to Athens' borderland fortresses, but more probably refers to the city itself. For this interpretation and an analysis of the grammatical difficulties involved in the passage, see Gomme et al. 1945–81, 1:458–59.

[23] Cf. Thuc. 1.143.4, 2.22.2, 4.12.3, 4.14.3. On Thucydides' narrowly military-economic view of sea power, see Starr 1979.

[24] Thucydides was convinced that city walls were necessary for civilized life: 1.2.2, 1.5.1, 1.7, 1.8.3; and showed a good deal of interest in the history of Athens' walls: 1.90–93, 1.107.1, 1.108.3.

Theoretically, therefore, Athens needed only to protect the walls and navy to guarantee the security of the empire and win (or at least avoid losing) the war. Unlike Pericles, Thucydides could choose to concentrate on theoretically achievable ends and to ignore the means of internal politics if the latter seemed unworthy. Several passages in Thucydidean speeches suggest that the desire to defend one's land was indeed an unworthy, even slavish, impulse. An Athenian envoy at Camarina told his audience that Athens' allies had been justly subdued, since, in the Persian Wars, they had not the courage to leave their homes (*ta oikeia*), but chose slavery (*douleia*) instead (6.82.4). Athenian ambassadors in Sparta in 432 noted that if Athens had medized "in order to save their *chōra*," all of Greece would have been lost (1.74.4; cf. Pericles' similar comments at 1.144.4). Archidamus warned the Peloponnesians in 432 that they must not expect the Athenians to be "slaves to their land" (1.81.6).

Pericles presumably conceded the strategic insignificance of local resources (which go unmentioned in his list of Athenian assets, 2.13.3–5), but knew that in order to implement his policies he had to make political compromises. To Thucydides, however, compromise with the demos was demagoguery—and the historian was determined to draw the distinction between Pericles and the demagogues as sharply as possible: Pericles made decisions according to his own opinion and controlled the demos; the demagogues, on the other hand, attempted to please the mob in all things and so were controlled by it (2.65.8–11). Thucydides' Pericles could not be depicted as making a deal with the rural citizens over a concern so negligible in the greater scheme of things as rural property. Rather, Pericles must be portrayed as having demonstrated to them the unavoidable logic of his long-range strategy, which was based on sea power and empire. If this was not the way Periclean Athens really *did* work, it was the way it *should have* worked.

The Thucydides I have described here is not the impartial and objective observer he claimed to be (1.22.2–4), but this does not mean he was a dishonest historian. In an insightful essay on Thucydides, Chester Starr meditated upon the problem of historical objectivity and concluded, "All that a true historian must keep steadily in mind is an effort to counter his *known* prejudices and to take into account all the known evidence; his unconscious attitudes will be detected by others as they judge his work."[25] Thucydides, like all historians,

---

[25] Starr 1983, 32. A good deal of the debate over both Periclean and Spartan strategy is ultimately based on decisions about the reliability of Thucydides' analysis. Cawkwell (1975, 69), who believes that "it is unthinkable that Thucydides sought to mislead," and Holladay (1978, 404), who is unable to countenance the idea that Thucydides could give a slanted interpretation, both argue that Pericles' strategy was purely defensive, just as Thucydides tells us it was. On the other hand, Wick (1979, 2), who suggests that Thucydides deemphasized Athenian strategic interest in Megara "almost to the point of being devious," and Kelly (1982, 54), who notes that generalizations in Thucydides "cannot be taken as literally true and universally applicable," are

had his biases and *idées fixes*, which emerge in the analytic passages and speeches of his history. Yet in his descriptive narrative of events, he presents enough discrete pieces of evidence (in this case at least) that later historians may reassemble the jigsaw puzzle for themselves and speculate as to why the picture they assemble looks somewhat different from Thucydides' own.

---

both able to use Thucydides' narrative statements in arguing against Thucydides' own strategic analysis.

Chapter 7

POWER AND ORATORY IN DEMOCRATIC ATHENS: DEMOSTHENES 21, *AGAINST MEIDIAS*

In 1991 Ian Worthington invited me to write an essay on "oratory and power" for a proposed volume of essays on classical Greek oratory and rhetoric. My initial goal in accepting the invitation was to answer a friendly challenge issued by Daniel Tompkins: could I apply the general perspective on rhetoric and rhetors developed in *Mass and Elite in Democratic Athens* to the reading of a single speech? *Against Meidias* was attractive as an object for analysis for several reasons. It is a personal favorite within the Demosthenic corpus, and (not unrelated) its content is particularly well suited to an analysis that focused on mass-elite relations. Moreover, it had recently been the subject of a fine text edition and important articles. The recent scholarship clarified some of the legal and stylistic dilemmas that had long obscured our understanding of the speech.

The topic assignment presented a significant theoretical challenge, in that it seemingly demanded a detailed discussion of what I meant by "power"—a concept that was obviously central to my research on democratic Athens and yet tended to resist categorical definition. After attempting to sort out two primary modern approaches to power (the juridical, associated with John Locke, and the discursive, associated with Michel Foucault), the essay focuses on the ways in which power was explored, explained, mediated, and enacted in Demosthenes' speech delivered (as I suppose) before the Athenian people's court. The speech is particularly revealing of the different ways in which power, in the democratic polis, related to equality and inequality, to the private and the public realms, and to the social environments inhabited by elite aristocrats and ordinary citizens. The speech suggests, in my reading, that the concepts of public and private cannot easily be separated from the social inequalities that accompany economic class distinctions; Demosthenes overtly pits the equal political standing of ordinary Athenian citizens in the public realm against the unequal social standing of elite Athenians in the private realm. A central point of the speech is that collective public power must be employed frequently and vigorously by Athenian juries if the hierarchies pertaining in private Athenian social life were not to spread into the public world of the citizen and thereby corrupt the freedoms, political equality, and sense of personal security upon which the democracy was predicated.

The Greek terminologies of freedom, equality, and security are all prominently marked in Demosthenes' speech. Taken together, these three abstractions (or rather,

This essay was first published in Ian Worthington, ed., *Persuasion: Greek Rhetoric in Action* (London and New York: Routledge, 1994), 85–108. All unattributed (single number) citations are from Demosthenes 21, *Against Meidias*. Translations are adapted from MacDowell 1990.

the practices to which they point) constitute what I suggest is best conceptualized as the citizen's "dignity"—a term I have borrowed from the work of Charles Taylor (see Taylor 1994). The freedom/equality/security triad is identical to the traditional triad of values that informs the modern liberal doctrine of rights. And this should mean that there are some significant parallels between the values essential to ancient and modern democracies. But it is, I believe, a serious error to suppose that Athenians embraced a doctrine of rights. Modern liberal theory attaches rights (conceived as substantives having an existence that is not context-dependent) to individuals by invoking premises of inherency and inalienability. The Athenians took a much more pragmatic approach to the construction and maintenance of citizen dignity. For Demosthenes in *Against Meidias* and for democratic Athens as a society, the dignity of the citizen was neither inherent or inalienable; it was enacted through a pattern of individual and collective practices. I return to the similarities and differences between liberal and Athenian democracies in Chapter 11.

The Athenians' pragmatic approach to dignity had juridical consequences. The citizen who failed to behave properly was subject to legal action that could remove from him some or all of the protections and privileges enjoyed by other citizens. Such a man was said to be *atimos*. The term *atimos* (and other terms within its semantic field: *atimia, timē, philotimia*, along with their various adjectival and verb forms) becomes a pivot on which the speech's argument turns. In the public realm, the *atimos* was stripped of his dignity by the collective and legal action of his fellow citizens. But in the private realm of wealthy aristocrats, the *atimos* was a man stripped of his personal honor by the unanswered self-consciously insolent act of a fellow aristocrat. The distinction between citizen dignity and personal honor seems to me to be an extremely important one for understanding the pragmatic consequences of democracy at Athens. Citizen dignity was protected by the ongoing and collective actions of the demos. Honor was an affair of individuals or of families—at least until fighting over honors threatened to disrupt the public peace.

Establishing this dignity versus honor distinction seems to me particularly important in light of the tendency among classical scholars to regard individual/family honor as a value capable of occupying the whole of the field denoted by the vocabulary of *timē*. This can quickly lead to an assumption that the values dominant in the Athenian public and the private realms were fully isomorphic. That assumption of isomorphism tempts readers to regard aristocratic values as primary in all realms and thereby renders democracy an empty institutional shell, incapable of changing or even challenging long-established power relations. As in other essays collected here, I argue that a close reading of the sources demonstrates the error of the assumption that aristocrats and their values were in control in democratic Athens. Demosthenes indeed suggests that the sort of isomorphism sketched above *could* come to pertain in Athens, and that it was the self-serving goal of certain wealthy Athenians to bring about that state of affairs. But Demosthenes also claims that aristocrats and their values did *not* currently dominate Athens and that, if the jury votes rightly, they will be prevented from doing so. The problem of honor versus dignity is discussed further in Chapter 11 and is the subject of recent and insightful articles by G. Herman (1993, 1994, 1995); see also Fisher 1992, now the authoritative work on *hubris*, and D. Cohen 1995, especially 90–101.

To STUDY politics and political life is to study power and the play of power. But what is power? A simple definition of a powerful entity might be "one with the ability to satisfy its own desires by instrumentally affecting the behavior of others."[1] This simple definition leaves a lot undecided: What sorts of entity are we talking about (individuals? corporate groups?), and what are their desires? These questions can be answered (at least in a preliminary way) by applying the definition to a concrete historical situation. In the case of fourth-century Athens, it is clear enough that there were powerful individuals within society— most obviously wealthy citizen men capable of affecting the behavior of workers (whether slave or free) and of satisfying their desire for material goods by appropriating the surplus generated by the labor of others. On the other hand, it is equally obvious that the fourth-century Athenian demos, as a collective entity, was powerful in that it was often able to satisfy its desires for (inter alia) autarky (in the Aristotelian sense) and autonomy by affecting the behavior of both Athenian citizens and others in a variety of ways (e.g., by levying taxes and paying soldiers to protect state interests and assets).

In Athens, as in other societies, the spheres dominated by different powerful entities sometimes came into conflict; notable among these conflicts was the clash between public and private interests. There was a high potential for discord between powerful Athenian individuals (e.g., rich men who wished to retain the use of their wealth to satisfy their private desires) and the demos (which was determined to put some part of that wealth to public use in ensuring autarky and autonomy). A good number of "individual versus community" conflicts were eventually adjudicated in the lawcourts of Athens. And hence dicanic (lawcourt) oratory was among the primary instruments whereby the power of the individual Athenian was tested against the power of the demos. The study of oratory in Athens should, therefore, be able to tell us something about how power worked in democratic Athens—and vice versa. But before we can hope to understand the instrumental role of oratory in negotiating the play of power in Athenian society, we will have to refine and expand our definition of power.

There is a large modern literature on the subject of power; here I will focus on two major paradigms. The first and more traditional approach to power, which we may call the "coercion" paradigm, sees power as centered in the

---

[1] Cf. Dahl 1957, 202: "A has power over B to the extent that he can get B to do something that B would not otherwise do."

state and fundamentally based on force or the threat of force, that is, the ability to deploy violent physical coercion.[2] The state, as sovereign authority, attempts to monopolize the right to use force legitimately within society (e.g., by police actions) and to deploy force externally (by making war). The state is the primary locus of power in that all holders of legitimate protections and privileges within society (e.g., property owners and citizens) look to the state to exert force when necessary to enforce those protections and privileges. Thus, for example, if my brother is murdered or my house is robbed, I must expect agents of the state to apprehend and punish the perpetrator, rather than take vengeance myself. And, on the other hand, as long as I obey the laws and fulfill my various duties and responsibilities as a member of society, I can expect to remain free from the operations of power. This model sees power as essentially juridical and repressive. Both those who approve of and those who oppose the state and its ideals can agree that according to the coercion paradigm, power is exerted in order to repress behavior that is deemed likely to threaten the sovereign authority of the state and that contravenes its laws.

The second approach to power, which we may call the "discourse" paradigm, is less interested in overt coercion, sovereignty, state apparatuses, and law as such. It focuses instead on how social and political knowledge is produced and disseminated throughout society.[3] According to this second paradigm, power is not centralized anywhere, and is neither "legitimate" nor "illegitimate." Thus sovereignty is not at issue, and a study of formal juridical institutions alone will not reveal the fundamental workings of power. Rather than seeing power as repressive, the discourse paradigm sees power as productive: it emerges through the production of social understandings regarding what is true and what behaviors are right, proper, even conceivable. As a consequence, the concept of freedom becomes problematic. Since power is productive and omnipresent (rather than repressive and located in the state), it is not simply a matter of my being free to do whatever is not prohibited. Rather, all of my social interactions, including my speech, are (at least potentially) bound up with a regime of power that is also a regime of truth. It is not easy to get outside power, since all forms of social communication (including

----

[2] Definition of "paradigm": see Chapter 2. What I am calling the coercion paradigm finds its philosophical underpinnings in seventeenth-century social contract theory, notably Hobbes' *Leviathan* (Hobbes [1651] 1950) and J. Locke's *Two Treatises of Government* (Locke [1689] 1970). Contract theory explains the ultimate basis of legitimate authority by positing an exchange of complete individual freedom for the security offered by voluntary submission to a political sovereign. Locke's definition of power (*Second Treatise*, sec. 3, p. 268) is succinct: "Political power I take to be a right of making laws with penalties of death, and consequently all less[er] penalties for the regulating and preserving [of] property, and of employing the force of the community, in execution of such laws, and in defense of the commonwealth from foreign injury; and all this only for the public good." On contract theory and its relevance to classical Athens, see also Chapter 11.

[3] The discourse paradigm, developed in the 1960s and 1970s, finds its most complete expression in the work of Michel Foucault, e.g., Foucault 1979, 1980a, 1980b.

speech) will depend upon generally agreed-upon truths (e.g., schemes of social categorization) as the fundamental premises of meaningful interchange. Coercive violence itself is thus part of discourse: the regime of knowledge will prescribe under what conditions one category of person may or may not perpetrate violence upon another and what constitutes violence (e.g., whether a free man may strike a slave; whether it is meaningful to speak of a husband raping his wife). The regime of knowledge/truth/power is thus maintained through discourse. A key question that faces the student of power working within the discourse paradigm is how, and by whom, social understandings are produced and reproduced—or challenged and overthrown.

Which of these two approaches is most useful in assessing the *dunamis* of the individual, the *kratos* of the Athenian demos, and their relationship to public oratory in the fourth century B.C.? The applicability of a coercion paradigm of power to the Athenian polis is, I believe, necessarily limited by its dependence on the notion of the sovereign state—a concept that seems to have been foreign to the demotic Athenian understanding of state and society.[4] There are, on the other hand, obvious affinities (some of which were discussed by Plato and Aristotle) between formal rhetoric and the broader realm of social and political discourse.[5] Thus, I will argue here that focusing on power as discourse will explain more about how persuasive public speech functioned in classical *dēmokratia* than would an exclusive focus on power as overt coercion.

If we describe the set of assumptions employed in decision making by most Athenians as a "regime of truth," it becomes apparent that one of the key "truths" upon which democratic Athenian society depended was that citizens were simultaneously equals and unequals. Citizens were equals in the public realm of political (including judicial) decision making. In the public sphere every citizen's vote had (in principle anyway) identical weight. The introduction of pay for public service and the use of the lot ensured that every citizen (at least those over age thirty) had equal access to the perquisites and the risks associated with most forms of government activity (e.g., magistracies).[6] In the fourth century most Athenians, including the elite, seemed willing to live with public, political equality—in any event, there was no systematic effort to challenge it between 403 and 322. Yet citizens remained unequal in private life. Despite the fears of elite critics of democracy, the Athenian demos never consistently employed its collective power to equalize access to desirable material

---

[4] See Chapter 8, especially 120–22.

[5] For Plato and Aristotle on oratory and discourse, see Halliwell 1994, 222–43. Cf. Kennedy 1991, 309–12; Vickers 1988, 83–147.

[6] The few exceptions (e.g., the Treasurers of Athena, limited to the highest wealth class: *Ath. Pol.* 47.1) are to be explained in terms of the demos' concern with maintaining fiscal accountability. General accounts of the opportunities and responsibilities of the Athenian citizen: Sinclair 1988; Hansen 1991.

goods.[7] Insofar as happiness is measured by ease of access to material goods, the rich Athenian lived a happier life than his poor neighbor. All Athenians knew that, and most seemed to be quite willing to live with it.

Why were elite Athenians willing to tolerate public equality, and why did ordinary Athenians, for their part, willingly countenance private inequality? Opacity is not an adequate answer; the Athenian regime of truth was unable fully to obscure the contradiction or the complexity of the balancing act: Theophrastus' "Oligarchic Man," who expresses his antidemocratic ideas in the Assembly (*Characters* 26.2) as well as to strangers (*xenoi*) and like-minded associates (26.7) and complains that it is shaming to have to sit next to his social inferiors in the Assembly (26.5), expresses in comic terms what we may guess was a fairly widespread sense of unease among the elite.[8] Aristotle (*Pol.* 1301a25–39, 1302a24–31) believed that it was the tendency of democrats to generalize equality (and so to oppress superior members of society), whereas the tendency of oligarchs was to generalize inequality (and so to oppress the poor); both tendencies, in Aristotle's view, were unjust and led to instability. In the *Politics* the philosopher unsuccessfully attempted a solution to the problem of balancing equalities by devising a system of mathematical proportions.[9] How did the Athenian regime finesse the problem?

In *Mass and Elite in Democratic Athens* I argued that powerful elite individuals and the mass of ordinary citizens who composed the demos struck and maintained a viable social contract in part through the discursive operations of public oratory.[10] In the Assembly and especially in the lawcourts, individual speakers employed the power of speech (sharpened in some cases by formal training in the art of rhetoric) in an attempt to explain themselves—their lives, their needs, their current circumstances, and their relationship to the demos— to a mass audience. The audience in turn assessed the form and the content of the speaker's address, sometimes responding vocally to specific comments. After the speeches had been delivered, the members of the audience exerted power through their collective judgment. In the ongoing dialectical give-and-take of public oratory, audience response, and demotic judgment, a set of common attitudes and social rules was hammered out. And thus Athenian ideology, the discursive basis of Athenian society, was not given from on high

---

[7] Elite fears: e.g., Aristotle *Pol.* 1318a24–26; cf. Ober 1989b, 197–98. There probably were cases in which juries convicted rich men out of greed, but there is no evidence that this was done consistently; see ibid., 200–201.

[8] For an earlier (second half of the fifth century) manifestation of antidemocratic sentiment, see [Xen.] *Ath. Pol.* Plato (*Rep.* 553a–c) suggests that oligarchic attitudes were stimulated by witnessing one's distinguished father punished by death, exile, or disenfranchisement in the people's court (*dikastērion*).

[9] Aristotle *Pol.* 1280a22–24, 1282b14–1284a3, 1287a13–17, 1296b15–34, 1301a25–1302a15; cf. Harvey 1965–66, 101–46, 99–100; Ober 1991a, 120–30.

[10] Ober 1989b, passim.

and was not a unique product of elite culture; rather, it was established and constantly revised in the practice of public debate.

The matrix of power within which oratory was practiced in democratic Athens made the *technē* of public speaking both dangerous and exciting. The Athenians were well aware both of the speaker's power—his desire and ability to sway his audience—and of the power of the audience—its willingness and ability to punish the speaker for rhetorical missteps. Furthermore, the content of many speeches was overtly concerned with issues of power. In the Assembly, the question was often how Athenian military strength could be increased and how it should be deployed. In the lawcourts, the issue was frequently whether or not a display of personal power by an individual Athenian had abrogated Athenian rules regarding appropriate social behavior.

The theme of "personal power versus social rules" was especially to the fore in cases involving charges of *hubris*. "Insolent outrage" is a reasonable enough translation for the term as it was used in Attic oratory, but Athenian law never spelled out exactly what behaviors constituted acts of *hubris*.[11] Because the law did not explain to him what *hubris* was, the juryman in a *graphē hubreōs* (or other action in which the law against *hubris* was invoked) had to judge the entire social context: the social and political statuses of litigant and defendant; their families, friends, and past behavior; the location and timing of the incident; and its ramifications for the whole of the demos.[12] This lack of nomothetic specificity is a problem for the coercion paradigm with its concern for "rule of law," but it makes perfect sense within the discursive paradigm of power. The Athenian *dikastēs* did not judge litigants according to an externalized, juridically "given" model of appropriate behavior. Rather, he judged within and through a regime of social knowledge and truth, a regime that his decision would participate in articulating—whether by strengthening existing assumptions about social categories and behavior or by revising them.

For the historian, the proof of any analytic paradigm lies in its practical explanatory usefulness. In *Mass and Elite* I applied discourse analysis to the corpus of Attic oratory; here I propose to focus on a single oration. Demosthenes 21, *Against Meidias*, is a particularly good example of the relationship between oratory and power that I have sketched out in abstract terms above. Whether or not it was formally a *graphē hubreōs*, the case was certainly concerned with a charge of *hubris*. Demosthenes' speech is openly concerned

---

[11] Definition of *hubris*: MacDowell 1990, 17–23, concluding (19) that "its [*hubris*'] essence consists of having energy or power and misusing it self-indulgently." See also Fisher 1976, 177–93; 1979, 32–47; 1990, 123–38. On the "open texture" of Athenian law and the social significance of an avoidance of strict definition, see Osborne 1985b, 40–58; Humphreys 1985a, 241–64; Todd and Millett 1990, 1–18.

[12] The seriousness with which the juror would have undertaken his task is underlined by Aristotle (*Pol.* 1311a1–2), who notes that the demos feared the *hubris* of the powerful, just as the *oligoi* feared property confiscation.

with defining the limits of behavior appropriate to the most powerful individuals in Athenian society—and with the public consequences of allowing those limits to be breached (8). Moreover, after years of neglect, a new critical edition of the speech has appeared, as have significant interpretive articles. This new scholarship has clarified (even where it has not resolved) issues of chronology, law, composition, and delivery.[13]

The specific incidents that led Demosthenes to bring charges against Meidias are laid out clearly in the speech's narrative (13–19): in the spring of 348 B.C. Demosthenes was *chorēgos* for his tribe, Pandionis. His preparations for the presentation of his tribal chorus at the Festival of Dionysos were hampered in various ways by Meidias, a well-known, wealthy politician who had an old personal quarrel with Demosthenes. Demosthenes persevered and presented the chorus, but at the Dionysia itself, in the orchestra of the theater, Meidias punched Demosthenes in the face. At the Assembly meeting held in the theater following the Dionysia, Demosthenes brought a *probolē* against Meidias, charging him with misconduct during the festival. The vote of the Assembly went against Meidias (6). This prejudicial judgment in a *probolē* did not entail punishment of the miscreant.[14] But it did give Demosthenes a boost in their future dealings in that it demonstrated that public opinion was behind him: the demos agreed that Meidias' behavior had been out of line. If Demosthenes wanted more than a moral victory, however, it was up to him to bring formal charges in a *dikastērion*. For whatever reason, Demosthenes did not immediately do so. Here certainty about the course of events ends.

Demosthenes 21, as we have it, purports to be a prosecutor's speech, delivered in a public lawsuit (not a *dikē idia*: 25, 28) before an Athenian *dikastērion* by Demosthenes in 347/6 B.C. Yet since antiquity (Plut. *Demosthenes* 12; Dionysius of Halicarnassus *First Letter to Ammaeus* 4), readers of the speech have expressed doubts about whether it was actually delivered. These doubts apparently stem from a passage in Aeschines (3.51–52) claiming that Demosthenes "sold" (*apedōto*) for thirty *mnai* both the "*hubris* to himself and the adverse vote of the demos given in the precinct of Dionysos against Meidias." It has often been supposed that this passage proves that Demosthenes accepted a bribe and so did not pursue the charge in the courts after the initial *probolē* in the Assembly. But then why did he write the speech? Several theories have been proposed attempting to reconcile the fact of the speech's existence with Aeschines' statement: it is claimed that certain passages show signs of incompleteness—and ergo that the speech was begun when Demosthenes still planned to prosecute Meidias but was never completed because the bribe subsequently induced Demosthenes to abandon his plan. Yet the stylistic argument for incompleteness

---

[13] Edition: MacDowell 1990; articles: E. M. Harris 1989, 117–36; Wilson 1991, 164–95.
[14] *Probolē* procedure: Harrison 1968–71, 1:59–64; MacDowell 1975, 194–97; MacDowell 1990, 13–17.

is not very convincing in and of itself; each of the supposed weaknesses, redun-
dancies, and inconsistencies has been vigorously defended by those who suppose that the speech does represent an essentially finished product.[15]

If left unfinished and never delivered, the publication of the speech against
Meidias (which concentrates on the prosecutor's bravery and steadfastness in
bringing the case before the jury: e.g., 3, 40, 120) would have been a political
and stylistic embarrassment to Demosthenes. Anomalous circumstances must
therefore be adduced to explain its eventual publication.[16] Furthermore, the
"no trial" hypothesis requires Demosthenes to have written a nearly complete
speech *before* ever bringing a formal indictment against Meidias: Demosthenes,
as prosecutor, would have suffered *atimia* if he had brought charges in a public
case before a magistrate and had then withdrawn them (103, and see below);
Aeschines could hardly have failed to mention that juicy fact. Yet, as E. M.
Harris points out, it would be very odd indeed for Demosthenes to have written the speech so early in the legal process. Harris concludes that there is no a
priori reason for us to believe Aeschines' claim. It was made in respect to
events that had occured some sixteen years previously, and few in the audience
at the trial of Ctesiphon in 330 would remember the exact course of events.
The fact that Meidias was not *severely* punished (as he clearly was not, since he
was politically active in the years after 347/6) allowed Aeschines to make up
the vague bribery story and leave his listeners to decide whether he meant that
bribery forestalled prosecution or that the prosecutor was bribed to propose an
excessively light penalty.[17] In sum, the case for supposing that *Against Meidias*
was never delivered is no more compelling than one that might be made
against other major public speeches in the Demosthenic corpus (e.g., 20, 22, or
23). I will proceed on the assumption that we are dealing with a speech that
was delivered in a *dikastērion* in more or less the form we have it, and was
subsequently published by its author.

The internal evidence of the speech indicates that the trial of Meidias took
place about two years after the incident in the theater. In 347/6, stung by an
(unsuccessful) attack launched by Meidias at his *dokimasia* (public scrutiny) for
the office of *bouleutēs* (111, 114), Demosthenes reopened the issue of the punch

[15] Review of history of the "stylistic weakness" argument (from Photius [*Bibl.* 491ab, citing
earlier opinion] in the ninth century, to A. Boeckh in 1818, through K. J. Dover in 1968): E. M.
Harris 1989, 119–20; MacDowell 1990, 24–27. Arguments against stylistic weakness: Erbse 1965;
E. M. Harris 1989, 121–29.

[16] Thus, Boeckh (1818, 60–100) suggested that the draft of the speech had been found among
Demosthenes' papers after his death and published only posthumously. Wilson (1991, 187) suggests that Demosthenes did circulate the speech himself.

[17] E. M. Harris 1989, 132–36. Wilson (1991), unaware of Harris' article, does not argue the
case, but speaks of the "likelihood" that the speech "was not risked in the public domain of the
courts" (165 with n. 12); by the end of his article (187), likelihood has evolved to certainty.

by lodging his complaint with one of the *thesmothetai* (presumably having sum-
moned Meidias to appear before the magistrate as well).[18] The indictment
would have been publicly announced by being posted in front of the Eponymous Heroes (cf. 103). There has been considerable discussion of what procedural category Demosthenes employed in his indictment. Although Demosthenes harps on *hubris* throughout the speech, MacDowell (among others)
has challenged the assumption that it was a *graphē hubreōs*, arguing that the
probolē procedure covered both the initial action in the Assembly and the subsequent trial in the *dikastērion*.[19] This point of law has little bearing on my argument; in either case we are dealing with a public *agōn timētos* (25: a guilty verdict
would be followed by a second set of speeches offering alternate penalties, any
fine levied went to the state rather than to the prosecutor, and penalties would
be imposed if the prosecutor withdrew the charge or failed to secure one-fifth
of the votes). If the jury trial was a continuation of the *probolē*, a court date was
probably set at the first hearing before the *thesmothetēs*; if a *graphē hubreōs*, there
would have been a preliminary hearing (*anakrisis*) before the magistrate at
which much of the evidence would have been presented.[20] As Harris points
out (see above), the speech was surely written between the time that the preliminary charge was lodged and the trial itself, and surely after the *anakrisis* if there
was one.

At the trial itself, Demosthenes and Meidias each used the power of oratory
in attempting to persuade the jury to vote in his favor. But that power depended on a close "fit" with audience expectations and presuppositions. This
meant adapting form and content of the rhetorical performance to the ideological context determined by an audience representing a cross-section of the
mature (over thirty) citizen male population of Athens—overwhelmingly men
who were not members of a social elite.[21] The two litigants, on the other hand,
were both celebrities, members of the same elite social category: both were
very wealthy, both highly skilled speakers, both *rhētores*, that is, members of
Athens' small cadre of expert politicians.[22] Thus, from the point of view of a
juror whose judgment was based on established social categories, there might
be little to choose between the two contestants. But social categorization would
not be the sole basis of his judgment. Both men would probably be known to

[18] Chronology: MacDowell 1990, 6–11. Indictment before the *thesmothetēs*: 3, 32, with Mac-
Dowell's commentary ad loc.

[19] The action was a *graphē hubreōs*: E. M. Harris 1989, 125, 130 n. 32 (with review of earlier
literature). Not a *graphē hubreōs*: MacDowell 1990, 16; Wilson 1991, 165 n. 11.

[20] Probably no need for *anakrisis* in cases of *probolē*: MacDowell 1975, 242; ergo the court date
would be set immediately upon the lodging of the complaint.

[21] Social composition of Athenian juries: Markle 1985, 265–97; Ober 1989b, 142–44; Todd
1990, 146–73.

[22] Definition of *rhētōr*: Ober 1989b, 105–12; Hansen 1991, 143–45.

him, at least by reputation—and he might well have heard them speak in the
Assembly or at previous trials.[23] The architectonics of each contestant's rhetorical self-presentation therefore consisted of building upon the audience's
existing opinion of himself, using his rhetorical skills as his tools. The building
materials included the facts of the case, the life histories of the litigants, and the
audience's social presuppositions.

Among Demosthenes' problems in constructing a persuasive case against
Meidias was the relative slightness of the offense, a problem that was exacerbated by the passage of time. The positive vote at the initial *probole* in the
Assembly was certainly in his favor, but two years later, who really cared if one
rich politician had bopped another in the nose? Given the existence of a
strongly antielitist streak in Athenian popular ideology, Demosthenes must
have worried that many jurors would see the incident as a silly intra-elite spat,
and one that could have been solved quickly enough if Demosthenes had just
been man enough to hit back. Demosthenes' central problem, then, was the
tendency of the jurors to lump himself and Meidias into a single social category
("over-powerful, elite politicians"). If that category were distinct from the one
in which the jurors placed themselves ("regular guys"), there was a dreadful
likelihood that the jurors would take on the role of spectators of a rather foolish
tiff among people for whom they felt no inherent sympathy. They might simply laugh the case out of court. Thus, among Demosthenes' rhetorical goals
was to draw a crystal clear set of distinctions between himself and his adver-
sary. Meidias is to be stranded on the far side of an unbridgeable gulf constructed by Demosthenes' oration; on the near side stands the prosecutor,
shoulder-to-shoulder with the demos. But it was more complex than that; Demosthenes must also remind the audience of his own continued possession of
elite characteristics, since on these characteristics rested his claim to the privileged political position accorded the *rhētōr*.[24] In sum, since the construction of
social categories was a key part of Athens' truth regime (i.e., the understandings the jury would use in their judgment), Demosthenes must work with a set
of assumptions about the category to which both he and Meidias belonged. At
the same time he must confound assumptions about the homogeneity of the
category. He must explain to the audience that "we are indeed both elite and
both powerful, but we are very different sorts of men in terms of our worth to
the demos."

The actual speech negotiates these difficulties with great finesse. The unbridgeable gulf between Demosthenes/demos and Meidias is brilliantly
sketched. In a number of passages Meidias is shown to be vastly wealthy and,

---

[23] Function of gossip in the making of a man's reputation: Dover 1988, 45–52; Hunter 1990,
299–325; D. Cohen 1992, 89–97.

[24] On the balance between elite and demotic claims on the parts of *rhētores*: Ober 1989b,
passim.

as a direct result of that wealth, arrogant (66–67, 96, 98, 100, 194) and scornful of the demos and those he regards as his inferiors (132, 134, 185, 193–95, 198, 203–4, 211). Worse yet, his wealth gave him considerable power within the society, power that he willfully used to destroy those ordinary citizens who stood in the way of fulfilling his desires (20, 98, 106, 109, 123–24, 137). In sum, Meidias was "rich, bold, with a big head and a big voice, violent, [and] shameless" (201). Meidias could be depicted as *sui generis*, isolated within society in willful self-exile (198). But elsewhere Demosthenes locates the entire class of the excessively wealthy across the gulf with Meidias. Here he suggests that Meidias' behavior is indicative of the antidemocratic attitudes harbored by the wealthy elite: they longed to gain control of the state, and if they ever did come to power, they would be merciless to the ordinary working man (208–10). In contrast to rich Meidias and his rich cronies, Demosthenes paints a picture of himself as a middling sort of man: a hoplite (not a cavalryman, like Meidias) who, along with his fellow soldiers, was shocked by lurid tales of Meidias' combined cowardice and grotesque extravagance during the Euboean campaign (133, cf. 1, 112).

In other passages Demosthenes presents himself rather differently: not among those who are weak or friendless, but indeed as a member of the Athenian elite, able and willing to use his elite attributes—wealth, speaking ability, standing in the community—to help defend the rest of the citizens against the likes of Meidias (111, 189, 192, 219). And thus he reveals himself as a powerful figure in his own right. Demosthenes must, of course, sidestep the appearance of arrogance. He avoids contradicting Athenian assumptions regarding the reality of popular control of affairs by pointing out that he is not alone in his heroic resistance to Meidias. Time and again, Demosthenes claims allegiance to and alliance with the laws—in one dramatic passage he literally takes the reified laws of Athens as his kin, asking the jury to contrast him, surrounded by the laws, with Meidias, surrounded by weepy relatives.[25] This striking image reveals a vital distinction Demosthenes establishes between himself and his rival: whereas Meidias depends on his family for support, Demosthenes is a public figure, devoted to the public good. He is, at least by implication, a powerful man only through the backing of the actively expressed will of the people—just as the laws themselves are just inscribed letters unless the people are willing to act boldly in their defense (223–25; cf. 37ff., 57, and see below). Demosthenes' wealth is meaningful to him only because it allows him to face down bullies like Meidias and to give generously to the public weal (156–57, 189). Meidias, on the other hand, is selfish with his money: he uses it in vulgar and offensive displays calculated to humiliate ordinary citizens (133, 158–59, 195–96). He never willingly contributes to public projects, and he arrogantly

---

[25] Pars. 186–188. I am indebted to Danielle Allen for drawing my attention to the key importance of this passage. See also par. 7.

believes that the special tax (*proeisphora*) he is forced to pay gives him the right to harangue and berate the rest of the citizenry in the Assembly (151–69).

So far we have touched on two of the rhetorical strategies Demosthenes employed in *Against Meidias* in order to distinguish himself from his rival. First he draws a line between the elite cavalryman and the ordinary hoplite; next, he contrasts styles of elite behavior: the selfish, antidemocratic man interested in his private goods versus the selfless public man who takes the laws as his kin. A third, more subtle tactic may have helped Demosthenes distinguish between the nature and function of his powers and those of his rival. At 154, Demosthenes specifically points out the differences in their ages: he claims to be thirty-two, while his opponent is "about fifty or a little less." The jury might suppose that there was an eighteen-year gap in the their ages. But Harris argues convincingly that Demosthenes was lying about his own age.[26] He suggests that Demosthenes' primary motive for the fiction was a desire to emphasize the disparity between the two men's liturgical records; Demosthenes' generous record looked even better if compressed into a shorter lifespan. There was, however, a pointed subtext: Emphasizing, or even, with Harris, overstating the age difference helps Demosthenes to depict himself as a young man confronting a man considerably his senior in years as well as in political strength. This contrast would have considerable resonance for Athenians, raised on stories of the youthful exploits of Theseus—mythical founder of the democracy.[27]

The youth versus powerful older man theme at 154 is no fortuitous bit of extemporaneous invention. Demosthenes had already, at 71–72, prepared his listeners to focus on the theme of age and power inequality by relating a pair of anecdotes. In the first, he "reminded" his listeners of a story, one that he claimed many of them would know well, of a youth's successful confrontation with an older, stronger, insolent man.[28] He followed up with another brief tale that linked the first story to his own situation and illustrated the serious consequences that could result from acts of *hubris*. Both *logoi* concern men who killed other men who dared offer them *hubris*. The first concerns Euthynos and Sophilos:

[26] E. M. Harris 1989, 121–25.

[27] The ideological underpinnings of the Theseus myth are discussed by Strauss (1993, 100–129). On the social and political significance of acting out a culture's central myths, see Ober and Strauss 1990, 245–46, with literature cited. Cf. also par. 69: Meidias' failure to demonstrate "youthful enterprise" (*eneanieusato*). Demosthenes pointedly mocks Meidias' pretensions to youthful machismo at par. 131: Meidias no longer thinks it *neanikos* to insult individuals, so he insults whole groups; and par. 201: Meidias falsely thinks it *neanikos* to ignore "you"—the people. The root meaning of *neanikos* is "youthful," and MacDowell's translation of *neanikos* as "macho" is on the mark.

[28] This is an example of the "everybody knows" topos: Ober 1989b, 149–50, 163. This is used elsewhere in the speech (e.g., 1, 16, 137, 149, 167) and helps establish Demosthenes' solidarity with popular knowledge and wisdom.

Everyone knows—or if not everyone, many people—that on one occasion Euthynos the famous wrestler, the young man (*neaniskos*), defended himself even
against Sophilos the pancratist. The latter was a strong man, dark—I'm sure
certain ones of you know the man I mean. They were in Samos, just passing the
time privately (*idiai*) with some friends; and because he [Euthynos] thought him
insolent (*auton hubrizein*), he defended himself so vigorously that he actually killed
him. (71)

The implied parallel to young, vigorous Demosthenes and older, stronger
Meidias is quite clear in the context of the oration.[29]

The second tale is equally instructive:

Many people (*polloi*) know that Euaion, the brother of Leodamas, killed Boiotos at
a dinner party (*en deipnōi kai sunodōi koinēi*) because of one blow. It was not the blow
that made him angry, but the dishonor (*atimia*); nor is being hit such a serious
matter (*deinon*) to free men (*eleutherois*), though it is serious, but rather being hit with
hubris. (71–72)

As in the case of the Euthynos *logos*, the story of Euaion is one of revenge for
insolence offered in a specifically private context (see MacDowell 1990, ad
loc.). But with Euaion—to whom Demosthenes pointedly compares himself
(73–76)—the speaker adds that hubristic assault brings with it the threat of
atimia, and points to the psychological effect of insolent assault on *eleutheroi*.
Demosthenes' follow-up to the double story is to point out that in his own case
the context of the insult was not private, but public: he was *chorēgos*, the assault
occurred in the theater at a public festival and was witnessed by citizens and
foreigners alike (74, cf. 31ff.). It is in the transposition of what might well have
remained a private affair between rival aristocrats to the public realm dominated by the demos that the stakes involved in the play of power and ideology
are most clearly exposed.

After relating the early history of his conflict with Meidias—a tale that
enables Demosthenes to emphasize his extreme youth (78)—the prosecutor
introduces the poignant figure of Strato the arbitrator. With the Strato *logos*,
the speaker confronts his audience with the implications of private-realm aristocratic arrogance spilling over into the public realm. When we combine the
salient points of the Euthynos and Euaion stories, we get a tale of justifiable
revenge executed by a brave young man against an older, stronger man in
order to redress the *atimia* associated with an act of *hubris*. Strato, by contrast, is
far from an aristocratic youth in the first flush of his strength: an older man (as
an arbitrator [*diaitētēs*] he was, by definition, sixty years old), he was a worker
and inexperienced in public affairs (*penēs*, *apragmōn*: 83). Moreover, says De-

[29] At par. 78 Demosthenes moves immediately to the story of his early problems with Meidias,
describing himself then as a "very young lad" (*meirakullion*) who was confronted by a violent and
profane break-in by Meidias and his brother.

mosthenes, Strato was no rascal (*ponēros*), indeed he is a useful citizen (*chrēstos*: 83, cf. 95): the exemplary ordinary Athenian who did his mandatory year's public service as arbitrator not because he was ambitious but because it was his duty.[30] Strato was assigned by lot to Demosthenes and Meidias when the former indicted the latter for slander (foul language used in the presence of Demosthenes' sister and mother, when Meidias and his brother broke into Demosthenes' home [*oikia*] demanding a property exchange [*antidosis*]: 78–80). On the day of the arbitration, Meidias did not (at first) show up, and so Strato reluctantly gave a default verdict against him. After Demosthenes had gone home in triumph, Meidias arrived at the arbitrators' offices and tried to bribe Strato to reverse his judgment. Strato refused. Meidias later vindictively and manipulatively gained a judgment against Strato, and so "he expelled and disenfranchised (*ekballei kai atimoi*) the arbitrator" (87). Strato, like Euaion, thus suffered *atimia* (cf. 92) at the hands of a hubristic man—and yet the meaning of *atimia* has shifted dramatically with the move from the private to the public sphere, as has the victim's power to defend himself.

The *atimia* that Euaion suffered when punched by Boiotos was personal and social dishonor: his worth was compromised in his own eyes and those of his fellows. This loss of honor (*timē*) carried with it no formal political disabilities and was evidently wiped clean by Euaion's vigorous self-defense. The meaning of *atimia* for Strato was quite different: rather than being stripped of private honor, the arbitrator lost his status as a citizen. Moreover, since Meidias had secured the judgment through the legal system, there was no recourse for Strato as there had been for Euthynos and Euaion—as an *atimos*, Strato became utterly powerless (92, 95). Having lost even the right to speak in public fora, he is put on display by Demosthenes as a mute example of the ghastly effects on an ordinary Athenian of hubristic power exercised in the public realm.

Taken together, the three *logoi* (Euthynos / Sophilos, Euaion / Boiotos, Strato / Meidias) illuminate a crucial difference between elite and demotic

---

[30] Interpretation of this passage: Ober 1989b, 209–11. I follow Goodwin (cf. MacDowell 1990, ad loc.) in translating *allōs d' ou ponēros* as "moreover not bad" rather than (per MacDowell and others) "but in other ways not bad." MacDowell (1990, loc. cit.) and Wilson (1991, 180–81, citing Thuc. 2.40.2) seem to me to get the force of *apragmōn* wrong. There is certainly an echo here of Pericles' Funeral Oration (Thuc. 2.40.1–2: τὸ πένεσθαι οὐχ ὁμολογεῖν τινι αἰσχρόν . . . μόνοι γὰρ τόν τε μηδὲν τῶνδε [sc. ἔργα τὰ πολιτικὰ] μετέχοντα οὐκ ἀπράγμονα, ἀλλ᾽ ἀχρεῖον νομίζομεν. Both Pericles / Thucydides and Demosthenes are manipulating traditional sentiments about the link between wealth, public activity, and usefulness to the community (cf., for example, the Solonian *telē*). But the point of the Strato story is that this ordinary man became Meidias' victim through no fault of his own. Strato's *apragmosunē* is his lack of overt political ambition, not an unwillingness to do his public duty. Since the Athenian laws require certain public duties, *every* Athenian (not just those who are ambitious) is at risk from the Meidas-type. Note, too, that *chrēstos*, which in elite discourse could mean "elite," here clearly means "man who is a positive asset to the state," in contrast to the *ponēros*, who is a public liability.

strata of Athenian society. On the one hand, the elite linkage of *hubris* with personal dishonor—what we might call the "economy of *timē*"—provides the appropriate context for private acts of *hubris* and for the quick, violent, personal revenge associated with those acts.[31] But the fate of Strato—the exemplary ordinary Athenian (*anēr politēs*: 88; *Athēnaiōn hena*: 90; *tōn pollōn heis*: 96) who became *atimos* in the process of doing his public duty—suggests that the willful exertion of personal power in the public realm has as its target not private or family honor, but a central quality of citizenship itself. The distinction revolves around the term *timē* and its associated semantic field: the language of *timē* clearly meant one thing in the world of aristocratic competition, quite another in the world of the ordinary citizen. Although there is considerable talk of *philotimia* in the speech (67, 159, 162), this attribute is associated specifically with the elite individual whose most precious possession was his personal honor. By contrast, the most precious possession of the ordinary Athenian was, for want of a better term, the dignity he enjoyed because he was a citizen.

By citizen dignity, I refer to the "basket" of privileges, immunities, duties, and responsibilities that the full citizen (one not suffering legal disabilities rendering him *atimos*) enjoyed by the simple fact of his possession of citizen status. Citizen dignity, in the sense in which I am using the term here, was a composite, a conglomeration of attributes that is not adequately captured by any one Greek word. Citizen dignity is perhaps most visible in its absence: Its negative, shadow-other is *atimia* in its political sense: the status of Strato after Meidias' successful legal attack. The positive content of citizen dignity is best captured by the several discrete elements that constitute the composite; it may most readily be defined by the intersection of individual freedom (*eleutheria*: 124, 180), political equality (*isotēs*: 67, 111), and security (*bebaiotēs*: 222; *asphaleia*: 227). It is in the triadic relationship between freedom, equality, and security that the ordinary citizen found and defended his place in the Athenian sociopolitical order. But that defense could not be carried out individually, or by reference to inalienable rights.

Private honor and citizen dignity had much in common: both implied a rejection of self-abasement and an immunity from degrading violations of the body's physical integrity (179, 180).[32] But in Greek aristocratic society, honor (as has often been pointed out) was a scarce resource in an endless zero-sum game. In the simplest two-player simulation, player A gains in honor only at the expense of player B's honor.[33] Although Athenian citizenship was highly exclusivist by modern standards, dignity was not in the same sense a scarce

---

[31] For the linkage of *hubris* with private dishonor, see esp. the work by Fisher: 1976, 1979, 1990.

[32] On bodily integrity, see Winkler 1990, 54–64; Halperin 1990, 96; Wilson 1991, 164–65.

[33] Zero-sum, honor/shame-based competition and its links to the "Mediterranean society" model: Winkler 1990, 45–70; D. Cohen 1992, 35–69.

commodity *within* the community of citizens. The dignity of citizen A was not ordinarily enhanced at the expense of his fellows. In the course of the fifth and fourth centuries, the Athenian citizenry radically augmented the material and psychic value of citizenship.[34] Thus, while the total number of players did not expand much, the total "quantity" of dignity available to the players *was* expansive. Dignity was a citizen's personal possession in the sense that it could be lost through individual acts (e.g., engaging in prostitution) or removed by legal judgment. Yet it was simultaneously a collective possession of the demos. The downside of this collective ownership was that the total sum of dignity could be reduced (and thus each individual's immunities, etc., lessened) if the citizenry failed to act to guard its possession. It was the power of collective action that had created citizen dignity in the first place;[35] a lack of collective defense in the face of threats offered by powerful individuals could result in its loss (45, 57, 124, 140, 142).

The chain of reasoning developed above helps to explain the argument that underlies Demosthenes' speech. It was one thing for powerful, honor-driven aristocrats to attack one another and to defend themselves in private. It was quite another thing when an aristocrat began to bring his *hubris* to bear on ordinary citizens. At this point, and especially when attacks were made upon citizens acting in formal public capacities (as *chorēgoi* or *diaitētai*: 31–34, 87), it was incumbent upon the collectivity to staunchly resist the deployment of individual power. Nothing less than the individual and collective dignity of the citizen was at stake: "If anyone who tries to stand up for himself when quite illegally assaulted by Meidias is going to suffer this [court-mandated expulsion and disenfranchisement] and similar treatment, it will be best just to offer *proskunēsis* [bow down] to hubristic men, as they do in barbarian lands, rather than try to resist them" (106). If the citizenry will not stand up to Meidias, they will cease to be dignified citizens and will devolve into salaaming subjects of the powerful few.[36]

In order to avoid this nauseating outcome, the jurors must see the situation clearly: Meidias is an exemplar (*paradeigma*: 76, 97, 227) of the powerful rich. The individual rich man, and the rich as a class, are desirous of forcing their hierarchical approach to private life and their hierarchical system of social categorization upon the whole of Athenian political society. Intolerant of equality and freedom, they long to humiliate and subjugate all ordinary persons, whom they regard not as dignified citizens but as subhuman (185, 208–9). Individually, ordinary Athenians were much too weak to stand up against the violence of the powerful elite. And the laws alone had no force capable of

---

[34] For the origins of this process, see Manville 1990; for its development in the fifth and fourth centuries: Ober 1989b, 53–103.

[35] See Chapter 4.

[36] Cf. par. 124: anyone who stands in the way of convicting Meidias "is simply taking away our enjoyment of free speech (*isēgoria*) and freedom (*eleutheria*)."

preventing their misuse by the elite. But acting collectively, in defense of the laws and customs of the democratic order, the demos was indeed powerful enough to force the elite to recognize the dignity of each citizen, and powerful enough to discipline any of those who dared to step out of line:

> All this [the tale of Meidias and his toadies], I suppose, is frightening to each one of the rest of you, living individually as best you can. That's why you should unite: individually each of you is weaker than they [the rich] are, either in friends or resources or something else; but united you'll be stronger than each of them and you will put a stop to their *hubris*. . . . If a man is so powerful (*dunasthai*) that he can prevent each of us singly from getting justice from him, now, since he is in our grasp, he must be punished jointly by all for all, as a common enemy of the state. (140–42)

A desirable outcome was thus possible: mass strength could trump individual strength. Yet, given the structure of Athenian legal procedure, in order for this desirable outcome to be realized, it was necessary that a brave and resourceful individual citizen be willing to stand up to the exemplary hubristic malefactor by dragging him into court. Enter Demosthenes, the man who (as he explains in detail) has what it takes to confront the monster and bring him to justice: the necessary elite attributes of wealth and rhetorical skill and the necessary allegiance to the public good.

Yet Demosthenes makes clear that prosecuting Meidias with the support of laws and demos and in defense of the dignity of the citizenry required more than just personal strength and bravery in the face of superior strength. It also entailed a willingness to sacrifice individual honor, since it meant that Demosthenes had to forego deadly private vengeance. This "sacrifice" meant, however, that he could have his cake and eat it too. By constructing an image of himself as a bold young elite, Demosthenes shows that he is the sort of man who *could* successfully have defended his *timē*, just as Euthynos and Euaion had defended theirs. But, happily for the demos, Demosthenes is also the moderate, middling citizen who sees clearly that the interest of the state (avoiding bloodshed, while simultaneously making a public example of Meidias and thus curbing the insolence of the rich as a class) must override his natural urge to dispatch his rival on the spot:

> I think my decision [not to retaliate physically] was prudent (*sōphronōs*), or rather it was providential (*eutuchōs*), when I acquiesced at the time and was not induced to do anything disastrous—though I fully sympathize with Euaion and anyone else who has defended himself when dishonored (*atimazomenos*). . . . When I exercised so much care to prevent any disastrous result that I did not defend myself at all, from whom ought I to obtain atonement for what was done to me? From you and the laws, I think; and an example (*paradeigma*) ought to be set, to show everyone else that all hubristic men should not be fought off at the moment of anger, but

referred to you, in the knowledge that you are the guarantors and guardians of legal protection for victims. (74–76, cf. 219)

Later in the speech Demosthenes underlines his selflessness by pointing out that it is not he who is most in danger from Meidias:

> You should all be equally angry, in view of the fact that the likeliest of you to suffer easy maltreatment are the poorest and weakest (*penestatoi, asthenestatoi*). . . . In my own case, no doubt, I repulsed lies and accusations . . . I haven't been annihilated. But what will you, *hoi polloi*, do, unless you publicly frighten everyone away from the misuse of wealth for this purpose [*hubris*]? (123–24, cf. 221–22)

We can now grasp the import of the peroration and see how it relates to the proem of the speech: Demosthenes, the elite *rhētōr* (cf. 189), had done his part by dragging Meidias, master of legal evasion, into court. The demos in the Assembly had done its part by condemning Meidias in the initial *probolē* (2–3). Now it was up to the jurors to be as true to their own interests and to the common ideals on which Athenian political life was predicated. They must use their collective power of judgment to destroy the dangerous individual and reestablish the authority of the demotic regime of truth:

> Before the case was proved you showed your anger, you called on the victim [Demosthenes] to take revenge, you applauded when I brought a *probolē* against him in the Assembly; yet now that the case has been demonstrated, and the demos sitting in a sacred precinct has given a preliminary condemnation of him . . . when it is in your power to deal with it all by a single vote, will you now fail to support me, to offer *charis* to the demos, to teach everyone a lesson (*tous allous sōphronisai*), and to secure a safe life for yourselves in future by making of him an example (*paradeigma*) to everyone? (227)

Finally, we need to consider the degree to which Demosthenes' oratory was, and could have been, independent of the discursive regime that forms its deep context. In a recent article on *Against Meidias*, Peter Wilson argues that in several key passages Demosthenes loses rhetorical control of his own text: although he hoped to depict himself as a loyal democrat, his speech is hopelessly subverted by established and elitist aristocratic norms.[37] Thus (in the terminology adopted above) social power in the form of a truth regime wins out in the end—and that regime was ultimately a product of elite, not demotic, ideals and discourse. Is this actually the case? While conforming in obvious ways to demotic ideals, does Demosthenes' oratory finally and helplessly serve to subvert them? Is the democratic ideology that is so prominent in much of the speech actually twisted against itself by the irresistible power of an overarching

---

[37] Wilson 1991, 170–71, 181–82, 186–87. In arguing that aristocratic norms subverted what was ostensibly democratic discourse, Wilson follows Loraux 1986.

aristocratic value system? I don't think so. Rather, Demosthenes' speech shows us how a central aristocratic ideal (*timē*) is at once transformed by and delimited within the public democratic environment. Demosthenes tells his audience an interesting and complex story about honor and its relationship to *hubris*. By invoking the examples of Euthynos and Euaion he shows the enduring importance of honor within the "realm of inequality" that characterized the subsociety of the elite. By exploring the two senses of *atimia* he shows how personal honor is transubstantiated into citizen dignity in the realm of equality that characterizes citizen society. The example of Strato, by demonstrating the danger that "a Meidias" represents to the individual dignity of the ordinary citizen, shows why a democracy must isolate and regulate elite behavior patterns. And Demosthenes' speech itself is an example of *how* the democratic regime can and should use the skills and attributes of the "good elite" speaker in reasserting order.

Demosthenes' speech participates actively in democratic ideals. Its persuasive power is overtly intended to allow the power of the people to find its target, that is, the powerful individual who embodies the continuing threat of "nontransformed" aspects of aristocratic culture to spill over into the public realm. Oratory is thus a lens that focuses the great but diffuse power of the Athenian truth regime upon appropriate objects. The pretrial lack of focus is symbolized by the avid but inchoate hissing and shouting against Meidias in the theater, by the many who approached Demosthenes to urge him to follow through on the prosecution (2, 23, 198, 216, 226), and perhaps even by the overwhelming but forceless initial vote at the *probolē*. Demosthenes implies that if the regime had been working smoothly, and Meidias had been a proper citizen, the latter would have listened carefully to these expressions of demotic dissatisfaction and would have conformed to the spirit of the laws without the need of a trial (61, 63). But Meidias is a rogue elite, who thinks he can ignore or override all signs of popular disfavor. In this situation, discourse must be translated into overt action (30). It is through the speech of the prosecutor and the subsequent vote of the people gathered as *dikastai* that the regime is reified. At this point, speech and judgment become concrete forces for action, in a way that a general regime of thought or law, that remains both everywhere and nowhere, never could. *Logos* becomes *ergon*, and thus the power of the people is manifested in the life of the citizen:

> For in fact, if you cared to consider and investigate the question of what it is that gives power and control (*ischuroi kai kurioi*) over everything in the polis to those of you who are jurors at any given time . . . you would find that the reason is not that you alone of the citizens are armed and mobilized in ranks, nor that you are physically the best and strongest, nor that you are youngest (*neōtatoi*) in age, nor anything of the sort, but rather you'd find that you are powerful (*ischuein*) through the laws. And what is the power (*ischus*) of the laws? Is it that, if any of you is attacked and gives a shout, they'll come running to your aid? No, they are just

inscribed letters and have no ability to do that. What then is their motive power
(*dunamis*)? You are, if you secure them and make them authoritative (*kurioi*) whenever anyone asks for aid. So the laws are powerful (*ischuroi*) through you and you
through the laws. You must therefore stand up for them in just the same way as
any individual would stand up for himself if attacked; you must take the view that
offenses against the law are common concerns (*koina*). (223–25)

Here, several of the key themes I have attempted to elucidate are set out
clearly: the power of the collectivity; the association of individual powerfulness
with youthfulness; the relationship between the individual acting in defense of
his own person and honor; and the need for common action in defense of
common dignity.

The movement from inanimate law to political action through the medium
of speech that is at the heart of the passage quoted above suggests that Athenian oratory, while deeply enmeshed in common assumptions about social
categories and proper behavior, is more than a ventriloquization of a truth
regime. The individual speaker, with his individual attributes and perspective,
was indispensable as the spark that fired the system. It was in this dynamic
relationship between truth regime and individual initiator / orator that Athenian democracy existed. Without the common assumptions I have dubbed the
"regime of truth," Athens would been no more than a mob of self-interested
individuals—and thus certainly would have fallen prey to the endless round of
debilitating *stasis* that characterized the histories of so many Greek poleis in the
fourth century.[38] Without the intervention of distinct voices and individual
histories into the matrix of social assumptions, Athenian society would have
been static and nightmarish—an Orwellian "1984" with the demos as Big
Brother. The balance of individual and social power was always uneasy; a
good part of the enduring fascination of Attic oratory is its depiction—at the
level of both form and content—of a highwire act with no net.

[38] Cf. Aristotle *Pol.* 1302a31–b3 (recalling much of the language of Dem. 21): men fight *staseis*
in order to gain *timē* and material goods (*kerdos*), and to avoid *atimia* and punishments. What stirs
them up in the first place is either seeing others increasing their share of *timē* and *kerdos*; or *hubris*,
fear (*phobos*), preeminence (*huperochē*), contempt (*kataphronēsis*), or disproportionate self-aggrandize-
ment (*auxēsis*).

Chapter 8

THE NATURE OF ATHENIAN DEMOCRACY

My long-running debate with Mogens Herman Hansen over how to interpret various aspects of Athenian democracy and how to characterize its nature has been very fruitful (see, for example, Hunter 1994, 185–89). The published version of that debate is inaugurated in this 1989 essay over the question of the primacy of ideology versus that of institutions; it is continued in Chapter 11, over the question of polis as state (a community of citizens) versus polis as society (a community embracing citizens and noncitizens). The dramatic acme of our dialogue occurred, however, a few years earlier, in December 1986 at a meeting of the American Philological Association.

Hansen served as commentator on a panel on social and ideological aspects of Athenian democracy in the fourth century B.C., at which I delivered a paper, "Elite Education and Political Leadership in Democratic Athens." During the discussion period, Hansen and I began disputing the question (which is central to this chapter) of how to define the term "demos." He advocated a limited, institutional definition; I proposed the broader definition defended here. Following the adjournment of the formal panel proceedings, the panelists and members of the audience initiated a symposium at the hotel bar. Hansen and I kept on about the demos; neither of us was able to make much headway with the other, and neither was willing to drop the subject. As the wine arrived, my interlocutor announced that there was only one way to resolve such disputes and placed his right elbow on the table. I accepted the challenge and we proceeded to arm-wrestle over the meaning of demos, to the startled amusement of our fellow symposiasts. That memorable physical encounter was no more decisive than, but just as convivial as, any of my subsequent, less literal wrestling matches with the man now generally acknowledged to be the dean of Athenian democracy studies. And the encounter seems an appropriate symbol for a discussion centering on the complicated relationship between theory and practice, discourse and deed.

This review essay points up a number of the issues of conceptualization, definition, and methodology that are at stake in contemporary discussions of ancient Greek democracy. The chapter tests the work of a scholar whose approach is highly empirical and positivistic against the historical method advocated in Chapter 2; that is to say, I begin by asking whether a given approach will yield conclusions that are useful and meaningful, and I posit that it will not do so unless the conceptual apparatus being employed is meaningful given the context of the society in question. This concern is

This review of Hansen 1987 was originally published in *Classical Philology* 84 (1989), 322–34. Page references within the text of this chapter are to Hansen 1987. Copyright © 1989 by the University of Chicago. All rights reserved.

illustrated by the discussion of "sovereignty"—a term that is, so I argue, seriously misleading when applied to classical Greek forms of political organization.

As in other chapters, the problem of how norms relate to practices takes center stage.
For Hansen, the normative logic represented by the established lawcode is ultimately
more important than the actual practices of Athenian society at any given point in its
development. Thus, on the issue of speaker and audience in the Assembly, if the logic of
the law points to a norm of one-way communication—from speaker to audience—then
historical evidence for audience-to-speaker communication points only to aberrations
and is not of fundamental importance in understanding the nature of the system. By
contrast, the norms that most concern me are those that constitute what I call popular
ideology; they are most clearly revealed in the discourse of Assembly and lawcourt
debate. That ideology is, in turn, intimately linked to contemporary practices: on my
reading, in a responsive direct democracy, institutional practices and popular ideology
cannot get too far out of balance, because institutions can be and are changed with
relative ease, and the experience of using institutions in turn results in changes in the
way citizens think about politics and society. Ideology is thus neither prior to nor opposed to sociopolitical practice; it is part of practice, just as in speech-act theory the
descriptive function of language is part of its performative function. The ongoing democratic process of norm-practice adjustment may or may not result in an actual change
in the laws—in some cases, laws that are no longer congruent with ideology may simply
be ignored or fall into disuse. And so, for me, the relatively abundant evidence for two-
way communication in the Assembly (and the lawcourts) points to the true nature of the
political process in Athens. Hansen offered spirited replies to my review (see, among
others, Hansen 1989a, 215–18; 1989b). He deals with the relative analytic value of
institutions and ideology in detail in Hansen 1991, 73–85.

———

THE CONSTITUTIONAL history of Athens is an increasingly popular topic
among historians, at least in part because of the groundbreaking work of Mogens Herman Hansen. Since the mid-1970s Hansen has published an impressive series of monographs and articles that have clarified many aspects of Athenian legal and governmental practice, especially of the fourth century B.C.
Furthermore, since it is possible to determine more about Athenian government in the fourth century than in any previous period, Hansen's fourth-
century studies have contributed to reassessments of fifth-century democracy
and its sixth-century antecedents.[1] His previous work has already earned

---

[1] On pp. 125–30 Hansen lists thirty-five theses that sum up his revisions and clarifications of
the traditional picture of the Athenian consititution. I tend to agree with sixteen of these (nos. 1, 3,
5, 10, 11, 14–21, 26, 34, 35). The five theses with which I tend to disagree in whole or in part (nos.
6, 23, 24, 29, 32) will be the main subject of this chapter. On the remaining fourteen I suspend
judgment, either because I regard them as possible but unproven or because I have not thoroughly

Hansen a place in the history of ancient constitutional studies; the publication of *The Athenian Assembly in the Age of Demosthenes*, written for both the specialist and the general reader, will bring him a wider audience and provides the opportunity to view his work from a broader perspective.

Hansen's oeuvre is voluminous, and his studies are invariably closely reasoned, copiously documented, and provocatively argued. His titles, which sometimes take an interrogative form (How often . . .? How many . . .? When did . . .?), leave the reader in no doubt about subject matter, and his conclusions leave no doubt as to the author's stance. In a typical study Hansen begins by narrowly framing the question to be asked. He defines the terms of the argument as accurately as possible, lists possible answers, and then presents all evidence that seems to bear on the issue. In conclusion he sums up the evidence, discards the possible answers that are not supported, and states the conclusion. The method is thus empirical and exclusive; it is the approach that, taken to a logical extreme, was favored by Sherlock Holmes, who claimed that "when you have eliminated the impossible, whatever remains, *however improbable*, must be the truth."[2] Like a Sherlockian solution to a criminal mystery, the typical study by Hansen appears to be an impartial collection of all the evidence that is accessible to anyone willing and able to make careful observations. Once it has been properly analyzed, the evidence is seen to point unerringly to a specific conclusion.

Although Hansen's work has provoked many challenges (which are frequently the subject of quick and vigorous replies; cf. 125–30 with nn.), most of the debate has centered on narrowly focused and (to the nonspecialist) often abstruse constitutional issues. There has been little concern with investigating Hansen's vision of the "nature of democracy," probably because he himself does not seem overtly concerned with the problem. In the absence of an explicit ideological point of view, his conclusions appear objective, and one seems safe in using them to construct one's own theses without fear of introducing unwanted bias. But adopting certain of Hansen's conclusions entails acquiescing in his specific understanding of political life. If the consequences of this acquiescence go unnoticed by students of social, cultural, and political history, Hansen may end up winning the war for the definition of the nature of Athenian democracy, despite any battles lost on technical grounds.

Empirical description and analysis are natural corollaries to Hansen's understanding of the relationship between government, politics, and society. But Hansen's conclusions are not necessarily more (or less) "objective" than those of other scholars who start, as Hansen (4) himself recognizes all historians must, with a set of a priori assumptions. Like all historians, Hansen poses

---

worked through the evidence. For the significance of Hansen's work for reinterpreting earlier Athenian history, see, for example, Ostwald 1986; Sealey 1987.

[2] Doyle 1967, 1:638 (*The Sign of Four*, ch. 6).

questions based on his own understanding of what is important. And, like all historiographic products, the form (if not the content) of Hansen's conclusions is predetermined by the questions he asks: his answers are necessarily structured, and their scope is necessarily limited, by the assumptions on which his questions are based, despite his determination to treat the evidence exhaustively and fairly. Therefore, a monograph or article by Hansen, like any other text, is best understood as a social construct, the product of the interplay between the writer's view of reality, his method of investigation, and his reading of the evidence.[3] If further justification for undertaking to analyze Hansen's methodology is needed, one may appeal to Hansen's oeuvre itself; for among his strengths as a historian is his concern with epistemology and the sociology of knowledge (2, 4).

The particularistic approach adopted in most of his previous studies has tended to obscure Hansen's point of view; the specificity of the questions he asks has rendered it difficult to see the forest for the trees. But in *The Athenian Assembly* he gives us glimpses of the forest. The importance of Hansen's work for those interested primarily in the details of constitutional history is undoubted. But in order to determine the value of Hansen's contributions to a more general understanding of Athenian democracy, one must ask not only whether his conclusions correctly answer the questions he has posed, but also whether he has posed meaningful questions in meaningful terms (i.e., in terms that are readily understood by readers and accurately describe ancient political and social structures; cf. Chapter 2 above). By attempting to define Hansen's conceptualization of Athenian democracy, I hope to assess the value of his methods and conclusions for readers who are interested in the topic, taken in its broadest terms: democracy as a central structure in a complex social and political system.

Perhaps Hansen's clearest a priori stance takes the form of a value judgment: he respects the Athenians and believes that Athenian democracy is an important subject with contemporary relevance (5–6). He defends the fourth-century democracy (123–24) against those who have claimed that devotion to the public good declined in the decades after the Peloponnesian War.[4] Hansen denies that the democratic government was parasitic upon on a slave economy, and instead points to the (usually overlooked) economic contribution of Athenian women (34, with nn. 232 on p. 123). He demonstrates that the state was not financially crippled by the provision of pay for widespread political participation, noting (48) that the military budget was far larger than the civilian. Hansen refuses to view Athenian government as an antiquarian relic, and cautiously employs modern parallels (especially the Swiss cantonal assemblies) to elucidate Athenian practice (2).

---

[3] See, for example, White 1973; Hedrick 1993.
[4] See, e.g., Garner 1987, 132; Carter 1986.

Equally fundamental, but in my view more problematic, are Hansen's converging assumptions that Athenian democracy is best understood as a "constitution," and that we can best understand this constitution and the principles on which it was based by analyzing relations between formal institutions of government. Students of Athenian history must come to grips with the constraints that these "constitutionalist" assumptions place upon the analysis of political life.[5]

A good example of Hansen's method is provided by his investigation of whether the *ekklēsia* and / or the *dikastēria* "embodied" the demos and his understanding of how this issue bears on the problem of the locus of sovereignty in the Athenian state. Hansen begins by considering the definitions and interrelationship of the terms *dēmos*, *ekklēsia*, and *dikastērion*. He collects a large number of texts (mostly passages from fourth-century orations) that show that citizens gathered in the Assembly were often addressed by speakers as *ho dēmos*. Conversely, jurors were seldom (or never) addressed by litigants as *"ho dēmos."* Hansen concludes that the *ekklēsia* did in fact embody the demos of Athens, whereas the *dikastēria* did not. This conclusion is then combined with the fact that the decision of jurors in a *dikastērion* could overturn (through conviction in a *graphē paranomōn*) a decision made in the *ekklēsia*. Ergo, the Athenian demos (embodied by the citizens gathered in the Assembly but not by jurors) was not sovereign, but the lawcourts were.[6]

The validity of Hansen's interpretation is contingent, of course, on the meaningfulness of the terms in which the original question was posed. Do the concepts "embodiment" and "nonembodiment" (or "representation," or "manifestation," two other constitutional concepts Hansen discusses in this context) best represent the relationship between demos, *ekklēsia*, and *dikastērion*? Is political power in Athens best conceptualized as legal sovereignty? Perhaps not; but Hansen's argument is likely to convince those who are used to thinking of good scholarship as objective and without ideological bias and of "the evidence" as transparent, neutral, and authoritative. If a scholar can show that most of the texts bearing on the question he or she has posed point to a certain conclusion, the tendency of empirically minded historians is to assume that the problem has been solved. Moreover, if a number of scholars have investigated a particular question, and if the majority of them agree about its solution, this may add to the conviction that the broader issues have been settled. The authority of the *communis opinio* of "objective" scholars, in conjunction with the authority of "objective" texts, reifies the assumption that the questions asked and answers offered by past scholarship—and the form and terms in which

---

[5] The constitutionalist model has been questioned by, e.g., Connor (1974, 32–40) and Finley (1985a, 99–103).

[6] Pp. 101–3; evidence collected in Hansen 1978, 127–46. Hansen also emphasizes the relationship between *psēphisma* and *nomos* in this context.

those questions and answers were cast—are self-evidently meaningful. But if both texts and a priori assumptions employed by scholars are social and ideological constructs, the issues of authority and meaning become much more complex.

As Hansen sees it, the fourth-century Athenian democracy was based on a set of abstract principles: moderation was desirable, the law should exist separate from and superior to social and political processes, the organs of government should be distinct in their powers, and, in general, all forms and forums of public decision and action should be defined by clear boundaries and restrictions. These principles were reflected in laws and institutions, which were changed over time in order to conform more precisely to the principles. The sum of laws and institutions, which embody and conform to prior principles, is the constitution. Hansen acknowledges that political realities require institutions to be somewhat more flexible than the ideal called for, so there is always a "gap between the constitution and how it works" (62), but he regards these exceptions as less important than the ideal represented by how the institutions *should* have worked.

The abstract principles on which the constitution was built are, for Hansen, in some sense exterior to the social matrix and to the realm of practical politics. Principles are apparently the covert force that causes change. Because of these guiding principles, one is to assume, constitutional development was linear, teleological, and "whiggish" in that it was aimed at a definite end, and that end was a good one. Thus, fourth-century constitutional evolution proceeded inexorably toward the creation of an orderly, legalistic, and moderate democracy. These constitutional and teleological assumptions are always implicit in Hansen's writing. For example: "Athenian democracy was, ideally, based on the principle of rotation. . . . The Athenian ideal is well represented by Aischines in his speech *Against Ktesiphon*" (61). "The debate [in Assembly] was a one-way communication from the speaker to the people. In principle there was no communication from the participants [Assemblymen] to the speakers [on the *bema*]."[7] "The Athenians of 403 wanted to replace the radical democracy of the fifth century with a more moderate form of democracy," and as a result "the powers of the *ekklesia* were somewhat reduced" (94).

Hansen emphasizes the centrality of institutions in defining the political order when he argues against the existence of a ruling political elite that used constitutional institutions to mask its true power (85–86). Hansen formulates the nonconstitutionalist argument as follows: "Don't believe that you understand Athenian democracy by learning about the *boule*, the *ekklesia* and the

---

[7] P. 71; pace Hansen, the text of Aeschines 3.2 (paraphrase of a "Solonic" law *peri tēs tōn rhētorōn eukosmias*) does not prove that comments from the audience were violations of "the letter of the law" (although this may be the impression Aeschines wished to convey): the clause ὥσπερ οἱ νόμοι προστάττουσι need only refer to τῷ πρεσβυτάτῳ τῶ πολιτῶν, and not necessarily to the words ἄνευ θορύβου καὶ ταραχῆς. The actual text of the law is, of course, lost.

dikasteria. Look instead for the real power exercised by leading politicians, influential families and political groups." Hansen argues that this approach is anachronistic; he outlines the constitutional decision-making process and concludes (86), "Behind this constitutional framework there are no traces of informal organizations corresponding to political parties or interest groups in modern democracies."[8] Yet this exclusionary argument is far from complete since parties and interest groups of the sort found in modern democracies hardly exhaust the roster of extrainstitutional forces that might have contributed to Athenian political life.

The Athenian elite need not have been a ruling elite, a political party, or a formally organized interest group in order to have influenced public decision making. The distinction between elite and non-elite citizens was of great concern to Athenian citizens of all classes. Athenians were very aware of the political significance of differences in economic class and birth status, as shown by both philosophical and rhetorical texts.[9] Hansen acknowledges in passing the "constant and important opposition between social groups" (86), but he normally chooses to ignore the influence of social tension or conflict in the public realm.

While Hansen understands the importance of the interrelationship of social realities and political practice, he generally subordinates sociopolitical questions to institutional concerns. For example, in attempting to solve the question of how many citizens attended a typical meeting of the Assembly, he does address the sociopolitical question of whether pay for attendence was adequate to allow laboring citizens to participate (11, 47–48). Yet Hansen (following [Aristotle] *Ath. Pol.* 41.3) assumes that the introduction of pay and subsequent increases in the rate of Assembly pay were motivated by the constitutional requirement of ensuring a quorum (114, 126). One might argue rather that the reform was motivated by the determination of the Athenian lower classes to ensure that the Assembly was not dominated by the upper classes—who were seen (rightly or not) as likely supporters of oligarchy.

Hansen usually conceptualizes the Athenian citizenry as a political institution: citizens are defined in relationship to the institutions of government, before which they were (for the most part and at least in principle) equal. Political equality was clearly a chief component of an Athenian's self-image, but an exclusively institutional definition of the citizen obscures an important political factor: the ways in which subgroups within the citizenry defined themselves in relationship to each other. A citizen of democratic Athens lived not only in a

---

[8] As an example of the nonconstitutionalist position, Hansen cites Connor 1971, 4–5. For a recent assessment of the influence of political groups in fourth-century Athens, see Strauss 1986. Neither Connor nor Strauss sees Athenian political factions as parties or interest groups of the modern type.

[9] The relevant texts are discussed in Ober 1989b. Cf. Seager 1973, 7–26; Welskopf 1965, 49–64.

constitutional realm in which political equality was the norm, but also in a
social matrix in which inequality predominated. The voters in Assembly, lawcourt, and Council were institutional equals, but social unequals; the disso-
nance between the two spheres was an important variable in political decision
making.

Much of Hansen's work has emphasized separation of powers between the
various bodies of government.[10] Central to *The Athenian Assembly* (especially ch.
4) is the attempt to define the scope of the Assembly's powers and to show how
those powers were limited by the powers of other bodies, especially the
people's courts. But Hansen's strong arguments (61–62, 114) for the prevalence of amateurism in Athenian government tend to weaken his separation of
powers thesis. If each body of Athenian govenment had been controlled by an
entrenched bureaucracy interested in maintaining its own position vis-à-vis
other bureaucracies, the separation of institutional powers would be a key
issue.[11] But since (as Hansen demonstrates) each powerful government body
was staffed by a large number of amateurs—citizens chosen more or less at
random from the whole spectrum of citizen society—the question of how
inter-class tensions were resolved *within* each institution (and ultimately within
the society as a whole) may be for many readers, and may have been for the
Athenians, a more consequential matter than the separation of powers *between*
institutions.

Looking at the function of democracy as a social as well as a political structure illuminates the ways in which the Athenians themselves thought about
and used their government. Such an approach suggests alternatives to the
linear causal relationship that Hansen traces between formal principles and
institutional change. Concentrating on the climate of opinion, and on the ways
in which opinions were formed and expressed, clarifies the social context
within which institutions operated and evolved. This is not to say that institutions were epiphenomenal; Athenian political ideology (the set of ideas about
the public realm common to most citizens, sufficiently coherent to lead to
action, but considerably less formally organized than theoretical principles)
evolved within an institutional, as well as a social, context.[12] Institutions and
the relationships between them are therefore only part of the story, and not
necessarily the fundamental part. Viewing Athenian democracy as a sociopolitical (rather than constitutional) phenomenon, and the primary "domestic
policy goal" of the democracy as resolution of tensions resulting from social
inequality (rather then the achievement of an orderly, moderate government),
entails asking a set of questions different from those Hansen poses. It suggests

[10] See esp. 98–124; cf. Hansen 1981, 345–70.

[11] As it is in modern governmental systems; see, for example, Tulis 1987, 9–12, with literature
cited.

[12] On ideology and institutions in ancient and modern democracies, respectively, see Finley
1983; Bowles and Gintis 1986.

alternatives to the ways in which Hansen uses rhetorical texts, and calls into question some of his conclusions about the meaning of the two components of the word *dēmokratia*.

Although Hansen is conversant with epigraphy and is able to control complex architectural arguments (e.g., 17–19), his most important set of sources is the corpus of Attic orations.[13] Most extant speeches were delivered by elite private litigants or public speakers (*rhētores*) attempting to influence large bodies of (mostly) non-elite citizens. Rhetorical strategies and *topoi* can reveal much about the social background of Athenian politics. But even a scholar primarily interested in institutional procedure must be conscious of the rhetorical context. Athenian public speeches were addressed to enthusiastic amateurs, not to judges or professional lawyers. The context demanded a rhetoric based on personalities and on appeals to class and status-group interests, to patriotic aspirations, to prejudices, hopes, and fears. Therefore, the discourse of the *dikastērion* and *ekklēsia* relied primarily not on the language of constitutional law, but on more subtle and less logically rigorous appeals to popular ideology.[14]

Descriptions of political and legal practice offered by the orators are seldom impartial accounts of constitutional procedure and precedent; and yet they are treated as such by Hansen. He is not unaware of the problem—in discussing a passage from Hyperides' *For Euxenippus* Hansen notes that the speaker uses the term *rhētōr* in two ways, as a legal term and in the sense belonging to "common usage" (62). But if ordinary usage of important words differed from legal definition (the way terms were used in sometimes archaic laws), and if the orators deliberately confused common usage and legal definition to suit their own purposes, then decontextualized rhetorical passages must be regarded as very tricky building blocks for restoring the details of a constitutional order.

A few examples serve to point out the dangers of divorcing rhetorical passages from their ideological context. Hansen states (39) that the nine *proedroi*, who (along with the *epistatēs*) presided over meetings of the Assembly, "seem to have wide powers. They could refuse to put a proposal to the vote." The source cited in support of this contention is Aeschines 2.84: Aeschines describes a meeting of the Assembly held a few years previously—a meeting he was sure the jurors would recall—at which Aleximachos proposed a motion. After the motion had been read out, "Demosthenes arose from among the *proedroi* and refused to bring the motion to a vote." So far so good, but Aeschines' description of the aftermath disproves Hansen's conclusion: "But you [i.e., the jurors, who are here simply identified with the Assemblymen]

---

[13] Cf. 3, and 230–41 (the "Index of Passages Cited"); citations of orations are about equal in number to all other sources combined.

[14] I do not mean to imply that public rhetoric was empty of content, or that speakers or audiences were unconcerned with arriving at good and just decisions, but that just decisions are not necessarily dependent upon legal language and precedent. Cf. Ober 1989b, 43–49; Humphreys 1985a, 241–64.

shouted and called the *proedroi* to the *bēma*, and so against [Demosthenes'] will the motion was put to a vote."

Aeschines relates the incident to demonstrate Demosthenes' undemocratic attitude, as well as to prove his opposition to a treaty. He casts Demosthenes in the role of the arrogant and headstrong individual who attempted to subvert the will of the people—and failed. There is no implication here that Demosthenes, as *proedros*, had the power to withhold from a vote a proposal on which the majority of Assemblymen wanted to vote. The incident is rather an example of the power of the people to override any attempt by a magistrate to use his position in an arbitrary way. If the passage proves anything about "constitutional" authority, it is that *proedroi* had no independent power to block proposals, and if they so attempted, the people could summon them to the *bēma* and force the vote. The "summoning" itself is an example of the sort of communication from audience to speaker that Hansen states was forbidden "in principle." In this case, emphasizing the putative constitutional principle at the expense of practice (which is discussed on pp. 69–72) obscures the fundamental importance of two-way communication in the praxis of the Assembly.

Hansen states elsewhere (139 n. 51) that "we know from Dem. 21.193 that garrison troops were not allowed to attend the assembly." In the passage cited, Demosthenes describes his opponent Meidias' intention to repeat the "slander" he had made at the *probolē*, defaming both the demos and the *ekklēsia* by claiming that the Assembly in which he was convicted "was composed of men who had stayed at home when they ought to have marched out, and who had left the fortresses deserted" (ὡς ὅσοι δέον ἐξιέναι κατέμενον καὶ ὅσοι τὰ φριούρι' ἦσαν ἔρημα λελοιπότες, ἐξεκλησίασαν). Here Hansen finds a formal legal prohibition in a claim that a partisan speaker has put into his opponent's mouth about what ought to have occurred but did not (the citizens in question ought to have marched out and ought to have garrisoned the fortresses, but instead were in the city and so were able to attend an Assembly). Even if we assume that Meidias really made the claim Demosthenes attributes to him, there is a significant difference between "should not have" (according to one speaker) and "were not allowed to" (according to law). Perhaps there was a law prohibiting garrison troops from attending the Assembly, but this passage does not demonstrate its existence, language, or purpose. Rather, the passage illustrates Demosthenes' tactic of attributing to Meidias a hatred of the demos (compare Chapter 7 above), here allegedly manifested in Meidias' willingness to insult the people by claiming they shirked their military duties.

In support of his theory that the powers of the lawcourts were separate from and superior to the powers of the Assembly, Hansen points out that "when *ekklesia* (or *demos*) and *dikasterion* are used as constrasting terms and mentioned in order of preference, *dikasterion* invariably takes preference over *ekklesia* (*demos*)" (105; cf. 91). In five of the six passages Hansen cites as examples, the speakers do indeed praise the quality of the decisions made by juries relative to decisions made in the Assembly.[15] But must we conclude that these comments were based on a constitutional separation and elevation of judicial power? Each of the passages Hansen adduces is a statement made by a litigant facing a popular jury. One might hypothesize that the speakers deliberately flattered their audience by making the most of the jurors' responsibilities. An Athenian *dikastēs* might well look kindly upon, and pay close attention to, a litigant who had just informed him that his vote represented the most authoritative decision made in the public realm.

The passages that emphasize separateness and superiority of *dikastēria* (versus demos or *ekklēsia*) should be read in conjunction with other passages that assume a congruity between decisions made by jurymen and those made by Assemblymen. Litigants sometimes warned jurors that their decisions would be closely monitored by the demos and suggested that jurors should make a decision that would please the demos.[16] The tendency of litigants to remind jurors of the decisions "you [jurors]" had formerly made in the Assembly likewise argues against a strict separationist interpretation.[17] But, as we have seen, Hansen believes (97) that "a proper understanding of the term *demos* disposes of the view that . . . the *dikasteria* were manifestations of the people (the *demos*) . . . only the *ekklesia* was a manifestation of the *demos*. . . . Neither the *nomothetai* nor the *dikastai* were believed to embody the *demos* (i.e. the whole of the people)."

Hansen has perhaps put too much weight on the habit of public speakers of referring to Assemblymen and not jurors as *ho dēmos*. The primary meaning of *dēmos* to the Athenians was not "Assemblymen," but "the whole of the Athenian citizen body." This latter meaning, which we might characterize as "capital-*D* Demos," was an ideological construct. This Demos was real, in that there were indeed some 20,000 or (8) 30,000 individuals living in fourth-century Attica who enjoyed full citizen rights; but Demos could not be perceived by the senses. No one had ever seen Demos; it was too big ever to gather in any one place. Therefore, the Athenian Demos was not, as M. I. Finley supposed, a "face-to-face society," but an example of what Benedict Anderson has called an "imagined community."[18] This imagined Demos was, however, a fundamental and vivid political concept: Demos could be personified (as a mature, bearded man).[19] An antidemocratic coup would result in Demos being over-

---

[15] P. 105 n. 675. In the sixth passage (Dem. 24.78) neither the term *dēmos* nor the term *ekklēsia* is used, and it is not certain that either is implied.

[16] Dem. 21.2, 227; Lys. 12.91, 22.19; Dinarch. 1.3, 106, 2.19, 3.16; cf. Dinarch. 1.84.

[17] E.g., Dem. 19.224, 21.214–16; Hyp. 1.17; Lys. 19.14; Aesch. 2.84, 3.125; Dinarch. 3.19; Isaeus 5.38. Hansen discusses, but does not resolve, this issue in Hansen 1978, 135–36.

[18] Citizen population: Hansen 1985. Face-to-face community: Finley 1983, 28–29, 82–83. "Imagined community": Anderson 1992. On the origins and development of "the multi-purpose word *dēmos*," see Whitehead 1986, 364–68.

[19] He is shown being crowned by the female deity Demokratia on the stele relief adorning the

thrown; *kataluein ton dēmon* was the commonest periphrasis for counter-revolution.[20] This imagined Demos was the demos assumed in the word *dēmokratia*—the entity that held power in the state.

A meeting of the Assembly was open to all citizens, and decisions made by those who attended—"the *demos* in the narrower institutional sense" (97)—certainly symbolized the will of Demos. But the participants at a given Assembly were not identical to Demos. Nor, certainly, were juries or boards of *nomothetai*, bodies that were limited in size and that excluded citizens under age thirty. These added restrictions may be responsible for the convention of addressing jurors as *Athēnaioi* rather than as *dēmos*, but decisions of *nomothetai* and *dikastai*, like decisions of Assemblies, symbolized the will of Demos.[21] Hansen argues that, unlike the *ekklēsia*, *dikastēria* did not manifest or embody *ho dēmos*, but rather were "representative of the *demos*" and were "assembled to act *on behalf of* the *demos*" (104; Hansen's emphasis). The distinction is, for Hansen, a meaningful one because "representation . . . implies distinction and not identity."

Hansen points out (102–4) that the concepts of "delegation of powers" and "committee" are problematic for analyzing Athenian government; but "representation," "embodiment," and "manifestation" are equally troublesome. "Representation," in a constitutional sense, implies delegation of authority and/or formal appointment or election.[22] Since Hansen argues that the authority of the lawcourts was not delegated, and since the Athenian juror was not appointed or elected to represent a larger constituency, "representation" does not seem the best way to conceptualize the relationship between lawcourts and Demos. "Embodiment" and "manifestation" imply identity, and the Athenians at least sometimes perceived a distinction between Demos and those who attended a given Assembly (e.g., Dem. 21.193, noted above; see other examples cited by Hansen, 138 n. 40).

I would suggest, as an alternative, the concept of "synecdoche," a figure of speech in which a part stands for and refers to a whole, or vice versa. Each of the various institutional "parts" of the citizen body (*ekklēsia*, *dikastēria*, *nomothetai*, *boulē*) could stand for and refer to the whole citizen body. Orators could speak of jurors as having made decisions in Assembly because both a jury and an

---

nomos against tyranny: *Supplementum epigraphicum Graecum* 7:87; cf. Raubitschek 1962, 238; illustration: frontispiece to Ober 1989b. Since the law was passed and the stele authorized by *nomothetai*, not by an Assembly, the figure must represent "capital-*D* Demos," not *dēmos qua ekklēsia*. Cf. also Aristophanes' *Knights*.

[20] See Ober 1989b, 299 with n. 14; Sealey 1973, 283.

[21] *Dikastai*: see passages cited above, notes 16 and 17. That Demos' will was symbolized by the decisions of *nomothetai* is demonstrated by the stele relief described in note 19 above.

[22] See *Webster's Third New International Dictionary*, s.v. representative: "Constituting the agent for another esp. through delegated authority . . . of, based upon, or constituting a form of government in which the many are represented by persons chosen among them usu[ally] by election."

Assembly were parts of the whole. The words *dēmos* and *Athēnaioi* (whose primary meanings denoted the whole of the citizen body) could be used to refer,
respectively, to the "part" of the citizen body that attended a given Assembly
or sat on a given jury. Synecdoche takes us from the vocabulary of constitution
to that of signification, but this should cause difficulties only for those who
assume that Athenians were more concerned with legal definition than with
symbolic reference. Close reading of speeches by fourth-century orators, which
Nicole Loraux has described as "the only [Athenian] texts genuinely inspired
by democratic thinking," reveals the importance of symbolic reference in the
Athenian public realm.[23]

Hansen tends to downplay the significance of the ideological construct
Demos, because his approach necessarily emphasizes institutions, ergo *dēmos* as
ekklēsia. But without the concept of Demos as the implied authority behind all
democratic bodies, an entity that transcended and undergirded all public institutions, Athenian political life is incomprehensible. In the passages I have cited
above, *dikastai* were reminded by the speakers of their duties to Demos both as
jurors and as Assemblymen. The *graphē paranomōn* procedure gave Demos a
chance to consider at a remove decisions made in Assembly. When a jury
overturned a *psēphisma* by convicting its proposer, this was a result of Demos'
having turned against the proposer and/or having reconsidered the original
decision; the jury's action did not override Demos' authority. We must keep in
mind the importance of informal (extrainstitutional) communication in
Athens.[24] If rumors circulating in the agora suggested that Demos was un-
happy with a *psēphisma*, some ambitious citizen might be encouraged to take
the risk of lodging a *graphē paranomōn* against the proposer, since a successful
indictment would be likely to gain him the sympathy of Demos, which would
stand him in good stead in future contests in the Assembly and the courtroom.

The primary principle involved in democratic decision making at Athens
was not separation of institutional powers, but demotic control of the public
realm. Demosthenes makes this clear in his speech *Against Timocrates*. The
speech emphasizes the importance of the laws and lawcourts (and so is cited by
Hansen some eighty-five times; cf. 235). But "what, then, is the only honest
and trustworthy safeguard of the laws? You: *hoi polloi* " (24.37). Demos was a
sociological construct (*hoi polloi*) as well as a political construct (*hoi politai*), and
democracy worked by balancing political equality against social inequality.
The consequences of social inequality and the power of the elite were amelio-
rated through the forms of debate and decision in both courtroom and Assembly. In both institutions the audience rewarded and punished speakers by re-

---

[23] Loraux 1986, 176. Loraux's book is a good example of the insights that can be gained by
looking at rhetorical texts as symbolic discourse that both refers to and helps to define national
ideologies.

[24] Praising the divinity of *phēmē*, Aeschines (2.145) defined it as "when *to plēthos tōn politōn* of their
own will . . . say that something is the case."

sponding verbally to them, that is, through *thorubos* (cf. 70–72), and by the final vote. The ordinary citizens were suspicious of elite pretensions; contestants in the Assembly and courtroom were constrained to devise rhetorical forms that would be acceptable to their mass audiences. Elite citizens' involvement in both institutions entailed their acknowledgment—in both the content and the structure of their discourse—that the will of the many was the will of Demos and that Demos was the legitimate political authority. The ultimate *kratos* of the Demos lay in this demotic control of the public processes of signification: the power of the many to participate actively in assigning political meanings to symbols deployed in public speech.

The imagined community, Demos, provides the missing subject that would allow Hansen's many passive clauses to be recast in the active voice: "Legislation was conferred on the *nomothetai* . . . the *ekklesia* was entitled to hear . . . the *ekklesia* was deprived of jurisdiction . . . the people were restricted to the passing of decrees and the election of officials . . . the power of officials was maintained . . . the people were entrusted with the *ad hoc* election of envoys."[25] Without the concept of Demos, there is no agent for these passives, other than the unsatisfactory (in this context) term *polis* (cf. 178 n. 664: "It is not the *demos*, but the *polis* which appoints the *dikasteria*," citing Dem. 21.233). *Polis* cannot be characterized as a political agent distinct from "the will of the citizen body." Through the operations of its parts, Demos effected the various institutional changes described by Hansen. These reforms, which Hansen has done much to clarify, changed the external forms in which power was deployed, but never limited the collective power of the Athenian citizenry.

Hansen has often conceptualized political power as "sovereignty," a term he has used frequently over the years and retains in the conclusions of *The Athenian Assembly* (129: "In fourth-century Athens the *ekklesia* was no longer 'the sovereign body of Government'"), even after he has pointed out some of the difficulties associated with its use (105–7, esp. 106: "Many problems are avoided if we dismiss the concept of sovereignty"). The reasons for this apparent ambivalence are not clear. But we must face the issue squarely: if "sovereignty" defined as unitary power with a specific institutional locus is a concept without meaning for Athenian democracy, then "Was the *ekklēsia* sovereign?" is no longer a meaningful question.[26]

The concept of sovereignty was developed in the sixteenth and seventeenth centuries by Western European political theorists writing on the institution of

---

[25] These examples, taken from pp. 107–8, could be multiplied.

[26] The problem is not solved by replacing the question "What institution is sovereign?" with "What institution is *kurios*?" since, as Hansen points out (106–7), the answer to the latter question (as supplied by rhetorical texts) varies with context. *Nomoi* are sometimes said to be *kurioi* (106 with n. 681), but *nomoi* had no independent power of action, and no effective enforcement apparatus existed apart from the will of the people: Dem. 21.223–24. Cf. Chapter 7 above.

monarchy.[27] Monarchical power is by definition unitary, since it is located in the person of the monarch. Absolute monarchs—those whose sphere of public action is unlimited—are therefore unitary sovereigns. English-language sovereignty theory was given its classical formulation by Thomas Hobbes, who specifically defined sovereign power as an institution that monopolizes the legitimate use of force and that is legitimately maintained by force.[28] Neither Hobbes nor any other early modern political theorist considered democracy, as *popular* sovereignty, to be either desirable or practical; these theorists conceived of sovereignty, properly so called, as unitary state power that resided, preferably, either in the person of the monarch or in a representative assembly. The traditional theory of sovereignty does not encompass the idea that legitimate power could reside with an abstraction such as "the People"; consequently it is of very limited utility in explaining democracy.[29]

The concept of sovereignty can usefully be applied to democracy only by replacing the idea of "sovereignty as located in institutions" with "sovereignty as the ability to change institutions." Adam Przeworski suggests that "people are sovereign to the extent that they can alter the existing institutions, including the state and property, and if they can allocate resources to all feasible uses."[30] I would add: "And so long as they also control the ideological symbols through which political agents make decisions." By this extended definition the Athenian citizenry was indeed sovereign: there was no entrenched ruling elite at Athens that could successfully oppose the desire of Demos to alter institutions or allocate resources, and the people controlled the means of public communication (especially the Assembly and the courts) in which ideological symbols were forged and deployed in open debate.[31]

Redefining sovereignty to include power over discourse residing in the citizenry, as opposed to legal power residing in a set of institutions, mitigates the problem raised by the concept of "the separation of powers." The separation of powers doctrine, an offshoot of the traditional, institutional theory of sovereignty, was enunciated in the seventeenth and eighteenth centuries, when English and French aristocrats attempted to limit the powers of absolute monarchs.[32] Since the separation of powers is predicated on a subdivision of unitary sovereignty and on the assumption that some of the sovereign's powers would pass into the hands of a ruling elite, the concept as traditionally defined

---

[27] Pp. 105–7; cf. Allen 1941, 247–70 (English theorists), 394–444 (Jean Bodin).

[28] Hobbes [1651] 1950, chs. 17–19, 28, 30.

[29] Ibid., chs. 17, 19; Allen 1941, 436–48; Bowles and Gintis 1986, 22–23, 167.

[30] On popular sovereignty, see Bowles and Gintis 1986, 181–83, quoting Przeworski on p. 182.

[31] Ober 1989b, esp. 293–339.

[32] The classic formulation is Montesquieu's *The Spirit of the Laws* of 1748, book 11: Montesquieu [1748] 1949, 1:171–209.

is not much more useful for our purposes than the traditional theory of sovereignty. And once we dispense with separation of powers as a central issue, we can deemphasize restriction and limitation as the operative terms in which we conceptualize the nature of Athenian democracy.[33]

None of the preceding discussion is intended to cast doubts on the importance of Hansen's overall achievement. That achievement is well represented (if not fully embodied) by *The Athenian Assembly*. Individual democratic institutions certainly had distinctly defined responsibilities in Athens, and these responsibilities were redefined over time. Hansen's question concerning "the extent of the sphere regulated by decrees of the people" (109) or by other constitutional instruments is valid, even if it does not define the nature of Athenian democracy. No student of classical Athenian political life (even one who has read all of Hansen's other, more specialized, articles and monographs) can afford to ignore this seminal book. Those who remain unconvinced by some of Hansen's conclusions will learn much from the attempt to refute them. It should be obvious to readers of this chapter that thinking about the implications of Hansen's theses has substantially aided my own attempt to understand Athenian democracy. Whether or not Hansen's institutional model of political life becomes the accepted paradigm, *The Athenian Assembly* will quickly establish itself as a classic in the field of ancient constitutional and legal history and deserves to find a broad audience.

---

[33] Foucault (1980a, 81–102) attacks the emphasis on restriction and limitation entailed in conceptualizing power as legal sovereignty. Collins (1989) argues persuasively that the association of political order with separateness and difference was a product of a seventeenth-century consciousness, and he demonstrates how this consciousness led to the idea of representative sovereignty.

Chapter 9

THE ATHENIANS AND THEIR DEMOCRACY

The assessment of the three books under review in this chapter may be read as a second installment of the discussion initiated in Chapter 8: How best to assess the relationship between democratic Athenian practice and political theorizing? And how best to negotiate the considerable distances that separate ostensibly similar ancient and modern concepts? As in other chapters, these concerns quickly become involved with the status of Athenian elites vis-à-vis the ordinary citizens. The essay's critical fire is primarily concentrated on Cynthia Farrar's *The Origins of Democratic Thinking* (1988), a book that I found particularly challenging. It engaged me deeply not least because its stated ambition—to explore the relationship between the thinking of important classical Athenian writers and the democracy of their own time, and to use the results of that exploration as a way to rethink contemporary liberal theory—is very similar to what I hope to accomplish in my own work on Athenian critics of popular rule (see especially Chapter 10). Moreover, I share with Farrar a deep intellectual debt to the "Cambridge School" of intellectual history associated especially with Quentin Skinner and John Dunn. Despite (or perhaps because of) the similarities I found myself in profound disagreement with elements of Farrar's approach and with some of her conclusions about the role of Athenian elites in the origination of "democratic thinking."

At the core of my disagreement with Farrar's approach is my conviction that the way she uses the terms "democracy" and "democratic" is not contextually meaningful. I argue that, given her intention to write intellectual history (as well as to do political philosophy), the democratic thinking whose origins she seeks should be democratic according to the lights of people living in the fifth century B.C.—the general date of the texts she explores. Instead, she appears to understand by "democracy" a political situation in which the significant decisions are made in advance by a wise, historically minded, tutelary elite. Thus, for example, Thucydides' interpretation is "democratic" because he successfully "controls the interpretation" of his readers. Control of interpretation may well be part of Thucydides' authorial goal, but it seems to me that elite control—of politics or of the interpretations by which political decisions are made— would be regarded as antidemocratic by fifth-century Athenians, both those who would applaud such control and those who would excoriate it. Farrar returns to some of her key arguments in Farrar 1992.

By contrast, this chapter's least-qualified praise is heaped upon Ellen Wood's *Peasant-Citizen and Slave* (1988), which is held up as a good example of how theoretical sophistica-

---

This essay—a review of Farrar 1988, Sinclair 1988, and Wood 1988—was first published in *Echos du monde classique* 35 (1991), 81–96. Page citations within this chapter refer to the books under discussion.

tion (Wood is, by professional training, a political theorist rather than a classicist) opens up interpretive possibilities that are closed by more narrowly positivistic approaches. In this case, Wood's revisionist-Marxist approach to the problem of exploitation and surplus value helped her to challenge (I believe quite successfully) some of the entrenched opinions of classical historians about the relationship between slave labor and democratic citizenship. It is only fair, however, to point out that Wood and I agree on a particularly controversial point: we reject the notion that Athenian democracy was fundamentally dependent upon slave labor. Wood argues at length that the democracy of Athens was founded on a "free peasantry"—a very rare historical phenomenon. Because the Athenian smallholders, unlike most peasants elsewhere, were not subject to heavy rents (exploitation by landlords) or taxes (exploitation by government), they had adequate time and energy both to farm their lands and to participate actively as citizens.

Wood's position (and mine, especially in Ober 1985a and 1989b) on peasants, subsistence, and the place of slavery in Athenian society, which was explicitly critical of an article by Michael Jameson (1977–78), has been the subject of considerable scholarly counter-fire, especially by Jameson (1992) and Victor Hanson (1992, 1995). The debate concerns a number of intertwined questions: Was agricultural slavery relatively common or relatively rare in Attica? What was the total number of slaves in Attica at any given time? What was the economic role of slaves, and how dependent was the Athenian economy, overall, on slavery as opposed to free labor? Are "peasants" and "subsistence farmers" accurate terms for free Athenian agriculturalists, or should we be speaking instead of "yeomen" and market-oriented "entrepreneurs"?

These are extremely important problems, central to our understanding of Athenian democracy (see also Chapter 11). Philological analysis can contribute to a better understanding of some of these problems—Wood is most vulnerable when she claims, for example, that the Greek term *oiketēs* is as likely to mean "free servant" as it is to mean "slave." Archaeological evidence may be able to offer some clues—although some of the claims about the relationship between plot size and economic structure, formulated on the basis of surface surveys (see, for example, Lohmann 1992, 1993), seem to me debatable in light of the nature of the evidence. In the end, given the extremely lacunary state of our evidence and problematic nature of our literary sources (especially Old Comedy), the debate is likely to remain centered on competing theoretical models. And hence, exercising the greatest care and self-consciousness in the use of analytic models remains essential. Among the strengths of Wood's book is her demonstration of how the long-paradigmatic "myth" of the idle Athenian mob originates in politically tendentious eighteenth-century British historiography. This and related issues are now discussed in considerable detail by Jennifer Roberts (1994). Wood herself remains very much engaged in the debate; see Wood 1996.

RECENT SCHOLARSHIP on the topic of classical Athenian democracy is remarkable both for its diversity of approach and for its sheer volume.[1] Moreover, this spate is highly opportune—if one assumes (as do the authors of the books under discussion in this chapter) that classical scholars should be aware of the worlds of ideas and political realities that exist outside the borders of their discipline. A number of (nonclassicist) political theorists have now rejected the arguments of the elitist school of political sociology (i.e., Pareto, Mosca, Michels, and their intellectual descendants), and are arguing that strong democracy (political egalitarianism of the sort that arguably characterized Athenian ideology and practice—rather than the "thin" conception of the negative freedom of the individual that is often equated with democracy in the modern Western world) is both desirable at the local and national level and, at least theoretically, feasible.[2] Meanwhile, dramatic political changes in Eastern Europe and elsewhere have helped to refocus attention throughout the world on what democracy means (or should mean) in both political and economic terms.

The coincidence of focus on Athenian and modern democracy is particularly felicitous in an era perceived by many classicists to be characterized by a pervasive disciplinary crisis.[3] Classical historians must surely welcome the chance not only to learn from other fields, but to contribute substantially to a cross-disciplinary debate with wide-ranging "real-world" significance. If classical historians are willing to keep in mind a potential audience that includes nonclassicists, the fruits of ongoing research into the nature of ancient democratic politics will be enthusiastically greeted in the wider intellectual marketplace. There is no doubt that many contemporary political theorists care about the history of Athenian democracy and Athenian ideas about politics.[4] Athens is not only the *earliest* democracy known to have evolved in a complex society, it is also the best-documented historical example of a (relatively) large-scale *direct* democracy operating over time as a state government.

It is thus gratifying to note that each of the three books discussed here is simultaneously a scholarly contribution to classical studies and accessible to Greekless scholars in other disciplines. Furthermore, although all three books deal with key aspects of Athenian democracy, there is relatively little overlap. Each author has a distinct approach and point of view; each asks different questions and refers to different bodies of evidence. Cynthia Farrar combines political philosophy with a history of ideas about politics. R. K. Sinclair offers a history of political institutions and those who used them. Ellen Wood uses economic and political theory to rethink political aspects of social history.

[1] See, for example, the bibliographies in Ober 1989b; Manville 1990. See also Develin 1989; Hansen 1989a; Stockton 1990; Meier 1990.

[2] Radical egalitarianism: Ober 1989b. Elitist theorists and their authoritarian view of leadership: Nye 1977. Barber 1984 and Gutmann 1987 exemplify recent trends in democratic theory. Negative freedom: Berlin 1969, xxxvii–lxii, 118–72; Sen 1990, 49–54.

[3] Culham and Edmunds 1989.

[4] See, for example, MacIntyre 1981, 131–45; Dahl 1989, 13–23.

Farrar's *The Origins of Democratic Thinking* is intended as a history of ideas (278) that will be simultaneously a contribution to democratic theory and a spur to political action. The first chapter is entitled "Ancient Reflections: A Force for Us"; her goal is to heal the "unease" (especially the hyperindividualism: 14) of modernity. According to Farrar, the political philosophizing of Plato and Aristotle has little to offer the contemporary world because these two writers "retreated" from practical politics; Plato "abandoned the claims of autonomy and fused man's social and his ethical identity" (256). Rather, "it is democracy, as conceived and lived by Athenians in the fifth century B.C., that offers at least the possibility of healing this spiritual and social fragmentation" (274). Fifth-century "democratic theorists" have much to tell us because they struggled in the real world of politics and citizenry with real issues, especially the freedom of the individual versus the community's collective good.

Farrar argues that the Western tradition of "democratic thinking" originated in fifth-century Athens. Thus democratic Athens is the context for the earliest examples of sophisticated theorizing about the political realm, and this theorizing has much to offer anyone interested in democratic political practice. To support this set of contentions, Farrar assesses the fragmentary surviving work of Protagoras, Thucydides, and Democritus. In her view, Protagoras, unlike Plato, refused to acknowledge the existence of a "real world" outside the world of seeming and appearance, and Farrar points out the linkages of Protagoras' epistemological stance with the processes of debate in the Athenian Assembly (62–64). Protagoras emphasized the beneficent socializing effect of polis life, and his "man-measure" doctrine saw ordinary men's experience and understanding as the "touch-stone of social values" (76). Protagoras is the world's first democratic political theorist (77), but his man-measure theory separated the political realm from the social and so raised the possibility that individual and collective goods are noncongruent (99). By contrast, Thucydides' text "shows that . . . well-being can be secured only in a political context and only by deploying principles of historical understanding" (130). It is a sort of moral education (137) that "does not merely express [democratic] principles; it embodies them" (133). Writing (in Farrar's view) to refute Protagoras, Democritus argued in favor of a basic reality "which eludes and must elude man's direct 'measurement'" (207). Democritus' atomism attempted to offer solutions to problems of objectivity, self-sufficiency, and individual will. His thought had a strong political/ethical dimension; he relocated "the source of freedom and order to within the individual" (241), and "he believed in the capacity of the human mind to know truth as well as to act autonomously" (205). But "as a result of this emphasis on individual good . . . Democritus has difficulty establishing a strong connection between personal well-being and a genuinely political order" (193).

Each of these three writers is taken by Farrar to be an exemplar of democratic thinking, but the political thought of Protagoras and Democritus was, in her view, fatally flawed. Her prize for the first, best democratic thinker goes to Thucydides, whose "historical politics" is regarded by Farrar (2, cf. 13–14, 128) as "the strongest, most stable version" of democratic theory. "The possibility of concrete reflection revealed by this history is that embodied in Thucydides' demonstration of the value of his own history and of Athenian politics under Pericles as modes of prudent self-understanding" (14).

Farrar's goal of rethinking serious problems of modern society in the terms of an ancient political model seems to me altogether admirable.[5] I find a number of Farrar's arguments convincing. But there are also some serious problems with her approach. First, and most superficially: this is not an easy book to read. Farrar's style is both dense and repetitive; she has a tendency to gnomic sententiae that may wear on the reader's nerves (e.g., "Prudence is historical and history prudential": 188).

A more serious problem (from the perspective of the history of ideas) is that the "way of living reflectively and politically" for which Farrar argues (14) cannot be equated with democracy as it was "conceived and lived" by most ordinary Athenians, nor was that "way of living" prima facie advocated by the elite authors of the texts she analyzes. If Farrar's preferred "way of living" is *neither* democratic by ordinary Athenian standards (as measured by their conceptions and practices) *nor* demonstrably the view advocated by the authors of the classical texts, the book's utility as a history of ancient ideas will be nugatory, although it may still be interesting as political philosophy.

An inquiry such as Farrar's must explain what the author means when employing terms such as "democracy" and "democratic." If Farrar were writing political philosophy per se, she might legitimately have employed definitions foreign to the experience of fifth-century authors.[6] But since she intends a history of fifth-century Athenian political ideas, her definitions must, it seems to me, be grounded in the texts and their specific historical context.[7] Farrar defines the experience of democracy, in the theories of her three exemplars, as "autonomous participation in the creation of order and unity under the tutelage of reason . . . guided by an elite in the interests of the whole" (267). If one were willing to grant a rather broad and loose definition of "reason," "elite," and "guided," this might work as a definition of Athenian democracy as the ordinary Athenians understood and lived it in the late fifth and fourth centuries (the period for which we have texts by which to test the proposition). Farrar's definition of the three terms in question tends, however, to be quite

[5] For the counter-argument, see Holmes 1979, 113–28, with the discussion of Euben 1990.

[6] In some passages (e.g., 126, 128) "democracy" apparently means for Farrar no more than "political"—and "political" means the reconciliation of personal autonomy with a self-reflective social order (274).

[7] This is not to say that readers should expect a single dictionary-style definition of *dēmokratia*, but they may legitimately expect the author to offer the approximate definitions (which may be complex and even contradictory) that were utilized within a text or group of texts.

narrow: although some forms of political reasoning can be taught to the many, the kind of reasoning necessary for true leadership is evidently accessible only to a highly intelligent and educated elite whose duty it is to shape and control (guide) the understanding of the mass of citizens.

As Farrar knows very well, educated elites will not always choose to guide the masses, and she supposes that without the guidance of reasoning elite leaders, democracy is impossible. This may explain why in some passages Farrar seems to imply that the Athenians lived democratically only for the twenty-some years of the *prostateia* of Pericles.[8] After the death of Pericles, a long decline set in, and democratic thinking itself soon died out: "Thucydides' successors as political analysts, like Pericles' political successors, lost their nerve and succumbed to the degenerative force of circumstances; they turned away from the demands of leadership and history" (191).[9] This statement seems to imply that Athenian democracy was the (rather fragile) product of Pericles' unique genius—just as true democratic thinking was almost uniquely the product of Thucydides' mind.[10]

How does such an analysis hold up historically? There are no texts to reveal how ordinary Athenians or their political leaders understood their government during the *prostateia* of Pericles. But the speeches of the Attic orators demonstrate that Athenian citizen masses and politicians *thought* of Athens as a *dēmokratia* long after the death of Pericles. Athenian political practice persuaded educated, upper-class residents of late fifth- and fourth-century Athens (e.g., Plato, Aristotle, Xenophon, Isocrates) that Athens was in fact ruled by the demos. Neither the orators nor the critics of democracy conceived of *dēmokratia* as a system wherein the citizen masses were effectively taught or guided (in Farrar's sense) by a benevolent, historically minded elite.[11] Thus Farrar's idea of "democracy" is not the same thing as *dēmokratia* as it was "conceived and lived" by ordinary or elite Athenians in the late fifth and fourth centuries B.C.

---

[8] See especially 130: Thucydides' history portrays "the effects of social and ethical disintegration" so that "a political understanding of man's interests" is no longer possible and his "capacity to act prudently to secure his real interests" is undermined. Cf. 14, 278 on "Periclean civic history."

[9] Cf. 129; 271–72: the fourth century seen as a long period of decline and fall. Farrar is not completely consistent; she sometimes imagines Athens as a polity, lasting through the fourth century, in which the masses of citizens were empowered, and in which they participated actively in rule (e.g., 273, 275–76).

[10] See esp. 278 for "the assimilation of Thucydides and Pericles."

[11] For a discussion of democratic ideology in the fourth century, see Ober 1989b, in which I argue that ordinary Athenians saw no need for formal education because they believed themselves and their institutions to be innately wise, good, and educative. Athenian public speakers, moreover, had to be very circumspect about appeals to history because they might be perceived by mass audiences as attempting to instruct their inferiors. There certainly was a role for elite leaders within Athenian democratic ideology, but it was not the paternalistic role Farrar seems to assign to Pericles.

But Farrar's is not a book about the fourth century, it is about the "Golden Age."[12] What of Farrar's three "democratic thinkers" themselves? The problem with Protagoras, as Farrar admits (53ff.), is that most of what we know of his thought comes through Plato, a very hostile source. Farrar coins the happy neologism "Platagoras" for the character of Protagoras in Plato's *Protagoras* and *Theaetetus*, and she demonstrates that the arguments of Platagoras and the historical Protagoras cannot be directly equated. Thus, the historical Protagoras' actual political theory can be approximated only roughly. Platagoras is too weak a reed to lean very heavily upon—we will have to look elsewhere for a proper explication of fifth-century democratic thinking. In the case of Democritus we possess numerous fragments, but few are explicitly political/ethical in content. Farrar argues persuasively that there is indeed much that is implicitly political in them, but because the original texts from which the fragments were extracted are lost, just what Democritus was driving at often remains obscure. Thus, despite Farrar's very evocative arguments linking phenomenological/cosmological theorizing with social/political ideas in pre-Socratic thought, she is still a long way from establishing that there existed a concept of "democracy" in atomist thinking that could be set up as a theoretical alternative to the "demotic" understanding of *dēmokratia* contained in fourth-century rhetorical texts, an understanding that, as we have seen, is incommensurate with Farrar's "democracy." This leaves us with Thucydides, whose substantial (if fragmentary) text deals extensively with political life and explicitly with Athenian *dēmokratia*.

Farrar argues convincingly that we will misunderstand Thucydides if we suppose that he is a historian in the modern disciplinary sense of the term. Rather, he is to be read as a political analyst who intended to teach a particular understanding of how politics works. He teaches both by a narrative account of events and by his associated analysis of the meaning of the events he describes. This must certainly be right, although Farrar seems to go rather too far in claiming that Thucydides' text was the theoretical equivalent of the practical functioning of Athens' teaching/guiding/controlling political elite: "In *controlling our interpretation* [my emphasis], he helps us to interpret" (188). This comment has rather frightening implications when viewed in Orwellian terms. Yet Farrar is especially good on the key issue of Thucydides' view of power as the ability of a people to act collectively (140). She is surely correct to say that in writing history, Thucydides "was responding to concerns raised by democracy," but is it equally correct to add that "his response was democratic: that is why he chose to write history" (126)? Were the social-political ideas expressed in Thucydides' history ever organized into a *democratic* theory of politics?

---

[12] On the question of the relationship between fifth- and fourth-century democracy, see Bleicken (1987, 257–83), who reviews the debate and argues for a unitarian position.

The obvious stumbling block in the way of Farrar's interpretation of Thucydides as a democratic thinker is that Thucydides' text never presents *dēmokratia* in a favorable light. Like Farrar, Thucydides admired Pericles. But he did not regard the Athenian *politeia* under Pericles as a true *dēmokratia*; rather, it was "in reality" the rule of one man (2.65.10: *ergōi de hupo tou prōtou andros archē*). Whether or not one accepts Thucydides' statement as a fair description of how Athens was actually governed in the time of Pericles (for the record, I do not; see Chapter 6 above), this passage certainly causes difficulties for Farrar's thesis that Thucydides was a democratic thinker who offered "a broader, deeper version of Periclean civic history" (278). It must be regarded as odd that democracy flourished most perfectly in Athens (according to Farrar) in just the period during which the finest political analyst of antiquity claimed that *dēmokratia* was a façade for a sort of monarchy.

Farrar discusses Thucydides 2.65.10 in the context of her argument that "the moderate blending" of the "Constitution of the Five Thousand" was the "institutional approximation" of Periclean leadership (186). Thucydides might well have agreed, but he did not call either regime democratic.[13] The government of the Five Thousand denied full citizenship to the great majority of free, native-born, Athenian males—men who were citizens when (before and after the regime of the Five Thousand) *dēmokratia* pertained. In order to regard the Constitution of the Five Thousand as a "moderate" regime, one must accept that universal free, native, male franchise is a radical extreme.[14] Because most Athenians did not accept this, the Constitution of the Five Thousand did not last long (cf. above, Chapter 5). Thucydides knew that the Constitution of the Five Thousand, although regarded as excessively democratic by extreme oligarchs, remained undemocratic by Athenian standards; that is why he approved of it and called it a mixed regime, a *xunkrasis*, rather than a *dēmokratia*.[15]

Dēmokratia, as understood by Thucydides, was the unstable rule of mob and demagogues; this is not democracy as understood by Farrar. Nor, as we have seen, does Farrar's democracy match *dēmokratia* as it was understood either by ordinary Athenians or by later Athenian political theorists. Thus Farrar's democracy cannot be equated with any understanding of *dēmokratia* that can be extracted from surviving ancient Athenian texts.[16] This has serious implica-

[13] Pericles calls the *politeia* of Athens a *dēmokratia* in the Funeral Oration (Thuc. 2.37.1), but this passage is certainly not Thucydides speaking *in propria persona*, however one comes down on the issue of the relationship between the speech that was given and the text as we have it.

[14] Despite the attempt of de Ste. Croix (1956, 1–23) to show that it was (sort of) democratic; cf. Rhodes 1972, 115–27.

[15] On the issue of Thucydides' approval of the Constitution of the Five Thousand, see Gomme, Andrewes, and Dover 1945–81, 5:331–39.

[16] The possible exception is Isocrates' ahistorical account of early Athenian *dēmokratia* in the *Areopagiticus* (not cited by Farrar). Although there is much in this text that is foreign to Farrar's analysis, Isocrates' vision of *dēmokratia* does incorporate a responsible, guiding, political elite.

tions for the book's intended force. Once it is generally accepted that "democracy" is the most desirable form of government, the definition of the term becomes a centrally important issue. Farrar's book purports to offer an ancient Athenian definition of democratic thinking in place of the deracinated liberal-democratic definition. The political notions of elite fifth-century Athenian writers might not seem to be quite so directly applicable to the political "unease" of the modern world if the book were called "the origins of thinking (much of it highly critical) *about* democracy." Yet this would more accurately describe the part of the book's content that is actually a history of ideas.

Farrar is admirably concerned with understanding ideas in their historical context (10–11), and she praises Thucydides' historical realism as the basis of his acute political understanding.[17] Yet she often seems to lose sight of the real context in which Thucydides wrote and of his real intended audience. Thucydides was not, in any ordinary sense of the term (ancient or modern), a "democratic" thinker. He was certainly not writing for a mass audience whose members might be taught how to think historically and/or act prudentially. Rather, Thucydides offered his elite audience a detailed explanation of what (in his view) was fundamentally wrong with *dēmokratia*.

Dēmokratia confronted Athenian elites with a political system that they could not control, and yet that *seemed* to work extremely well. I would readily concede that Thucydides intended to teach his (elite) readers and that he hoped to "control [their] interpretation." But the lesson he intended to teach, the interpretation he hoped to demonstrate as inescapable, was that *dēmokratia* was an inherently unstable form of political organization, one that, more or less predictably as a result of its own internal contradictions, pulled itself apart under the stress of a long struggle with a hostile nondemocratic power. The intended force of Thucydides' political analysis of *dēmokratia* is critical. This is far from saying that Thucydides was a revolutionary oligarch; he was capable of equally sharp criticism of oligarchs.[18] Thucydides' political-theoretical project (or part of it) was to challenge the way his elite audience—both those who were willing to live with democracy and those who hoped to overthrow it by force—thought about political power. In its critical stance, the intended force of Thucydides' historiography is akin to that of Plato's and Aristotle's political philosophy—as well as to that of Farrar's text, which cogently criticizes the failings of modern ways of thinking about the political order.

The validity of Farrar's criticism as political philosophy is for others to judge—I for one find it stimulating even when I disagree with it. But the book seems to me flawed as a "history of ideas" because it in some places ignores, and in others distorts, the broader context in which the ideas in question

---

[17] E.g., 128: "Thucydidean history appealed to what man is actually like, and the way the world actually is."

[18] See the passages cited in Pope 1988, 276–96.

developed—the many and various private and public discourses, practices, and rituals that contributed to the construction of a stable and usable democratic ideology among the ordinary Athenians.

For Farrar, the ideas expressed in great texts take on an autonomous reality of their own. The reification of ideas may not be a problem for philosophers, but it is deadly for historians when it leads to the double-forked intellectualist fallacy—the suppositions that intellectuals are influenced only by one another's texts and that political change (for better or for worse) is the direct and exclusive result of a trickle-down of thoughts generated by the educated elite.[19] The intellectualist fallacy can have serious consequences. It reinforces the apparent "naturalness" of unreflective and uncritically hierarchical models of political behavior: "followers" become powerless and mindless consumers of the notions tossed at them by their "leaders," and significant communication between leaders and followers is regarded as a one-way affair. The reader persuaded by a narrowly intellectualist approach to the texts is likely to end up imagining that there were only a few "real" people in ancient Athens—the "thinkers" and "leaders"—while the other quarter-million or so inhabitants of Attica fade away into an amorphous and uninteresting mob of sheep-like "followers." This sort of conclusion fits all too neatly into an elitist model of political behavior.

R. K. Sinclair's *Democracy and Participation in Athens* focuses on public practices, rather than ideas about the public realm, and so provides a valuable antidote to intellectualist readings of Athenian political life. Those readers who are well up on recent scholarship on Athenian democratic institutions (especially the magisterial studies of M. H. Hansen and P. J. Rhodes) may not find a great deal that is startlingly new here, but this well-organized, clearly written book is the obvious place for everyone else to begin. Chapter 1 is a brief overview of the historical evolution of democratic institutions at Athens. Chapter 2 deals with political leaders. Sinclair argues that the difference between Pericles and his political successors is less sharp than Thucydides would have us believe, since Pericles, like his successors, depended on wealth and rhetorical skill. There was a split between spheres of activity of *stratēgoi* and *rhētores* in the fourth century, but Sinclair warns against overestimating the practical significance of the split. Chapter 3 treats the responsibilities (military, religious, political, judicial) of the citizen and shows that Athenian politics cannot be explained in terms of elite political leaders alone; we must also seek to explain the high level of active participation by ordinary citizens. Chapter 4 deals with the relative powers of major and minor *archai*, along with the *boulē*, *ekklēsia*, and *dikastēria*. The Council of 500 is scrutinized particularly carefully and is shown to have been an impor-

---

[19] See, for example, 99: by studying politics, Protagoras allowed the link of society and state to be questioned, and so disintegration quickly followed; cf. 106.

tant institution, but the *bouleutai* were, according to Sinclair, not a ruling elite, and the *ekklēsia* remained sovereign. Chapter 5 concerns demographics and the ideological factors that he feels could have led to, or might have discouraged, large-scale participation. Chapter 6 demonstrates that both politicians and generals in Athens faced serious risks, due especially to the legal procedures of *eisangelia* and *graphē paranomōn*. Chapter 7 looks at the rewards of leadership: the chance of obtaining personal wealth was a factor, but more important was access to honor and power.

Many of these positions, and others that Sinclair brings up in passing,[20] now appear to be on their way to achieving the status of orthodoxy. But these positions were far from orthodox at the time that Sinclair was working on his book, and his detailed arguments will help to cement the new orthodoxy. Moreover, those who have not been following the (often abstruse) literature on these subjects will find Sinclair an excellent introduction and guide. Among Sinclair's virtues as a guide is his tendency to take self-consciously middle-of-the-road positions on controversies (e.g., 113–14). But taking the middle ground does not always work. There seems to be an unresolved tension in this book between a conception of institutions (especially the *boulē* and the *dikastēria*) as substantive entities that govern in their own right (the analogue is modern government bureaucracies) and a view of institutions as conduits for the expression and enactment of the unitary political will of the Athenian demos.[21] There is, of course, some overlap between these two positions. Modern government bureaucracies gain legitimacy both because they claim to rule by the consent of the governed and because they may be (at least partly) staffed by officials chosen (directly or indirectly) by the citizenry. Yet the two conceptions "institutions as government" and "institutions as direct conduits for the expression of popular will" cannot be fully harmonized.

The first, "institutionalist" approach regards political and judicial institutions as primary loci of power, and sees the sum of institutional powers as the government. This approach thus leads to, even requires, an analysis of how institutional "powers" were "balanced" within the political system and lends itself logically to a prosopographical analysis of the (often self-perpetuating) elites who staff institutions. Sinclair sometimes leans in an institutionalist direction (e.g., 132). The second, "ideological" approach emphasizes the directness of democratic decision making. It regards collective, popular ideology as more

---

[20] E.g., the important sociopolitical effects of face-to-face interaction between citizens in the demes; the ideas that Athenian democracy worked quite well, and that its relative stability, not its ultimate failure, is what needs explanation; the theory that the system of liturgies and *charis* was key to social stability.

[21] The first, institutionalist, approach is exemplified by work of Mogens H. Hansen, which Sinclair criticizes on occasion, but is very indebted to. See Hansen's defense of this approach in Hansen 1989b. It is only fair to point out that I am an advocate of the second approach: see Chapter 8 above; with Hansen's reply in Hansen 1989a, 215–18.

important than either institutions qua institutions or the personal histories of the individuals who staff them.

"Consent of the governed" and "separation of powers" are relatively meaningless concepts in the view of this second approach, because it supposes that in a direct democracy the citizens are not "governed" and political power is not subdivided.[22] In the place of an analysis of institutions and prosopography, it demands a close study of political language, in order to show what it was that constituted the will of the demos, and in order to trace how the popular will was translated into individual and collective action within the evolving framework of institutionalized political structure. Sinclair leans toward this second approach in places (e.g., 138), but his analysis of Athenian ideology seems constrained by an over-reliance on "common sense" arguments, by which I mean that he assumes that the Athenians tended to think pretty much like us.[23] Maybe they did—sometimes and on some issues. But often the Athenians did not think like us; an appreciation for the *foreignness*, as well as the familiarity, of Athenian culture is necessary for understanding classical political life. Because this tension is never fully resolved, the book cannot *explain* why or how democracy worked at Athens; it remains a description of a political system. Of course, this need not be a bad thing; a clear and judicious desciption is what many readers want and need.

A few minor complaints: there is a fair amount of unnecessary redundancy (e.g., we are told four times in three pages (107–9) that the Council of 500 met on about 260 days out of the year); and Sinclair sometimes states his own opinions as fact.[24] The extended discussion of the Council's influence (84ff.) attacks a straw man: the position that the Council was politically irrelevant and that the *bouleutai* never discussed important business. Who ever thought that? The footnotes (85 n. 34, 102 n. 107, 103 n. 113) seem to point especially toward A. W. Gomme's short article on the Athenian Council as the source of the silly heresy, but Gomme never argued that the *boulē* was irrelevant.[25] Gomme may have over-weighted the fact that only a few speeches delivered in the *boulē* have survived. But if Sinclair corrects Gomme on this (102), he should also acknowledge the strength of Gomme's central argument: that the Council

[22] This understanding fits Berlin's model of "positive" freedom in that it sees citizens as establishing a collective mastery over the political realm. The institutionalist reading of politics, by contrast, demands an emphasis on "negative" individual freedom from governmental interference. Notably, Berlin (1969, xl–xli, 129) argues that the concept of negative freedom did not exist in classical antiquity; although see below on Wood's assessment of *eleutheria* as freedom from coercive appropriation.

[23] See, for example, 132–33 on stage fright; and 18, where the emphasis on Athens as a competitive society seems to obscure important aspects of unselfish cooperation (e.g., in phalanx and trireme).

[24] E.g., 19 (the archaic *hēliaia*), 35 (Persian maritime strategy in 469 B.C.), 127 (whether Demosthenes 21 was or was not delivered).

[25] Gomme 1951, 12–28. Sinclair also cites Jones 1957; Headlam 1933.

never came to dominate the Assembly because the *bouleutai* never developed a corporate identity. Sinclair emphasizes the anticorporatist argument (102–3) without ever acknowledging it as Gomme's. Sinclair also manifests an occasional tendency to what might be called the "nuggets" mode of argumentation: picking out an individual and claiming his behavior in a certain instance was "typical,"[26] or pulling a couple of passages out of their context in order to use them to demonstrate (for example, and I believe wrongly) that wealthy Athenians were less likely to serve as jurors on the people's courts than to attend the Assembly.[27] Finally, although Sinclair is very interested in comparing how many wealthy and poor citizens participated in political activities, his emphasis on institutional powers seems to preclude delving into the question of how the life experiences of Athenians of various classes related to their tendency to participate or not to participate in the democratic processes of government.

It is the everyday life experience of ordinary, and especially rural, Athenians that forms the subject of Ellen Meiksins Wood's groundbreaking study, *Peasant-Citizen and Slave*. Wood deploys a model of historical explanation that borrows from a materialist Marxist tradition in its emphasis on the historical importance of the mode of economic production. However, Wood's analysis diverges sharply and self-consciously from orthodox Marxist materialism in regarding political relationships as coexisting with production in the "base" of Athenian society, rather than seeing politics and ideology as "superstructure" and the result of "false consciousness."[28]

Wood posits that an exploited peasantry, whose labor produces a surplus that is subject to coercive appropriation by politically sanctioned authorities (landlords and/or the government), is the standard model of preindustrial, precapitalist production. The Athenian social-economic system does not fit this pattern—Athenian "peasants" were subject to only minimal appropriation of their surplus agricultural production. This historical anomaly requires an explanation: what factors conspired to keep the Athenian elite off the Athenian peasant's back? Wood's thesis is that in classical Athens the political rights of citizen-peasants limited the degree to which they could be exploited (i.e., their surplus production appropriated). Because Athenian peasants were politically active citizens, the Athenian elite (the potential appropriating class) could not monopolize power. In Athens the political regime was discontinuous from the economic regime. Instead of a seamless "reality" in which the elite was perceived as "naturally" and thus legitimately possessing a conjoined and interwoven political power and power over the labor of dependents, the political

---

[26] In one case (134), the exemplar is Plato—surely the worst possible choice for a "typical Athenian"!

[27] P. 124; cf. Ober 1989b, 134–38, 142–44.

[28] Wood is relentless in attacking orthodox Marxist dependence on the "slave mode of production" as an explanation for ancient economy; see especially her discussion of the theories of G.E.M. de Ste. Croix: 64–80.

power of the Athenian peasants allowed them successfully to challenge the elite's right to surplus production.

As a result of the splitting off of political from economic power, the Athenian smallholders enjoyed a way of life that in some ways approximated the peasant utopia described by Eric Wolf: "The free village, untrammelled by tax collectors, labor recruiters, large landowners, officials."[29] The Athenian peasant-citizen, unlike other peasants, was free from the duty to perform coerced labor; he was free from enforced dependency, and this, according to Wood, is the root meaning of the democratic term *eleutheria*. Moreover, this freedom had remarkable results: Wood argues that the stimulus for much of Athenian culture can be found in the freedom of the peasantry and the consequent reaction of the Athenian aristocracy to that freedom.

This is an original position. Classical historians may ask, if Athenian society is essentially a *peasant* society, a regime of smallholder agriculturalists, why has the view of the Athenian masses as an urban "mob"—often out of work and therefore eager for employment in the trireme navy—prevailed since the early nineteenth century? Wood offers an answer in her first chapter, where she traces "the myth of the idle mob" to the political debates of late eighteenth- and early nineteenth-century England. Wood points out that the prevalence of chattel slavery in Athens was depicted in William Mitford's influential *History of Greece* (1784–1810) as an evil that led to underemployment among ordinary citizens. Too much leisure among the lower classes led to the "turbulence" of radical democracy, which fatally disrupted the "natural" hierarchical relationship between classes and so brought on decay and decline. As Wood shows, Mitford's notion of the linkage between slavery, citizen idleness, and democracy caught on fast, and was not limited to reactionaries: Karl Marx and his followers incorporated it in the theory of the ancient "slave mode of production." The "idle mob" thesis tended to be accepted uncritically as a given by Greek historians.

The ideological roots of historians' dogmas are complex and draw upon factors both external and internal to the discipline.[30] Wood emphasizes external factors (especially Mitford's conservative political views). But we should remember that the idle mob thesis is "supported" by numerous passages in the ancient sources (e.g., Aristophanes and Plato) and that it gained wide currency at a time when the disciplines of both philology and history were realizing their modern forms.[31] One might speculate that a growing philological tendency to see properly established ancient texts as authoritative may have conjoined with a growing historiographical concern to "respect the sources." The method of source criticism was not a useful corrective in this case, since most of the sources were closely contemporary to the phenomena they described, and they

[29] Wolf 1971, 272; cited by Wood at 126.

[30] See Novick 1988.

[31] Although see Roberts (1989, 193–205), who argues that the antidemocratic tendency in British historiography on Athens much preceded the American and French revolutions.

were mutually reinforcing. Thus the "scientific" tendencies of evolving disciplines, as well as a legacy of partisan, antidemocratic scholarship, kept the
myth of the idle mob afloat. Only an analysis willing to separate "knowledge
and honesty of the sources" from "history as it actually happened" could expose the myth. A more detailed historiographical assessment thus might nu-
ance Wood's scenario, but this chapter proves that historians must struggle
with (rather than accept the dogma of past scholarship upon) issues of production. We must understand how both free persons and slaves worked and what
their labor meant to the society if we are to understand the nature of Athenian
democracy.

In her second chapter (based on her important article in the *American Journal
of Ancient History* 8 [1983]), Wood discusses slave labor and production. Though
the attempt to estimate the absolute number of slaves in Athens is probably
futile, Wood demonstrates that it is wrong to suppose that lower-class citizens
could not have participated in political life unless they owned slaves. Particularly important here is Wood's discussion of the analytical weight that must
be given to the issue of surplus appropriation relative to intensification of agriculture. Wood does not deny that there is a link between democracy and
slavery in Athens; indeed, "the relative unavailability of Athenian free producers for exploitation was itself a critical factor leading to the growth of slavery" (61). But most slaves worked for rich men, and the countryside remained
preeminently the domain of the peasant smallholder. The textual evidence
that has been brought to bear on this issue remains ambiguous, but Wood has
shifted the balance of the debate. It is up to those who suppose that there *was*
widespread slave-ownership among non-elite Athenian farmers to make a positive case, by deploying either new theoretical arguments or new texts.

In her Chapter 3, Wood considers some of the implications of "charac-
teriz[ing] . . . Athenian democracy in terms of its exclusion of dependence
from the sphere of production, instead of emphasizing . . . chattel slavery. In
comparison to the conditions of other advanced civilizations of the ancient
world . . . the absence of a dependent peasantry and the establishment of a
regime of free smallholders stands out in sharp relief" (83). To explain how this
anomalous state of affairs came about, Wood sketches a (rather hypothetical)
historical evolution of the relationship between politics and production from
Mycenaean times to the classical period. Key for her scenario is the idea that
the existence of exclusive "communities" of laborers and appropriators could
not survive the collapse of Mycenaean palace economies. In the absence of a
political basis for exerting coercive force, landlords had to deal with laborers as
individuals and classes within the same community (98). This system, which
preserved hierarchy without preserving the ideology that had legitimated it,
proved unstable and led to the crisis of the early sixth century. Solon solved the
crisis by stripping the elite of the remnants of their extra-economic superiority.
Thus he strengthened the civic community while leaving intact the economic

dominance of landed wealth. Subsequent reformers, Peisistratos and Cleisthenes, worked according to the same logic, and the result was the breakdown of opposition between village and state—a breakdown that Wood considers the foundation of democracy. Ironically, this development of an autonomous civic realm, while serving to protect the male peasant-citizens from dependence and appropriation, also hardened the distinctions between free and slave, and between male and female Athenians. Obviously an admirer of Athenian democracy (see especially 4), Wood is nonetheless careful not to fall into the trap of polis nostalgia.

Chapter 4 argues that the peasant conception of freedom as absence of coercion and appropriation informs the central ideals of Athenian culture—even Platonic and Aristotelian philosophy: "The small producers of Athens were its cultural mainspring . . . in the challenge which they represented to aristocratic dominance" (169). If Wood is right, this suggests that Plato and Aristotle did not (pace Farrar) "retreat" from politics; rather, they actively engaged in an ongoing debate with democratic ideology. Wood's discussion of political philosophy (Protagoras, Plato, Aristotle) is rather impressionistic, but she shows clearly the need to read philosophical texts against the ideological context in which philosophers lived and to which their texts may have responded. This approach turns the intellectualist fallacy on its head. Rather than supposing that the masses respond to ideas offered by an intellectual elite, Wood suggests that Athenian elites were forced to respond to the ideas of the masses.

In explaining aristocratic literary culture as oppositional to democracy, Wood notes the fruitfulness of the debate between democracy and its elite critics. And in looking at aspects of this debate, she attacks some long-cherished shibboleths of modern scholarship. There was no assumption among the masses of Athenians that labor was in and of itself demeaning: "Freedom as most Athenians conceived it implied, among other things, the freedom of labour, in contrast to the freedom *from* labour" (137). The search for an explanation for Greek "technological stagnation" is shown to be misguided (150ff.), since a high rate of technological innovation is a modern development that can be attributed to the unique production (and, one might add, consumption) needs of a capitalistic society.

Few classical historians will accept all of Wood's general propositions. Textual evidence to support many points is lacking, and she has depended overmuch on a few secondary works. Much of her argument remains to be proved, and some of Wood's positions may not stand up to detailed philological scrutiny. A few readers might be tempted simply to reject Wood's conclusions out of hand because she is not a classicist and because she works from unfamiliar models. That would be a great shame indeed: basing her work on a mastery of political and economic theory, Wood has made a major contribution to the development of a new paradigm for explaining the evolution and historical meaning of ancient Athenian democracy. This paradigm sees material (production / consumption) and ideological (culture / discourse) factors as inextricably intertwined and as fundamentally important to processes of sociopolitical change and stability. It is a paradigm that should keep students of Greek history productively at work—testing, building upon, refining, and challenging its premises and claims—for years to come.

Chapter 10

HOW TO CRITICIZE DEMOCRACY IN LATE FIFTH-
AND FOURTH-CENTURY ATHENS

This essay was adapted from a frequently rewritten introduction to a book-in-progress on Athenian critics of popular rule (see Chapter 1). Various drafts were undertaken in Washington, D.C., at the Center for Hellenic Studies, in Armidale (Australia) at the University of New England, in Montana, and in Princeton. It was presented in somewhat different forms at a 1992 Cambridge University colloquium, "The Greek Revolution," and as the first of my 1994 Martin Classical Lectures at Oberlin College. I am indebted for constructive criticism to many scholars, notably to John Dunn (my Cambridge respondent), Paul Cartledge, Quentin Skinner, Peter Euben, and John Wallach.

The essay attempts to explain a vexing problem that I became aware of in the course of my work on popular ideology and democratic authority: If, as I suppose, Athenian democracy was in practice predicated on popular ideology, and if Athenian popular ideology had a tendency to hegemonic status (i.e., it tended to reify and naturalize existing power relations, monopolize the political landscape, and drive out alternative approaches to thinking and talking about politics and social relations), then is it fair to call Athens "democratic" in any but Athenian terms? Was Athenian *dēmokratia* nothing more than the tyranny of the *ideas* of the citizen mob? If so, Athenian democracy becomes, in normative moral terms, no better—indeed, perhaps considerably worse—than various sorts of elite rule.

The comparative historian may simply shrug at this point and express a lack of interest in normative problems: he or she may legitimately claim that it is how Athens developed as a society and how Athens was similar to or different from other societies, not whether Athens is better or worse than other societies, that matters to a properly historical perspective. But from the perspective of the historian overtly concerned not only with historical *realia* of a given society, but with deploying those *realia* as part of an attempt to test established political ideas, the moral status of Athens as a society is important. In this chapter I consider the extent of ideological hegemony within the citizen body and the possibilities opened within the society of citizens for challenging the hegemony of democratic thinking. In Chapter 11, the scope of the analysis is expanded by comparing the moral standing of the society of citizens to the moral standing of the whole society.

This essay was rewritten so often because I found the question of how to juxtapose the critic of democracy with democratic culture complex and, initially, baffling. I sup-

This essay was first published in Euben et al. 1994, 149–171. Copyright © 1994 by Cornell University. Used by permission of the publisher, Cornell University Press.

posed that I had a good grasp of how rhetorical texts worked (Chapter 7). And I felt fairly comfortable in assessing Thucydides as a historian with theoretical leanings (Chapter 6). But I felt much less clear about how to generalize the issue of political criticism: was there some overarching design that would encompass the critical voices of Ps.-Xenophon, Plato, Aristotle, Aristophanes, and Isocrates? Attempting to find my footing over this new terrain led me into a deeper examination of certain postmodern theorists (notably Michel Foucault on power) and revisionist Marxism (especially Antonio Gramsci on hegemony). These writers offered sophisticated descriptions of how problems of power and ideology related to hegemony and thereby helped me to establish the appropriate terms for setting out the first part of my question. But these continental traditions offered less purchase on the second part of the question, which pertains to the ways in which a specifically democratic hegemony might be distinctive and how resistance to hegemony might take literary form. I subsequently worked my way back through critics of postmodernism to the democratic pragmatism of John Dewey, the speech-act theory of J. L. Austin, and the concern with the politics of language that pervades the novels of George Orwell. These three well-known early to mid-twentieth-century writers (along with some of their more recent interpreters) seemed to me to provide the necessary concepts for setting out the second part of the equation.

The most remarkable thing about demotic Athenian political culture, when viewed from the perspective of various strands of contemporary thought (whether modern or postmodern), is its lack of an adequate formal foundation: the Athenians simply did not have resort to final authority (e.g., a constitution, the revealed word of God, or metaphysical Platonic Forms) when doing their political business. In the Assembly, the lawcourts, and other public forums, they made things up as they went along; or, rather, they predicated their decisions on (conceptually messy and often internally contradictory) ideology rather than established doctrine or scientific principles. Athens' democracy operated on the basis of opinion, not truth. This state of affairs did not, however, seem to bother the Athenian masses; their own opinions and established public practices served as a set of reasonably wise and consistent values, and they supposed that this set of values (this ideology) was an adequate guide for effective decision-making. But as soon as the democratic edifice's trick of aerial suspension without benefit of foundations was noticed by critics of democracy, the issue of how to establish foundations for belief and action became a central issue for Athenian political thinking—and hence for much of subsequent Western thought.

The Athenian political order thus emerges as a form of pragmatism that skirted the two extremes of value-free relativism and absolutist positivism; political theory emerges as an attempt to demonstrate the problems of politics without foundations. The upshot of the argument is that classical democracy and its fiercest literary critics existed in a close symbiotic relationship: Athenian democracy and the beginnings of the Western tradition of critical political theory were codependent, and political theory arose in the context of an unresolved and yet relatively nonviolent struggle over the means of production of political knowledge.

The issue of the relationship between Athenian democracy and political theory produced in Athens has been addressed from several perspectives in recent studies. Along with the pioneering work of Farrar (1988, 1992), see Roberts 1994; the essays collected in Euben et al. 1994 and in Ober and Hedrick 1996; and Yunis 1996.

———————

SOME 2,500 YEARS after the revolution that made it possible, democracy is widely regarded as the most attractive form of practical (as opposed to utopian) political organization yet devised. Among democracy's virtues is revisability— the potential of the political regime to rethink and to reform itself, while remaining committed to its core values of justice, equality, dignity, and freedom. How is this highly desirable flexibility achieved in practice? The *willingness* to contemplate change may be regarded as an innate characteristic of democratic political culture, and the *capacity* for nondestructive political change can be institutionalized in a democratic constitution. But I will argue here that actual revisions generally require interventions from critics, and major revisions require critics who stand, in some sense, outside the dominant political culture. Because actualizing a democratic regime's latent capacity for major revision is predicated on the identification of structural problems by cultural critics, the regime that is to maintain its flexibility must allow social space exterior to itself: if a political system could ever encompass the whole of society and the whole field of discourse, it would lose its capacity for internally generated change; no one would be able to point out that "the emperor is naked" or that "2 plus 2 does *not* equal 5." Though this degree of encompassing may be impossible except in the realm of dystopic fiction, the claim that revisibility is among democracy's attractions and strengths suggests that it is actually in the self-interest of a democracy (unlike brittle, nonrevisable authoritarian regimes) to defend and even to seek to enlarge space for criticism. Moreover, a democratic regime must allow the cultural critic to maintain his or her distance, to remain a partial outsider, if it is to remain truly democratic and avoid the totalizing tendencies inherent in every value-based system of social organization. In a direct democracy on the Athenian model, therefore, not only is freedom of speech a good idea, but the power of the people exists in a symbiotic relationship with resistance to that selfsame power.[1]

If, in late fifth- and fourth-century Athens, *dēmokratia* meant "the political power of the ordinary people," and if power includes control over the development and deployment of systems of meaning (including popular ideology and the rhetoric of public communication), then, for Athenians, criticism of the

———

[1] Impossibility of complete suppression of resistance: Large 1992. The need for an "outside": Codrescu 1990. Revisability and cultural criticism: West 1989.

language of democratic government and of the assumptions of popular ideology could be a means of resisting political power.[2] It seems probable that critics of the status quo existed at every level of Athenian society; it is not hard to imagine that in each village and neighborhood of the polis there were men and women who could be counted on to interrogate, humorously or angrily, various aspects of the current order of things. The voices of these "local critics" are now lost, and we cannot say to what extent they were able to (or desired to) get outside that order. But a number of Athenian intellectuals committed pungent and profoundly critical opinions to writing, and in the process they contributed to the construction of what we might well call an "outside." Studying classical Athenian literature critical of the democratic regime thus offers access to one very important fragment of what was probably much more diverse and widespread resistance to political power. We may regret the loss of nonliterary forms of criticism. But if we hope to gain even a partial understanding of the link between Athenian democratic politics and unease with how the people's political power was manifested and deployed, we must come to grips with the texts we have.

Exploring the symbiosis of democracy and criticism should be significant for intellectual historians and political theorists alike. For historians, it promises to furnish part of the deep context for some of the works of Ps.-Xenophon, Thucydides, Aristophanes, Plato, Isocrates, and Aristotle, among others. For the political theorist, looking at how classical democracy was criticized offers an alternative to the long-dominant but increasingly problematic paradigms of state socialism and rights-oriented liberalism. The history of political criticism in late fifth- and fourth-century B.C. Athens helps to explain how an attractive (in at least certain respects), revisable system of popular authority that was neither truly liberal nor truly socialistic could be sustained, and how such a system might be resisted. Given the differences between ancient and modern styles of politics, studying Athenian democracy and its critics certainly will not offer the late twentieth century an off-the-shelf technique for reconstructing a theory of politics. But if the complex relationship among justice, political power, and resistance to power no longer seems adequately explained by paradigms of liberalism and socialism (either alone or in combination), then trying to understand politics in classical Athens may be worth our while.

There is, of course, nothing particularly original in studying "the critics of Athenian democracy," and the ancient texts that lend themselves to such a

---

[2] I emphasize that the texts I address (with the exception of Ps.-Xenophon, *The Constitution of Athens*, sometimes dated as early as ca. 440 B.C.) were completed after the end of the Peloponnesian War (431–404 B.C.)—that acid test of democratic practice. This is a deliberate choice, made because my approach requires the prior establishment of the ideological context through analysis of public speech, and the surviving corpus of Attic oratory is overwhelmingly postwar. The relationship between democracy and "political" texts may have been rather different during the floruit of Attic tragedy in the fifth century; see, for example, Euben 1990.

study are well known. Some forty years ago A.H.M. Jones pointed out the two key issues:[3] First, while we have a good many classical texts in various genres that are critical of democracy, we have no surviving texts written with the explicit intention of explaining the principles on which Athenian democracy was predicated. Second, in the absence of theoretical defenses of democracy, understanding the "positive" argument an Athenian would make for democracy depends on a close reading of Athenian public rhetoric. While I am deeply impressed by Jones' fundamental insights, I find his approach to "criticizing democracy" problematic. Jones argued that Athenian democracy was stable because it was dominated by "bourgeois" or "middle-class" citizens.[4] I view *dēmokratia* rather as a dynamic system through which the mass of ordinary citizens (*hoi polloi*, *to plēthos*, *hoi penētes*) (1) maintained personal dignity and political equality, (2) restrained the privileges and power of elites (*hoi oligoi*, *hoi chrēstoi*, *hoi plousioi*), and (3) thereby protected themselves from certain forms of socioeconomic exploitation and political dependency.

Furthermore, Jones saw the debate over ancient democracy primarily in instrumental terms—for him, democracy was criticized and should be defended on the grounds of whether it allowed for rational decision-making about issues of state policy and whether it provided a secure environment in which civil society could flourish and in which private goods (especially material prosperity) could be enjoyed by individuals. Jones argued persuasively that democratic equality and freedom neither led necessarily to poor policy nor threatened civil society and, thus, that the ancient critics were wrong to cast aspersions upon the democratic government. But classical Athenian political life cannot be explained by a model of political behavior that assumes either a neat subdivision of the political realm into discrete categories of state, citizenry, and government, or a hierarchical differentiation between the (primary) private and (secondary) public spheres.[5] The Athenian did not engage in political activity solely as a functional means to gain the end of guarding against threats to his property or to his private pursuit of happiness. Rather, the values of equality and freedom that he gained by the possession and exercise of citizenship were substantive, were central to his identity, and provided a measure of meaning to his life.[6]

It was this noninstrumental aspect of Greek political life that attracted the attention of Hannah Arendt, who provides a noteworthy example of a modern theorist looking to classical Greece to construct a political theory that was neither traditionally liberal nor socialist. For Arendt, the polis provided

---

[3] Jones 1957:41–72, originally published in *Cambridge Historical Journal* 11 (1953), 1–26.

[4] See Markle 1985 for a detailed criticism.

[5] I explore this issue in more detail in Chapter 11.

[6] On identity, see, for example, Taylor 1989; Euben 1990; Manville 1990.

an ideal and explicitly public/political sphere for free human action and speech, for the "appearance" of human individuality through extraordinary deeds, and for the creation and collective maintenance of historical memory.[7] To focus on the role of public action in creating the identity of the free and equal citizen, and on public speech as a form of political action, is both historically defensible and theoretically useful.[8] But Arendt's Greek model cannot be adopted wholesale by the intellectual historian or by the political theorist interested in an empirical test of alternative models of politics. Arendt's polis, strictly divided between the private realm of necessity and economics and the public realm of freedom, action, and politics, had no place for social interaction that blurred the distinction between the citizen-warrior and the laborer-householder. Arendt's polis was an ahistorical ideal, based in large part on her own reading of Aristotle's *Politics*. Arendt's access to the polis was through ancient texts both critical of democracy and written in the context of the democratic regime. But, in common with many other readers before and since, Arendt largely ignored the context and accepted the criticism as a description of reality.[9]

If there is anything new in my approach to Athenian criticism of democracy, it is a concentration on the context in which critical texts were produced, that is, Athens' dominant political ideology and sociopolitical practices. I attempted to delineate that ideology and those practices in *Mass and Elite in Democratic Athens*. There I was concerned with how the ordinary citizens of Athens gained and held power through a form of ideological hegemony that constrained the public and private behavior of the elite (the wealthy, highly educated, and wellborn). Here I am concerned with how a few elite Athenians opposed democratic ideology through critical discourse. I hope that this meditation on the problem of "how to criticize," which is intended to prepare the way for a much more detailed assessment of the substance of individual ancient works of criticism, will hold some interest both for intellectual historians and for political theorists concerned with the "founding generations" of the Western political tradition. To focus on the critical force of works by Thucydides, Plato, et al. as resistance to a socially constructed regime of power and discourse—rather than as instrumental critiques of how and why democratic governmental institutions malfunctioned—is to suggest that Western political theory first emerged in a context of a fruitful and relatively nonviolent struggle over the means of the production of political knowledge.

---

[7] See Arendt 1959, 1963, 1968. Cf. Kateb 1983, esp. 1–51, for discussion of Arendt's view of Greece, and why it is disquieting and even threatening from the liberal point of view; Tlaba 1987, ix–x, 1–35, 38–42; Holmes 1979.

[8] Compare, from their different perspectives, Vernant 1982 and Meier 1990.

[9] There is some question whether Arendt actually believed in the polis she presents; see Tlaba 1987, 41–42.

CONTEXT

Athenian political texts (e.g., Thucydides, Plato's *Republic*, Aristotle's *Politics*) provided foundations for what was to become the dominant Western tradition of political philosophy. Origins are necessarily discovered (or invented) only in retrospect.[10] Yet as a result of their post eventum designation as foundational, Athenian political texts are typically read backwards: from the perspective of the philosophical tradition that eventually grew up from and around them, rather than against the political context in which they were written. Teleology is fatal to the enterprise of the intellectual historian, but the study of Athenian political texts (at least qua political texts) has long been the preserve of theorists and philosophers with a disciplinary tendency to be disinterested in original context. When it is noticed, the historical context for Athenian political writers is extrapolated from these selfsame authors. Thus the cockeyed picture that Thucydides, Plato, and Aristotle offer of Athenian democracy as an inherently foolish system gone wrong is sometimes taken at face value and read as an "objective" description of Athenian practice.

Though "historicist" readings are often frowned upon in literary and theoretical circles, the primacy of context is a point of convergence for several analytic traditions. The so-called Cambridge School of intellectual history focuses on how political terminology is used and revised by writers in arguments with their literary predecessors and contemporaries. Even the most innovative writers appropriate preexisting vocabulary for discussing problems, but they often deploy that vocabulary in self-consciously innovative ways. In some periods (e.g., the eighteenth century A.D. and the fifth century B.C.) the ways in which terms are used in arguments change very rapidly. But even a text produced during a revolution can and should be situated in its own proximate context. Political writing thus becomes historically meaningful when read against the backdrop of terms, assumptions, and ideas hammered out in earlier and contemporary discussions. That backdrop is typically best illuminated by the writings of lesser (because less innovative and original) intellectual lights.[11] A "Cambridge School" reading of Athenian political texts would require a reconstruction of the fifth-/fourth-century intellectual context, that is, the conceptual apparatus available for modification by the authors of our surviving texts. This sort of contextualist approach to political thought is not entirely foreign to classical scholarship; something like it is, for example, employed by

---

[10] By "Athenian political text" I mean a text that was written by an author who spent formative years in Athens and so wrote within a context defined in part by Athenian political discourse. Thus Aristotle (though he was not an Athenian) and Thucydides (though he did not necessarily write his history in Athens) both qualify as authors of Athenian political texts. For a critical assessment of the concept of foundations, see Barber 1988. Origins as retroactively constructed: Said 1975.

[11] See Skinner et al. 1988.

the "Begriffsgeschichte" school of Christian Meier.[12] But an approach that presupposes that the context for surviving texts was defined primarily by *literary* discourse cannot fully explain Athenian political texts if it ignores the role played by the Athenian demos.

An exclusive emphasis on the elite literary context (or, alternatively, on "intertextuality") will make it difficult for historians to link ideas with practices and events. It may lead them to fall into the habit of supposing that more or less fully worked out political theories must precede political practices. In the Athenian case, democratic practices were established well before any (surviving) text discussed democracy in abstract terms. A second consequence is that historical crises may come to be defined by elite perception: When the historian can show that contemporary intellectuals agreed that a crisis was occurring, are we then to assume that a real and general crisis pertained? Fourth-century B.C. Athens was long seen as beset by decline and disorder at least in part because Plato, Isocrates, et al. described it as such. The hypothesis that fourth-century Athens was characterized by a pervasive malaise is much harder to sustain if we look beyond the opinions of the literary elite to the social and political conditions of Athenian citizen society as a whole.[13]

The "climate of intellectual opinion" approach is doubly problematic in the Athenian case. First, we possess few "lesser light" texts of the sort that have allowed students of early modern political thought to define in detail the context of the major luminaries of the Renaissance. Moreover, as Jones pointed out, we have a number of important classical texts critical of democracy but no surviving texts that sympathetically and systematically enunciate the theory on which Athenian democracy was predicated. If we accept that in order to comprehend how political vocabulary was employed in classical Athens we must read our surviving political texts contextually, as interventions in an ongoing debate about politics, the question necessarily arises: Who defined the other side of the dialogue? If Thucydides, Plato, and Aristotle can be characterized as critics of democracy, with whom were they arguing? The absence of formal democratic theory in the text record has long bothered classical historians of ideas and has led to inventive efforts (e.g., by Eric A. Havelock and Cynthia Farrar) to find expressions of democratic theory lurking in extant elite texts. While interesting as theoretical exercises, these efforts are unsatisfactory as intellectual history.[14] The simplest hypothesis is that there are no surviving texts to explain democratic theory because few such texts ever existed. And

---

[12] Cf. Meier 1984, focusing on the revolution of the conceptual universe in the fifth century B.C. and the comparison with the eighteenth century A.D. Meier 1970 and Raaflaub 1985 are good examples of the genre.

[13] Mossé 1962, a book that remains fundamentally important, nonetheless tends to focus on decline and fall. The issue of Athens' "decline" is not, one might point out, identical to that of the "crisis of the polis."

[14] Havelock 1957; Farrar 1988. Cf. my comments in Chapter 9.

one needn't travel far to find the reason for this lacuna: In Athens democratic ideology so dominated the political landscape that formal democratic theory was otiose.[15] The climate of opinion to which the authors of critical political texts were responding was defined less by the reasoned positions of pro-democracy elite intellectuals than by democratic popular ideology and public rhetoric.

To understand Athenian political literature we must extend our contextual scope beyond the circle of Athens' intellectual elite to explore the linkages between public discourse, knowledge, and power. The idea that texts can fruitfully be read as products of complex matrices of social relations that are in turn formed through the play of power[16] helps to define the relationship between Athenian political texts on the one hand and the modes of discourse and the social practices typical of Athenian political society on the other. In short, the historian cannot hope to understand Athenian political texts outside the context of their production, nor can he or she grasp the context without a prior analysis of late fifth- through late fourth-century Athenian social practices, political ideology, and public speech.

IDEOLOGY, POLITICAL KNOWLEDGE, SPEECH ACTS

In *Mass and Elite* I argued that Athenian political ideology and significant aspects of Athenian social practice were formulated through, maintained by, and revealed in the processes of public speech. Because Assembly and lawcourt debates were particularly important forums, a careful reading of Athenian symbouleutic and dicanic rhetoric allows us to reconstitute in some detail the tenets of the popular political ideology of the very late fifth and fourth century B.C. In brief summary, among the central holdings of that ideology were:

1. A belief in the autochthonous nature of the Athenians, their innate intellectual superiority vis-à-vis all other peoples, and the necessity of maintaining the exclusivity of the citizenry;

2. An assumption that the ideal of political equality could be achieved and maintained in the face of existing and legitimate social inequality;

3. A conviction that both consensus and freedom of public speech were desirable;

---

[15] Although it is worth noting that Athenian dicanic (lawcourt) rhetoric may actually be more "theoretical" than often realized, and may have functioned as a way of discussing democratic values in abstract as well as pragmatic terms; see, for example, Chapter 7. I hope to pursue this notion in more detail in future studies.

[16] This approach to power is particularly associated with Michel Foucault; see Foucault 1979 and 1980a, and the essays collected in Foucault 1980b. It is worth noting, however, that in his own late work on Greek society (Foucault 1986), which focuses on how prescriptive philosophical and medical texts "problematized" sexuality, Foucault made what E. Said (1988, 8) has called a "particular and overdetermined shift from the political to the personal."

4. A belief in the superior wisdom of decisions made collectively by large bodies of citizens;

5. A presumption that elites were simultaneously a danger to democracy and indispensable to the political decision-making process.

The general acceptance by most Athenians of these ideological premises allowed democratic Athens to work in practice, as a society and as a state. Ideology mediated between the reality of social inequality and the goal of political equality, and thereby arbitrated class tensions that elsewhere in Greece led to protracted and destructive civil wars. It provided a role for elite leadership within a political system that was based on frequent public expressions of the collective will. But it also required elite leaders to remain closely attuned to popular concerns and prevented the formation of a cohesive ruling elite within the citizen body.

In democratic Athens there was no very meaningful separation between the realms of politics, political society (citizenry), and government. In the Athenian democracy, major government decision making (by *boulē*, Assembly, lawcourts, and boards of *nomothetai*, or "lawgivers") was legitimate specifically because it *was* political. And thus there was no meaningful separation between supposedly objective and scientific truths of the sort used (so we are told) by modern political rulers when making "serious" decisions, and the subjective political truths of the sort modern politicians find it expedient to present to the citizenry during elections and occasional plebiscites. In Athens, the general understanding held by the citizenry regarding the nature of society was the same understanding employed by decision-making bodies in formulating government policy for deployment in the real world. For most Athenians, the shocking "postmodern" conclusion that all knowledge is political (i.e., implicated in relations of power) was simply a truism; neither the possibility nor the normative desirability of apolitical forms of knowledge about society or its members ever entered the ordinary Athenian's head.[17]

In the decades after the Peloponnesian War, this relationship between ideology and political power provided the grounds for a remarkably stable sociopolitical order. Athenian democracy was not founded on a formal constitution or on a set of metaphysical/ontological/epistemological certainties, but rather was undergirded by a socially and politically constructed "regime of truth" (i.e., an integrated set of assumptions about what is right, proper, and true).[18] I

---

[17] Definition of postmodern: Hoy 1988. The modern horror at the politicization of knowledge is perhaps still best summed up in Orwell 1949; note that in Orwell's dystopia there remains a distinction between ideology ($2 + 2 = 5$) and brute reality ($2 + 2 = 4$), a distinction that is recognized by the rulers of society.

[18] Foucault 1980b, 131: "Each society has its régime of truth, its 'general politics' of truth: that is, the types of discourse which it accepts and makes function as true; the mechanisms and instances which enable one to distinguish true and false statements, the means by which each is

propose calling that regime "democratic knowledge." The existence and practical functioning of democratic knowledge depended on the implicit willingness of most citizens to accept the political verities they lived by as "constative"
(by which I mean that political and social "truths" were brought into being by
felicitously performed speech acts) rather than as absolutes denoted by a tran-
scendent natural or divine order. The authority of the demos was legitimated
neither by "divine right" nor by "natural right"—which distinguishes it from
the dominant early-modern and Enlightenment European explanations of
sovereignty.

The Athenian political order was grounded in democratic knowledge. And
democratic knowledge was predicated, in the language of J. L. Austin's speech-
act theory, on the "conventional effect of a conventional procedure" rather
than on an objective, metaphysical, or "natural" view of social reality; it was
created and re-created through collective practices of public communication,
rather than given by an external authority or discovered through intellectual
effort. In the terminology of semiotics, democratic knowledge did not need to
suppose that signifiers attached directly, permanently, or naturally to referents,
only that signifiers pointed to commonly accepted codes and socially constituted meanings. This democratic and (in modern philosophical terms) pragmatic position allowed the Athenians to avoid the epistemological traps (and
the political ugliness they can entail) of value-free relativism on the one hand,
and positivist absolutism on the other.

Athenian political culture was specifically based on collective opinion,
rather than on objectively verifiable, scientific truths. By this I do not mean
that the Athenians supposed that their collective opinion could cause the sun
to rise in the west, or alter other "brute" physical facts. But they regarded
social facts as conventional and political, not as homologous to the brute facts
of nature.[19] The expression *edoxe tōi dēmōi*—"it appeared right to the citizenry"
that such-and-such should be the case—defines the democratic approach to
the relationship between social knowledge, decision, and action. A politics
based on common opinion can be built from the bottom up, and potentially
allows for the integration of "local knowledges" (e.g., the specific practices of
village, cult, or family life) within the broader community of the polity. As a
result of the complex structure of Athenian political institutions, there was a
constant give-and-take between center and periphery, between specific local
understandings, local critics, and the generalized polis-wide democratic ideology.[20] This "system" (keeping in mind that it was not designed by any

---

sanctioned; the techniques and procedures accorded value in the acquisition of truth; the status of
those who are charged with saying what counts as true."

[19] Brute versus social facts: Searle 1969, 50–53, with the comments of Petrey 1990, 59–69.

[20] Local knowledge (as a possible source of criticism and resistance): Foucault 1980b, 80–85.
Complexity of the "grammar" of Athenian institutions: Hansen 1989b.

single authority, nor entirely rational in its workings) integrated Athenian processes of discussion and decision into a public way of knowing about society
that was simultaneously a way of being a citizen, doing politics, and making
policy.

The Athenian sociopolitical order was relatively stable because of the integrative tendencies and deep-rootedness of popular ideology. Ideological equi-
librium allowed the Athenians the luxury of a degree of epistemic continuity
adequate to provide a basis for collective decision making—Assemblymen and
jurors employed as the premises of their deliberations opinions that were generally accepted as valid by the citizenry as a whole. Yet, in practice, the democracy was flexible, dialectical, and revisable. The frequent meetings of Assembly and people's courts allowed (even required) contrasting, critical views
to be aired publicly, and this process in turn periodically forced constative
meanings (the assumptions used in decision making) to change in response to
changing external circumstances. Thus democratic knowledge evolved over
time (sometimes very rapidly) without precipitating a political revolution.
Meanwhile, democratic ideology and institutional procedure allowed for practical decisiveness: reasonably intelligent, binding (although open to legal challenge at the initiative of any individual citizen) decisions on internal matters
and foreign policy were made in the Assembly by the Athenian demos in the
absence of ruling elites, a genuine consensus, or complete and objectively verifiable scientific knowledge about details of political affairs.[21]

The complex relationships between democratic knowledge, social practice,
and critical political writing are, I believe, clarified by Austinian speech-act
theory. Austin argued that speech is not only descriptive, but also performative.
To the linguistic categories of locution (speech itself) and perlocution (the effect
of speech on an audience), Austin added "illocution"—the intended force of
speech that enables speakers to do things in the world. Austin showed that in
ordinary language, description and enactment are not easily separated. The
constative role of speech (to state what is so) is in practice inseparable from and
a product of speech's illocutionary, performative function (to make something
happen). If description is a subcategory of performance, then the production of
meaning and "truth" is a social process, accomplished by "felicitous" speech
performances that are necessarily carried out within the context of accepted
social and linguistic conventions. Sandy Petrey, who applies Austinian theory to
the study of literature, points out that these conventions are revisable: to the
degree that they are politically determined, conventions can be contested, or
even overthrown by revolutionary action. But once again, even in the midst of a
revolution, people do communicate. For speech to act, for human communication to be possible, conventions of some sort must pertain.[22] Returning to

---

[21] The sheer volume of political business done in this manner is overwhelming. Hansen (1991,
156) suggests that some 30,000 decrees of the Assembly were passed in the period 403–322.

[22] Austin 1975. Exactly how speech-act theory deals with reference has thus been the subject of

Athens, we can now see how the citizens enacted social, legal, and political realities when they voted in the Assembly and lawcourts: that which *edoxe tōi dēmōi* was constituted as true, for all social and political intents and purposes, through felicitously performed acts of collective decision and proclamation. When the Assembly votes for war with Sparta, a state of war is caused to come into existence by the Assembly's proclamation; when the jury votes that Socrates is guilty, he is constituted a guilty man.

In speech-act theory, as in intellectual history, context takes center stage. The successful performance of a speech act depends on existing social, political, and linguistic protocols: a courting couple would not be made man and wife by a child's proclamation that they were so; a judge's statement does things that a child's does not do because it is performed within the context of a set of conventions that are accepted as valid by the participants.[23] The felicity of the speech act is demonstrated by perlocutionary effects: the subsequent behavior of the relevant members of society. If, after the ceremony, our hypothetical couple acts like a married couple and is treated as a married couple by their society, we may say that the act of the judge who said "I pronounce you man and wife" was felicitous. And likewise in the case of a declaration of war by the Athenian Assembly or the conviction of Socrates. Thus the felicity of an illocutionary speech act is context-dependent and sociopolitically determined.

But what of the situation in which a speech act is felicitous within a local subcommunity, and infelicitous in the larger community, as in the case of a homosexual couple who enact a marriage ceremony?[24] This potential conflict between "local" and "national" spheres was not discussed by Austin, but it is important for the historical analysis of critical discourse as resistance. The act of performing a speech act that the speaker knows will be infelicitous within the larger community can be read as an intentional act of resistance.[25]

---

an ongoing debate, notably between J. Derrida (1988) and J. Searle (e.g., 1969, 1977), both of whom owe much to Austin's work and criticize certain aspects of it. The interpretation of Austin I advance here is very close to that enunciated by Petrey (1988, 1990). Petrey emphasizes the breakdown of the distinction between constative and performative but also points out that Austin tended to underestimate the role of politics in the construction of the conventions that permit speech acts to perform felicitously.

[23] This is explained by Austin's Rules A.1 and A.2 (1975, 13–14, 26–35). A.1: "[In order for a speech act to be felicitously performed,] there must exist an accepted conventional procedure having a certain conventional effect, the procedure to include the uttering of certain words by certain persons in certain circumstances." A.2: "The particular persons and circumstances in a given case must be appropriate for the invocation of the particular procedure invoked."

[24] I owe this hypothetical example to Charles Hedrick.

[25] Note that felicity here is clearly separate from the issue of "sincerity" and "comprehensibility." The two gay persons were presumably sincere in their intention to be married. What they intended is more or less comprehensible to members of the wider community, but their act was nonetheless infelicitous in the context of the wider community, which does not acknowledge the validity of the status change asserted by the ceremony.

The act brings the conventions valid within the local community into overt conflict with the conventions of the larger society and thus exposes the partial and socially constructed nature of the broader context. This exposure is dangerous (and thus meaningful as an act of resistance) because it challenges the tendency of the larger society to equate convention with human nature (in Greek terms, *nomos* with *phusis*), to see social facts as brute facts. Likewise, the promulgation of a system of knowing about society that a thinker recognizes will not be accepted by most within his community can be read as resistance to the dominant system of power and knowledge.[26]

An "Austinian" analysis of politics may help us to understand why traditional Marxist theory, with its essentialist commitment to the basic reality of economic and historical "laws," has been unable to explain the continued viability of capitalist societies in the face of the "contradictions" implicit in capitalist production: contradictions and class interests must not only be "revealed," they must be felicitously performed if they are to have perlocutionary effects. Applying Austin to politics leads to an emphasis on political power as control of the means of symbolic production. It points to rhetoric as a form of political action, and to criticism of discursive context as a central project of political theorizing: those in power seek to create and maintain a stable context in which rhetorical statements by appropriate speakers will act in predictable ways; theorizing this relationship points out the contingency of the context in question and thus the possibility for major revisions in what speech acts will be felicitous and who will be an appropriate speaker. If, in a democracy (unlike most other forms of government), political power (i.e., the control of the means of symbolic production) is at least *potentially* discontinuous with economic power (i.e., the control of the means of economic production), then the sort of approach I am advocating might be particularly well suited to the historical study of democracy and its critics.[27] In Athens, where the ordinary people held political power, members of the wealthy elite could be genuine political critics.

In *Mass and Elite* I attempted to define the conventions whereby the debates and proclamations performed in the Assembly and courtroom could and did "do things" within Athenian society. In trying to understand the relationships of power between elites and masses of ordinary citizens it is important to decide whether those conventions were the product of elite or demotic discourse. Was democratic knowledge simply a form of false consciousness or mystification that enabled an elite to control and exploit the lower classes of citizens?[28] I argue to the contrary, that the sociopolitical conventions dominant in late

[26] Cf. McClelland 1989.

[27] By "traditional Marxist theory," I mean studies that focus on economic production and deemphasize the state and ideology, e.g., G. A. Cohen 1978. Other forms of Marxist analysis (e.g., that of A. Gramsci, F. Jameson, T. Eagleton, and L. Althusser) do, of course, focus attention on politics and ideology.

[28] Cf. Eagleton 1991: 29–30, ideology types four and five.

fifth- and fourth-century Athens were the product of a historical development whereby the citizen masses *defined themselves* as Demos and the Athenian political order as *dēmokratia*.[29] As a result of this process, the demos gained control of the public language employed in classical Athenian political deliberations. Thus the primary context for felicitous speech performance in Athens was defined by popular, not elite, ideology. And hence democratic knowledge and demotic social conventions sought to extend a form of rhetorical and even epistemological hegemony over all members of Athenian citizen society, including the elites.

The hegemony of popular ideology and public discourse was the basis of Athens' political order. Athens was a democracy, not just because the ordinary citizen had a vote, but because he was a participant in maintaining a political culture and a value system that constituted him the political equal of his elite neighbor. Through publicly performed speech acts, democratic institutions were implicated in an ongoing process of defining and redefining the truths used in political decision-making and of assimilating local knowledges into an overarching democratic knowledge. It was that process and that overarching knowledge that elite Athenian critics sought to expose as problematic.

POWER AND RESISTANCE

Though my respect and admiration for certain aspects of the Athenian political regime are by now clear, it is obviously essential to avoid adulation. Accepting that ideology is an important part of historical context, socialist theorists since Antonio Gramsci have emphasized the roles of ideology (often defined as the ideas of the dominant classes) and cultural hegemony in obscuring "objective" material interests and in promoting stability within repressive regimes, a stability that primarily benefits the ruling class.[30] Whether or not we adopt Gramscian categories, it is clear that the Athenian citizen did benefit materially from the democratic regime in ways denied to noncitizens.[31] Thus, even if she accepts that demotic values operated to control the behavior of and to limit exploitation by elites *within* the society of the citizens, a modern critic might well argue that Athenian society as a whole was elitist, unjust, and unattractive, by defining what I have described as "democratic knowledge" as a hegemonic ideology that maintained the privileged position of a minority population of native-born, adult males at the expense of oppressed noncitizens.[32]

[29] For "capital-*D*" Demos, as the whole of the "imagined" citizenry, see Chapter 8.

[30] Eagleton 1991 offers an overview; on cultural hegemony, I have found Femia 1981 particularly useful.

[31] E.g., by his virtual monopoly on the right to own land (and thus to secure loans on land), and to be paid for various forms of government service. The advantages of citizenship were multiplied during the imperial era (Finley 1985b, 76–109), but were always considerable.

[32] See Chapter 11 for further discussion of the issue of social justice.

How would an Athenian critic have responded to this line of reasoning? Plato famously suggested (*Rep.* 562b–563c) that the excessively liberating tendencies of democratic culture extended well beyond the citizen body, to women, slaves, and even domesticated animals (cf. Ps.-Xenophon, *Ath. Pol.* 1.10–12). And in the *Ecclesiazusae*, Aristophanes comically turned over control of the Athenian state to citizen-women. It must, however, be said that on the whole, Athenian critics of democracy (at least those who wrote texts that survive) were only peripherally concerned with the oppression of noncitizens. Although they were not primarily concerned with the problem of noncitizen oppression, various Athenian critics of democracy *were* concerned with showing that democratic ideology was a sort of mystification that obscured truths about the world—truths that were historically objective (Thucydides), natural (Aristotle), or transcendental (Plato). The attempt to establish disjunctions between knowledges founded on these various forms of "real" truth and democratic knowledge, with its emphasis on socially constructed truth, played a key role in Athenian political criticism. Thus, although the Athenian critics were far from "politically correct" by any conceivable modern (or postmodern) standard, documenting and assessing the success of their diverse and sustained criticism of knowledge-as-power might contribute to current political debates by establishing that literary resistance to political power need not be futile.[33] Athenian critical texts may therefore be extremely important subjects even for students of political history and theory who remain utterly unconvinced by the ideas developed in those texts.

If critical resistance to *dēmokratia* was not ultimately futile, neither was it easy. For the prospective Athenian author of a text systematically critical of democratic culture (as opposed to the local critic of democratic practice), the issue was not how best to describe "what is functionally or instrumentally wrong with how this regime works." Rather, faced with the democratic tendency to monopolize the terminology of politics, he confronted the more basic problem of finding a vocabulary and a literary genre capable of being adapted to the expression of his criticism.[34] How to break free of the equation between democracy and legitimate political rule? How to explain why a rational reader should not find Athens' political system any more attractive than does the writer? How to articulate an alternative politics that the reader could be persuaded to prefer and (perhaps) actively to support?

---

[33] Cf. criticism of Foucault's lack of attention to the problem of resistance: Taylor 1986; Said 1986; Wolin 1988. There is a growing interest among students of Foucault's work to point out that he did in fact account for resistance, especially in his later work; see, for example, Gordon 1991. For Foucault himself on the problem of resistance, see, for example, 1981; 1991, 82–86.

[34] It will be clear by now that I disagree with the theory (of, e.g., Loraux 1986) that Athenian democracy itself was subverted by the continued power of aristocratic discourse; see Ober 1989b, 289–92.

Modern political theory might seem to suggest that the obvious starting point for the Athenian critic of democracy was the issue of sovereignty: "Who actually rules and in whose interest?" versus "Who *should* rule and in whose interest?" But the ugliness of the oligarchic governments of 411 and 404, regimes that in fact attempted to narrow the criteria for citizenship in Athens, may have tended to encourage late fifth- and early fourth-century critics to seek other lines of approach.[35] Although Aristotle was crucially interested in the question of who did and should constitute the political authority, Plato focused on the *source* of popular authority: democratic knowledge itself. He offered a fundamental challenge to democracy by bringing into question the basic assumptions on which democratic knowledge rested; he questioned the validity of mass wisdom as a basis for judgment, the efficacy of public rhetoric as a prelude to decision making, and the felicity of the speech acts performed by public bodies. A second line of approach, emphasized especially by Thucydides, was to query the nature and function of the demos' *kratos*—namely, political power itself. Given the interrelationship of knowledge and power, these two approaches can be seen as closely related; an attack on democratic knowledge undermined the demos' *kratos*, and an attack on the nature of or use of *kratos* by the demos might in turn destabilize democratic knowledge.

Before the Athenian critic of democracy could offer an alternative to democratic knowledge and practice, he had first to identify a *point d'appui* that would be recognized by his intended readers (probably elite, but not necessarily antidemocratic) as legitimate. The problem was most frequently addressed by attempting to exploit the audience's recognition of incongruities within the matrix of assumptions and values that constituted democratic knowledge (as in the Socratic elenchus) or of contradictions between democratic ideals and the outcome of democratically arrived-at decisions (e.g., Thucydides' account of the Mytilenian Debate). Closely related was the search for new genres in which criticism could adequately be expressed. Finding a gap, or a "lack of fit," in democratic knowledge, and developing (or adapting) a literary genre suitable to the exploitation of inconsistencies, were difficult tasks in light of the democracy's hegemonic tendency to obscure contradictions and its close relationship to the existing genres of drama and public oratory.[36] Various solutions, only gestured at here, were devised by individual authors in the last decades of the fifth, and especially in the fourth, century.

In the short pamphlet entitled *The Constitution of Athens*, Ps.-Xenophon took as his *point d'appui* the gap between the "real" interests of the elite and the interests protected by the democratic regime. Employing the trope of irony, he worked within (and perhaps originated) an editorial genre: a here-and-now

---

[35] The centrality of the issue of sovereignty in modern theory is, in any event, largely an artifact of the political conditions of early modern Europe; see Chapter 8.

[36] Cf. Ober and Strauss 1990.

discussion of actual political action and policy that freely employed the existing language of the democracy, and that allowed the logic of the democracy to "speak for itself." In the hands of this author, at least, editorial irony proved problematic. Ps.-Xenophon's irony seems unable to stand up against the democratic discourse he introduces into his text. The reader comes to feel that the author has nothing better to offer than the system that he claims he will not praise, but evidently cannot help admiring. Not surprisingly (to those who take the power of ideology seriously), the tactic of allowing the vocabulary of democratic discourse and the assumptions of the dominant democratic ideology free rein in the text leads to a general collapse of the intended force of the author's criticism.

Thucydides took over from Herodotus the embryonic genre we call historiography, and gave it a definitively political and critical stamp. By claiming to have reconstructed the "real" meaning and objective causes of the dramatic course of events that began in the mid-430s, Thucydides attempted to demonstrate the comparative ignorance and foolishness of the collectivities that made Athenian policy, as well as the incompetence of the democratic politicians who misled the masses and were misled by them in turn. Thucydides' political history sets up a contest between his austere, seemingly objectively based, historical way of knowing and emotion-laden, hopelessly contingent democratic knowledge; between his difficult, closely argued written text and the easy-listening, illogical orations of Athenian politicians; between his readers, who were in the process of being educated in the complexity of political *realia*, and Athenian Assemblymen, who thought only of power and their own pleasure. The narrative describes the horrors attendant upon the confrontation between the great force (*dunamis*) generated and wielded by a *dēmokratia* and the stubborn, brute realities of a protracted war.

For Aristophanes, genre was less of a problem, since the forms of comedy were well established. Moreover, the comic poet's audience expected him to criticize Athenian society. In *Ecclesiazusae* Aristophanes takes as his point of departure a comic "alternate Athens" and the incongruity between politically constituted identities and perceptible referents. He asks a funny question that has profound critical bite: could Athenian women be constituted "males" if the Assembly enacted a decree that they, rather than biological men, were to have the privileges and responsibilities of citizenship? The play exposes the contradiction between Athenian belief in the power of the citizenry to constitute political realities by legal enactment on the one hand, and in the naturalness of a world in which men alone were empowered political agents on the other.

Plato took the debate over politics to a more exalted plane. In the *Republic* he shifts from Socratic elenchus (in book 1), a form of debate that assumes an interlocutor with real opinions (i.e., an organic connection to the ideological context) and that owed something to Athenian traditions of public debate, to a

new generic variation of the dialogue form (in books 2–10).[37] In the later
books, Socrates expounds to students a metaphysical and ontological argument for a utopian, authoritarian political order ruled by a class of philosophers who had "left the Cave" and so had gained a rigorous and accurate
knowledge of reality. This approach enables Plato to work out a positive political program based on a formal distinction between mere opinion (*doxa*) and
actual knowledge (*epistēmē*). Viewed from the perspective of the *Republic*'s ontological epistemology, the problem was not merely that democratic knowledge failed to account for objective facts accessible to the careful observer (per
Thucydides). Rather, the problem was that democracy's claims to be a legitimate way of knowing about society and a just system for making decisions
were false because it had no way of testing appearances by reference to an
external, metaphysical Truth (i.e., the Forms). A political regime based on
mass opinion (the lowest sort of *doxa*) was thus not only likely to be sloppy in its
judgments and capricious in its behavior, it was also wrongly constructed by
definition. The entire performative process of the speech act is ruled out of
court and replaced by a reference-based morality. Justice becomes a fixed and
absolute standard. Politics becomes a matter of foundation (an unrevisable
although not indestructible order is built on the foundation of Truth), rather
than a matter of practice (a revisable order exists in the action of felicitously
doing).

Isocrates' *point d'appui* in the *Areopagiticus* is his fellow Athenians' nostalgia for
the better conditions widely assumed to have pertained in the days of their
ancestors. His approach is in some ways similar to that of Ps.-Xenophon in
that he adopts the overtly democratic genre of symbouleutic oratory and borrows political language from democratic ideology. But like Thucydides and
other Athenians involved in the "ancestral constitution" (*patrios politeia*) debate,
he employs a "historical" perspective. His ostensible goal is to recuperate
Athens' pristine and ancient form of government and society—which turns
out to be a highly hierarchical and paternalistic system that he specifically
names *dēmokratia*. In appropriating genre, vocabulary, and name from the regime he intended to criticize, Isocrates demonstrates an audacious pride. He is
confident that his rhetorical *technē* will allow him to transubstantiate democratic political slogans into an essentially aristocratic system of political values.

In terms of genre and critical stance (as in other ways), Aristotle's *Politics* is a
work of synthesis. His point of departure is human nature. The final goal of the
text (as we have it) is to derive the best possible regime from widely accepted
postulates about human nature. While granting democracy a relatively high
level of instrumental success in the regulation of class tension and recognizing
the validity of mass wisdom in certain sorts of decision making, Aristotle's

---

[37] I owe this insight into the distinction between the literary forms taken by book 1 and books
2–10 to a paper by Mary Blundell, delivered at Princeton University in March 1992.

teleological naturalism allows him to conclude that workers simply cannot achieve true political virtue. The citizens of the best polis will thus naturally have to be an association of leisured aristocrats, thereby obviating the need to solve the intractable problem of proportionate equalities. The citizens' formal and normative education will ensure that decision making is based on formally rational "practical reasoning" (rather than democratic knowledge) and that their society, having achieved the telos toward which the polis naturally was tending, will not require revision.

Even after a much fuller exposition of the content of Athenian political criticisms than I have sketched here, we will be left with two supremely difficult questions: What were these texts *meant to do*—what was their intended effect on readers? And what *did they do*—what practical effect did they have on the form or content of Athenian democracy? The general term "critic" covers a broad range of intentions. Are we dealing with an irreconcilable enemy of the democratic order, or a democrat who believes that current practice is inconsistent with the highest democratic ideals? I would tend to push Ps.-Xenophon and Plato in the direction of the first category, Aristophanes toward the second, and leave Thucydides, Isocrates, and Aristotle somewhere in between. But attempting to fix authors on a hypothetical political spectrum is hazardous: Athenian political texts are complex and multivocal; the illocutionary force of a critical text need not be limited to the hortatory, admonitory, subversive, or openly revolutionary. Aristophanes (for one) manages to fit all of these voices and more into the scope of a short play.

The lines of communication between elite critics and the demos, between those partially outside and those who remained comfortably within the bounds of the democratic regime, remain obscure.[38] Yet our current inability to trace simple cause-effect relationships between text and political change does not (in and of itself) invalidate the proposition that criticism is a precondition to revision. It has often been pointed out that Plato's utopia in the *Republic* could never have been realized in the real world. But the "practical" workability of theoretical notions is beside the point. By describing a hypothetical counter-regime or a counter-knowledge, based on a set of counter-truths, the critical theorist helped to establish and maintain a discursive space outside the dominant regime. The literary speech act performed felicitously within the society of elite intellectuals might or might not ultimately achieve felicity within the broader political society of Athens. The actual effect on democratic practice of a given author's criticism can seldom, if ever, be measured. But just as the Assembly brought into being a particular reality through the performative act of enunciating a *psēphisma* (decree), so the critic expanded the ground in which resistance to ideology was possible and fundamental change conceivable. And

---

[38] Cf. Chapter 7. I hope to explore this issue in future work on the theoretical content of other Athenian dicanic orations; see above, note 15.

thus (perhaps unwittingly) the critic helped to guarantee the potential revisability of the democratic regime through the performative act of constructing an alternative political paradigm. Once again, a comparison to Marxist
theory may be instructive. Whether or not the theorist succeeds in changing
society in accordance with her own ideals, she provides conceptual resources in
the form of original and challenging uses of existing terminology. Those cultural resources may be found useful even by advocates of change who reject
the substance of the theorist's argument in that they help to make (or keep)
thinkable the possibility of a world profoundly different from the one we now
inhabit.

Finally, what does the phenomenon of criticism of democracy in late fifth-
and fourth-century Athens have to tell us about critics of modern democracy?
Does the history of Athens lead us to conclude that conservative complaints on
the subjects of "democratic hegemony" and popular culture should be read as
part of a grand tradition of resistance? Should the conservative critic of democracy therefore be regarded as a particularly admirable, even essential, feature
of modern political life? This would be the case *only* if modern societies were
democratic in an Athenian sense of the term, that is, if the mass of ordinary
citizens maintained an active control over most aspects of ideology, public
discourse, governmental institutions, and the political agenda. Given the sovereign authority of the modern state, the thinness of modern practices of citizenship, and the top-down structure of mass communications and media, the
idea that the citizenry could exert any sort of hegemony in a modern liberal
democracy seems, on the face of it, chimerical.

Yet the notion that "democracy" once *did* and still *should* mean "the power
of the people" is remarkably stubborn. And that notion may provide exactly
the *point d'appui* needed by the truly essential critics of modern democracy:
those who refuse to accept that ever-expanding, hierarchical governmental
and corporate power (and the knowledges they produce) are an inevitable and
natural outgrowth of social complexity—or that they are desirable for a citizenry that hopes to live in a society characterized by justice, freedom, dignity,
and equality. Given the residual revisability of democratic culture, it is perhaps
not excessively utopian to hope that criticisms by educated elites of "democratic hegemony" might, some day in the future, once again be read as productive forms of resistance.

Chapter 11

THE POLIS AS A SOCIETY: ARISTOTLE, JOHN RAWLS, AND THE ATHENIAN SOCIAL CONTRACT

In July of 1992, Mogens Hansen hosted a symposium in Copenhagen on "The Ancient Greek City-State." Paper topics were assigned in advance by Hansen with the aim of defining some of the outstanding problems associated with employing "polis" as a descriptive term and as a category of analysis. I was asked to discuss "the polis as a society"; my paper was intended to contrast with Wolfgang Schuller's assessment of "the polis as a state." We were all asked, in writing our papers and comments, to keep in mind the passage from Aristotle with which my essay begins. I am grateful to the other participants at the Copenhagen symposium for comments and suggestions. Special thanks are due to Barry Strauss for his thoughtful formal commentary and to Mogens Hansen for the chance to continue our dialogue. My difference with Hansen over Aristotle's definition of *polis* is in part attributable to my "unitarian" conviction that books 1 and 2 of the *Politics* should be read in conjunction with the rest of the text as it has come down to us.

Once I had undertaken the preliminary work of developing contextually meaningful definitions for the terms "state" and "society," it became clear that Aristotle used the term "polis" in two senses: as a community of citizens (a "politico-polis") and as a community including those residents of a clearly defined territory who were not citizens (a "geo-polis"). The main argument of the paper is that these two senses of "polis" did not remain and could not have remained hermetically sealed off from one another. Both in actual state practice and in Greek political theory, the tangled relationship between the political society of citizens and the whole society, between the public and the private spheres of activity and ideology, was a central political issue. Moreover, in Aristotle's theory of politics, the state / society problem quickly and necessarily (given his premises) becomes enmeshed with an assessment of Athenian (or Athenian-style) democracy.

Aristotle begins with a few simple postulates: (1) human society originates as a collection of those natural nuclear families (including slaves in at least some cases) inhabiting a certain area, and (2) humans are by nature political beings—they have a natural impulse to perform the functions of citizens (i.e., to rule and to be ruled in turns—

This essay was first published in Mogens H. Hansen, ed., *The Ancient Greek City-State*, Historisk-filosofiske Meddelelser 67 = Acts of the Copenhagen Polis Centre, vol. 1 (Copenhagen: Royal Danish Academy of Sciences and Letters, 1993), 129–60.

which is why [3] political society is not a family writ large) within (4) a polis, which is the most natural, in that it is the smallest autarkic and largest "eudaimonic" form of human organization. In the simplest model of the natural society, then, every human being would act as a citizen in a polis. This was (in Aristotle's experience) nowhere the case, and he explains why: Among certain categories of humans, the impulse to citizenship is "short-circuited" by psychological deficiencies. Aristotle explains (in ways that are notoriously unsatisfactory to many modern readers, including myself) that children, women, and "natural" slaves cannot be, and should not want to be, citizens.

Aristotle's psychological process of reduction leaves, as natural citizens, all free, native, adult males (most of them "heads of households"). Ignoring for the moment the status of *atimoi* (see Chapter 7), it is just this subgroup of society that, in an Athenian-style democracy, enjoyed citizenship. In Athens, then, the two sets "natural citizens" and "actual citizens" were essentially identical. And thus Athenian-style democracy should be the most natural form of government for the most natural form of human political organization. The proposition can be tested empirically: As the most natural form of political society, democracy should be (by Aristotle's lights) the most stable. In other political societies, ones in which significant numbers of natural citizens were denied actual citizenship, we should expect to find evidence of considerable tension and unrest, as the demands of nature contested for dominance with established political culture. And this, in the empirical sections of the *Politics*, turns out to be the case: the problem of civil unrest (*stasis*) is frequently caused or exacerbated by the actions of unenfranchised natural citizens. Democracy is, according to Aristotle, both more stable than oligarchy and more likely to arise in conditions pertaining in his own time. Much of the interest of the *Politics*, from my perspective, lies in Aristotle's attempt to work himself around the logic of his own argument: although both teleological logic and empirical evidence suggested to him that democracy was the most stable, most natural, and therefore most desirable form of commonly existing polis government, Aristotle was certainly not ready to accept that democracy on the Athenian model was the best form of politics that Greeks could aspire to, or even the best they could reasonably hope to encounter.

The essay's second major concern returns to issues raised in Chapter 3. There I argued that classical Athens was at once stable and democratic, but I intentionally skirted the issue of whether classical Athens should be regarded by a modern liberal interpreter as an attractive society. Here I attempt to face the latter question more squarely: what is the moral standing of Athens as a state and as a society? Answering this question requires establishing that which I claim (Chapter 10) Athenian democratic practices avoided worrying about: a "foundational" external standard. This undertaking makes me somewhat uneasy, given my conviction that fixed foundations and genuine democratic practice are mutually exclusive. But it also seems important for anyone who may have to face interlocutors impatient with purely contextualized, pragmatic, historicized descriptions and explanations.

I therefore set out to test Athenian democratic society, along with Aristotle's "best possible" polis (as described in *Politics*, book 7), against the liberal standard set by John

Rawls' *A Theory of Justice*. Employing elements of modern game theory, Rawls develops his theory by setting up a thought experiment intended to yield a set of social and political rules that will be agreeable to all players. The outcome of the experiment is to be the best possible human society: a formally and procedurally just social contract. My own understanding of Athenian democratic society is likewise contractarian and owes something to simple forms of game theory. Moreover, and more controversially, I suggest that there are important contractarian elements to Aristotle's political theory. The essay concludes by comparing the society of book 7 of the *Politics*, Athenian political society, and Athenian whole society to Rawls' just society.

This sort of undertaking seems to me to be worthwhile for two reasons. First, it establishes a common (contractarian) ground for assessing ancient and modern politics in theory and practice. Second, it allows us to measure the similarities and differences between a particularly influential and well-defended modern liberal vision of justice on the one hand and ancient political theory and democratic practices on the other. If it is worthwhile, however, it is far from a panacea. Rawls' theory of justice is dependent upon the premises of his thought experiment; its claim to define the best possible (as opposed to best liberal) society is susceptible to criticism. The undertaking sketched in this essay will not, in the end, tell us in any definitive way what sort of society the Athenians should have developed or what sort we should want for ourselves. But it may help to expand the range of historical examples and theoretical notions available to us when we try to talk seriously about normative questions of politics, society, and justice.

Recent studies on Aristotle's *Politics*, bearing on the issues discussed here, include Swanson 1992 and Miller 1995. Rawls returns to the questions raised in *A Theory of Justice* in Rawls 1993; the spate of scholarly work on Rawls' theory and its implications continues unabated.

IN A KEY SENTENCE from book 3 of the *Politics*, Aristotle (1276b1–2) suggests that the polis may be a *koinōnia* (frequently translated as "community") of *politai* (citizens) arranged in respect to the *politeia* (citizenship or constitutional order). What is at stake in this claim? The *Politics* is typically (and fruitfully) read as a teleological theory of the state as a natural entity. Moreover, M. H. Hansen has argued that the term *polis*, when used of a "community" rather than of a physical "city," means state and not a fusion of state and society. Here I will argue that when analyzing the polis, neither the state/society distinction nor the community/city distinction can be fully sustained at the level of either Aristotelian theory or Athenian practice. Viewing the polis as at once society and state can, I think, contribute in meaningful and useful ways to our understanding of Aristotle's polis and the historical polis.[1]

[1] The society/state distinction became prominent in Western political thought in the late

First, definitions: If we posit a human population inhabiting a given territory, "society" is the sum of participants in the overall set of rules, norms, and
practices whereby social goods (e.g., rights, privileges, powers, property) are
produced and distributed. This larger society will encompass subsocieties with
specialized rules and norms; the interaction between subsocieties helps to determine the structure of the whole society. "State" denotes the arrangement by
which formal political power (legitimate coercive authority backed by physical
force) is distributed among recognized institutions and deployed by them.
Thus the procedural rules of governmental institutions fall largely outside the
purview of this paper, but some "political" aspects of production and distribution are within its scope.[2] I will attempt to make three points. First, when
Aristotle uses the term *polis*, he always assumes the existence of, and sometimes
refers specifically to, the society at large. Second, in the *Politics*, in modern
liberal democratic theory, and in Athenian practice alike, the problem of stabilizing the political regime is inseparable from issues of social justice. Third,
though fourth-century Athenian social practice did recognize a distinction between state and civil society, that distinction was far from clear-cut, and interchange between the public and private spheres was constant and meaningful.

ARISTOTLE

In several passages from book 3 Aristotle seems specifically concerned with the
state:

> The *politeia* is an ordering (*taxis*) of the polis in respect to various powers (*archai*)
> and especially [in respect to the power] that is authoritative over all (*tēs kurias
> pantōn*). For what is authoritative (*kurion*) everywhere is the governing body (*po-
> liteuma*) of the polis, and the governing body is the *politeia* (*politeuma d' estin hē
> politeia*). I mean, for example, that in democracies the *dēmos* is authoritative (*kurios*),
> while by contrast it is the few (*hoi oligoi*) in oligarchies; we say that the *politeia* too is
> different in these [two] cases (1278b8–12). . . . *Politeia* and *politeuma* signify the

---

eighteenth and early nineteenth centuries, especially in Hegel's *Philosophy of Right* (1821). For a
review of the issue as it applies to the polis, see Murray 1990a with bibliography. Polis as neither
state nor society, but as a political sphere that renders the former irrelevant and the latter marginal: Meier 1984, 7–44. Polis as state only: Hansen 1989c, 16–21; 1991, 55–64, taking his
definition of "state" from the fields of international law and jurisprudence. What I mean by useful
and meaningful is explained in Chapter 2.

[2] My definitions leave much in abeyance (notably issues of how meanings and identities, collective and individual, are constructed—see conclusions, below). They should be regarded only as
starting points for distinguishing an understanding of "polis = both state and society" from "polis
= state only." In other work I employ a more extensive definition of the term "state." On civil
society, see Bobbio 1989, 23: the "complex of relations not regulated by the state and so the
residue once the realm in which state power is exercised has been well defined."

same thing (*sēmainei tauton*), and *politeuma* is the authoritative element (*to kurion*) in *poleis*, and . . . it is necessary that the authoritative element be one person, or a few, or the many.[3] (1279a25–28)

The abstraction *politeia* is thus identified with the *politeuma* (cf. 1308a6–7), which is the element (either an individual or a sociological part, e.g., *hoi oligoi*) of the polis that is authoritative (*kurion*). If the polis is only a state (according to the definition used above), "authoritative over all" would mean the monopoly of legitimate authority to deploy force both internally (within the polis, e.g., by inflicting legal punishments) and externally (e.g., by dispatching military expeditions).[4] This formulation leaves aside the question of social goods, and yet the *Politics* is deeply concerned with how social goods are produced and distributed.

When Aristotle uses *politeia* as an abstraction that "signifies the same thing" (has the same root meaning) as the authoritative governing element, he is not merely defining the institutional "locus of sovereignty." In book 2 Aristotle noted (1273a21–25) the intimate connection between the ideological predisposition (*dianoia*) of *hoi polloi* (regarding wealth requirements for office) and the form taken by the *politeia*, and states specifically (1273a39–b1) that whenever the authoritative element (*to kurion*) assumes something to be worthy of honor, by necessity this opinion (*doxa*) will be adopted by the rest of the citizenry.[5] The authoritative element is (at least in a democracy) the sociologically defined segment of the polis that takes the lead in establishing and maintaining the terms by which the members of a *koinōnia* as a "community of interpretation" (in the terminology of Stanley Fish) will discuss the world and will (in the terminology of J. L. Austin) perform, through felicitous speech acts, social realities within the world. Ergo, the term *politeia* embraces not only the constitution (legal arrangement of governmental institutions), but the ideology (the system of beliefs by which actions are organized) and social practices promoted by the dominant subsociety within the polis.[6]

---

[3] The plural *archai* is here better translated as "powers," or "authorities" (LSJ s.v. II.1) than the more usual "magistracies" or "government offices" (LSJ s.v. II.4) because *dēmos* is used here as a sociological or a political term ("the mass" or "the whole of the citizenry" compared with *oligoi*), rather than as an institutional term ("the Assembly"). Cf. 1289a15–18: *politeia* is an arrangement connected to public offices (*taxis . . . peri tas archas*), in what manner they are distributed (*nenemēntai*), what element is *kurion* in respect to the *politeia*, and what is the *telos* of each *koinōnia*. Translations of *The Politics* are adapted from Lord 1984.

[4] Cf. Hansen 1989c, 41 n. 126: "The *polis* was a legitimate political power which—apart from a few survivals of legitimate self help—monopolized the use of force."

[5] On the problem with the concept of sovereignty, see Chapter 8. For the ideological nature of *politeia*, cf. 1294a19–20: it is liberty (*eleutheria*), wealthiness (*ploutos*), and virtue (*aretē*) that "contend for equality" within the *politeia*.

[6] Fish 1980; Austin 1975. For a fuller definition of what I mean by "ideology," see Ober 1989b, 38–43. Cf. 1286a2–3, where Aristotle makes a sharp distinction between the study of *nomoi* and the study of *politeia*; 1289a13–15: *nomoi* are and should be enacted *pros tas politeias* and not vice

And hence, "*politeia* is the particular way of life (*bios tis*) of the polis" (1295b1).[7]

For Aristotle, that way of life is founded on social relations. Sociological articulation into "parts" (*merē, moria*: especially economic classes [e.g., 1303a1–2, 1318a30–33], but also occupational groups, families, etc.) defines a polis' *politeia*, just as physical attributes determine an animal's species (1291a23–38).[8] Governmental powers (*archai*) are distributed according to preexisting relations of power (*dunamis*) among the parts (1290a7–13). Thus, while Aristotle surely does have the state in mind at 3.1278b–1279a, his discussion presumes that the state will be embedded in a matrix of preexisting social divisions and practices.[9] We may now hazard a more elaborate restatement of the key sentence: "The polis is a *koinōnia* of citizens whose practices and norms are arranged in respect to the beliefs and powers of the dominant subsociety (i.e., *politeia/politeuma*)." Turning from general to specific, "the polis of Athens is a *koinōnia* of Athenian citizens; because the demos is the authoritative element in this polis, the Athenian *koinōnia* is arranged in respect to the ideology of the mass of ordinary citizens."

The definition of the polis as a *koinōnia* of citizens might seem to exclude noncitizens from consideration.[10] And yet Aristotle devotes much space in the *Politics* (especially in book 1) to categories of noncitizens: children, women, slaves, and free males. The tension between conceptualizing the *koinōnia* that is the polis as a society of citizens and as a more heterogeneous entity that includes noncitizens is evident in the beginning of book 3: Aristotle begins by stating that for one investigating the *politeia*, it is necessary to decide "what the polis is (*ti pote estin hē polis*)." He then points to a dispute among those who use the term *polis*: some say it was not "the polis" that performed some action (*peprachenai tēn praxin*), but rather "the tyrant" or "the oligarchy" (1274b32–36), on the grounds that such regimes exist through domination (*tōi kratein*) rather than for the common advantage (*to koinēi sumpheron*: 1276a12–13).[11] But

---

versa; 1289a18–20: distinctly different *nomoi* are among the things (ergo *not* the sum of distinguishing characteristics) by which a *politeia* is distinguished (*tōn dēlountōn*), according to which *archontes* rule.

[7] Compare 1292a32–34: ideally *nomos* should rule overall (*archein pantōn*), yet in specific cases *archai* and the *politeia* itself (*tautē politeia*) should judge (*krinein*). In practice, the reality of power (ergo who rules [*kratousi*]) is sometimes quite different from the existing *nomos*: 1292b11–21.

[8] Compare 1289b27–90a8, 1290b38–91a10.

[9] On the embeddedness of politics in society, see Finley 1983, and the references gathered in Ober 1991a, 113 n. 2.

[10] Cf. Hansen 1989c, 19: "The *polis* did not comprise all who lived within its borders, but only the *politai*, i.e. the citizens."

[11] Since Aristotle (1276a13–16) then attempts to refute the distinction by pointing out that certain democracies exist through domination, it is clear that the "some" in question were supporters of democracy against oligarchy or tyranny. *Politeiai* that look to the common advantage are in accord with unqualified justice; *despotikai politeiai* look to the advantage of *archontes* alone (1279a17–21).

if the polis is not simply equated with its government, then it must be equated
with the territory and its residents (or some part of them), and therein lies the
problem:

> We see that the entire activity of the politician (*politikos*) and the legislator is
> concerned with the polis, and the *politeia* is a certain ordering of those who inhabit
> the polis (*tōn tēn polin oikountōn esti taxis tis*). But since the polis belongs among
> composite things (*tōn sugkeimenōn*), and like other composite wholes is made up of
> many parts (*moriōn*), it is clear that the first thing to be sought is the citizen (*politēs*);
> for the polis is a certain multitude (*plēthos*) of *politai*. (1274b32–41)

In this brief passage, Aristotle uses *polis* in two different ways: first, when explaining that *politeia* is a certain ordering of "those who inhabit the polis," he
clearly means *polis* as a geographical term (polis as city or territory: "geo-
polis"), and here the "inhabitants" so ordered must include noncitizens.[12] In
the second part of the passage, "the polis is . . . the citizens" (polis as community of citizens: "politico-polis"). The difficulty of separating the affairs of the
politico-polis from the larger society is intrinsic to Aristotle's understanding of
political affairs (*ta politika*). His primary concern was with the citizens (those
who "had a share" in the polis) and with how the *politeia* was affected (sustained
or threatened) by sociological subdivisions within the citizenry. Yet he could
not ignore the fact that citizens and noncitizens (those lacking a share) cohab-
ited within the geo-polis. More to the point, he saw that explaining the terms
of their cohabitation was fundamental to a comprehensive understanding of
what sort of *koinōnia* the polis was. Aristotle could distinguish "the advantage of
the entire polis" from "the common (*koinon*) advantage of the *politai*."[13] Thus,
while he focused on the citizen-society, he assumed the existence of a broader
society (*koinōnia tēs zōēs*: 1278b17) of which the citizenry formed only one (key)
part. In the opening passage of book 1, the polis is described as a *koinōnia politikē*
that is "most authoritative of all and encompasses (*periechousa*) all the other
[sorts of *koinōnia*]" (1252a5–6). One of the purposes of the *Politics* is to explain
how the broader society could be encompassed by the narrower citizen-
society. If we translate *koinōnia* as "society," then in the key sentence Aristotle is
asking "what sort of society is the polis?"

But why "society" rather than (e.g.) "partnership?"[14] The answer is Aris-

---

[12] Aristotle cannot be using *oikountes* as a synonym for *politai* in light of the discussion in book 1,
esp. 1252a20–21: we must investigate "what the polis is composed of (*ex hōn sungkeitai*)," followed
by a discussion of the relationship between free men, women, and slaves. See also 1277a7–10: the
polis is made up of (*sunestēken*), inter alia, husband and wife, master and slave. Cf. below, note 26.

[13] πρὸς τὸ τῆς πόλεως ὅλης συμφέρον καὶ πρὸς τὸ κοινὸν τὸ τῶν πολιτῶν (1283b40–
42), taking the *kai* as conjunctive rather than explanatory: "and the common advantage" rather
than "that is to say, the common advantage."

[14] Lord and Jowett translate "partnership"; Sinclair, "association"; LSJ s.v. includes "society"
among various possibilities, including "communion" and "fellowship."

totle's concern with the fundamental significance of difference, inequality, and autarky in the definition of the polis. Autarky, which demanded both an ability to defend against aggression and a sufficiency of material goods, was the end (*telos*) of the polis and was best for it (*beltiston*).[15] Defense required military service; material sufficiency required productive labor. Depending on the *politeia*, the citizens themselves (or some of them) might work productively, but much of their time and energy was devoted to "political" affairs: deliberation, rule, and military service. Thus it was unlikely that the citizens could, by themselves, produce enough substance to maintain the polis' autarky. Noncitizen residents of the geo-polis were not distracted from production by direct participation in politics, and the surplus value of their labor was necessary for the polis to remain autarkic. Thus the presence of noncitizens in the polis was foundational rather than epiphenomenal; were they removed from the *koinōnia*, the polis could not exist.[16]

Moreover, the primary productive unit of polis society was the family unit (*oikos*). Within the confines of the *koinōnia* that was the *oikos*, the (adult free male) citizen was master (*despotēs*: 1260a7–10). But to produce the material goods that sustained the *oikos* itself (on the microeconomic level) and the polis as a whole (on the macroeconomic level) he relied upon cooperation (based on a recognition of mutual interests) as well as coercion in dealing with noncitizen *oikos* members (his wife, children, and slaves—if he had them: 1252b9–12, 1323a5–6). The productive *oikos* was the basic building block of the polis (1253b2–3); in Aristotle's naturalized developmental scheme, *oikoi* banded together into villages and villages into a polis in order to achieve autarky (1252b15–16, 27–29).[17] Thus, at the fundamental level of the productive activity that allowed the polis to achieve its *telos*, the interests of citizens and noncitizens were conjoined.

Aristotle claims that the *oikos* was characterized by "masterful" and "economic" relationships and the polis by "political" relationships, and he describes the society-building process as natural. Yet only the first of the three steps in this process (formation of first *oikos*, then village, then polis) did not

---

[15] Definition of *autarkeia*: 1252b27–53a1. Aristotle's ideal of autarky does not imply a degree of self-sufficiency that would obviate all interest in trade (e.g., 1321b14–18: trade is the readiest way to achieve *autarkeia*), but rather an absence of dependence upon any foreign power; cf. Nixon and Price 1990.

[16] See 1277b2–3: "[It is] not [the case that] all those are to be regarded as citizens without whom there would not be a polis" (with specific reference to children and *banausoi*); 1252a26–34: the polis is built up of union between "those who cannot live without one another": men and women, masters and (natural) slaves. I do not mean by this that polis is necessarily "based on" slavery; but it is (materially) "based on" the labor of noncitizens—including women, children, and metics. For discussion, see Wood 1988; with Chapter 9.

[17] At 1280b33–35, the building blocks of the polis that will live well and autarkically are *oikiai* and *genē*, which I take to be the equivalent of *oikoi* and *kōmai*.

involve human choice (*ouk ek proaireseōs*: 1252a28).[18] The society-building process may be regarded as quasi-contractual in that it was rational and consensual. It was rational in that even the involuntary first stage (which brought together master and slave, man and woman into an *oikia*, or household) furthered the common material and security interests of all parties. The second stage was consensual because the relevant parties (masters of *oikiai*) are assumed to be capable of recognizing and acting in their own interests: their households were joined together in part in order to gain a long-term (*mē ephēmerou*: 1252b16) necessity—the avoidance of unjust treatment.[19] Thus, while natural, the society-building process is not automatic or naturally predetermined. Although Aristotle's theory does not aim at the social contract, it is founded upon a contractarian assumption: the polis could not exist without the prior agreement of households to live together justly and profitably.[20]

Aristotle's polis is logically prior to the individual or *oikos* (1253a18–19), but it is neither historically prior to nor a precondition for human existence. Although Aristotle knows of no historical period in which men ordinarily lived outside *oikoi*, he states that "in antiquity (*to archaion*)" families were scattered, and each was under the sole authority of the head of household (1252b23–24). Man is the most "political" of animals (1253a7–8), but living together and cooperating in human affairs is always difficult (*chalepon*: 1263a15–16, cf. 1286b1). Thus, although "there is in everyone an impulse (*hormē*)" to live in a *politikē koinōnia*, nonetheless he who first brought men together (to live in a polis) was the cause (*aitios*) of the greatest of goods.[21] Moreover, once achieved, the

---

[18] Cf. 1280a32–34: intentional choice (*proairesis*) is a precondition for the existence of the polis.

[19] 1252a34–1253a1; I identify the long-term necessity as avoidance of injustice on the basis of 1280a25–1281a1, where avoidance of injustice is linked with material prosperity as concerns of living, and contrasted to the *telos* of living well.

[20] What I am calling Aristotle's social contractarianism differs substantially from modern versions (e.g., Hobbes, Locke, Rousseau). First, since the process of polis formation is natural, the parties are impelled to join together. Next, Aristotle puts little emphasis on individuals. After the first step (forming the natural partnerships of man-woman, and slave-master), the parties to the contract are heads of *oikoi* (along with *kōmai* and *genē*). Moreover, though living together ensures justice and material security, these are not the ultimate purpose of the *koinōnia*, nor are they sufficient conditions for the existence of the polis (1280b23–1281a1: a passage taken by J. Barnes in Miller 1991, 21, as an explicit rejection of "the view that the state's authority rests on any 'social contract'"). Yet these are *necessary* conditions (1280b30–31). Finally, while *eudaimonia* is the highest good of the *politai* and of the polis as a *koinōnia politikē*, living under a regime of justice and enjoying material security is (at least by implication) the highest good accessible to women, slaves, and other noncitizens.

[21] 1253a29–31. See also 1285b6–9, where the process of being brought together (*to sunagagein*) is one of the benefits that members of a *plēthos* willingly (*hekontōn*) received from heroic monarchs of the past. Thus the process was voluntary, rather than imposed. Cf. 1286b34–40: the coercive power of constitutional monarchs should be inferior to that of *to plēthos*; once again underscoring the consensual nature of the political order.

polis can be destroyed by improper, unjust actions by its members (*phtheirousi tēn polin*: 1281a18–20, book 5 passim). In sum, the desirable natural *telos* of the polis is (unlike an oak, a horse, or an *oikos*) predicated upon human agency, consent, and practice, even though not predicated upon the free choice of each individual.[22]

Slaves were obviously problematic from the point of view of consent: it was difficult for anyone living in a society that valued freedom (*eleutheria*) as a primary good to argue plausibly that a slave would recognize his best interests in the productive practices organized by his master. Enter Aristotle's elaborate theory of natural slavery: the assumption that being ruled as a human possession was a natural condition for certain people allowed Aristotle to postulate that "the same thing is advantageous for the master and slave" (1252a34) and that slavery was therefore just (1255a1–3). This explained affection between slave and master (1255b12–15). Despite his innate inability to deliberate about or to choose the circumstances of his life (1260a12, 1280a34), the slave was rational and could be expected to understand that his best interests were furthered by his membership in the *koinōnia* of the *oikos*.[23]

Women were, collectively, a part of the polis constituting half of its population (1269b15–17) and were necessary to *oikos* and polis alike for biological reproduction (1252a26–31). No woman could be a *politēs*, but a woman's interests were conjoined to those of her *politēs*-husband through the institution of marriage. Although (unlike the slave) she possessed deliberative ability, her lack of citizenship could be justified by the "lack of authority" of the deliberative element in her nature (1260a12–13).[24] Male children were (potential) future *politai*. When properly educated (i.e., after he had been coerced into mastering and internalizing the principles of the *politeia*), and after his deliberative faculties had matured (1260a13–14, 31–32), a male child would come to understand his true interests clearly. Ensuring through education that children understood their interests to be one with those of previous generations of *politai* guaranteed the political and cultural reproduction of the polis.[25] Aristotle con-

---

[22] Cf. 1278b15–30. Whereas modern contract doctrine postulates the social contract as a way of escaping the state of nature, Aristotle assumes it as a precondition of attaining a natural state. The modern contractarian begins and ends with the contract; Aristotle imports an implied contract to get his developmental scheme off the ground (to transform a scattering of *oikoi* into a polis) and retains it as a means to achieve the stability that is a precondition to the end of living well. The contract, for Aristotle, thus conjoins two natural conditions (*oikos* and autarkic, eudaimonic polis). These important distinctions must not obscure the common element: the necessity of human agency and consent in the formation of a complex society. Harris (1993) points out the links between Hobbesian contract theory and classical theory's natural teleology.

[23] The slave was assumed to be capable of rational understanding (1259b28, 1260b5–7) and (unlike the *banausos*) was part of the *koinōnia* of the *oikos* (*koinōnos zōēs*: 1260a39–40).

[24] For Aristotle on women and their role in the polis, see Saxenhouse 1991.

[25] Gently coercive nature of education: 1259b10–11; education *pros tas politeias* is the greatest of those things which preserve the polis, although the most overlooked: 1310a12–14. Cf. the legal

cludes book 1 with a general suggestion that, since the household as a whole (*oikia . . . pasa*) was a part (*meros*) of the polis, and since women made up fully half the free population and children were future sharers in the *politeia*, it is clear that both wives and children of citizens should be educated "looking toward (*blepontas pros*) the *politeia*" (1260b15–20). Here noncitizens are connected to both polis and *politeia*, and so are surely to be regarded as encompassed by the *koinōnia* of the polis.[26]

Aristotle emphasizes the necessity to the polis of the concept of difference when, at the beginning of book 2, he refutes Plato's *Republic* as a valid description of a polis on the grounds that it was based on a higher level of commonality (or sameness) than any actual polis could tolerate. Aristotle points out that Plato's polis

> attempted as far as possible to be entirely one. . . . And yet it is evident that as it becomes increasingly one it will no longer be a polis. For the polis is in its nature a certain sort of multitude (*plēthos*), and as it becomes more a unity it will be an *oikos* instead of a polis and [then] a human being instead of an *oikos*. . . . So even if one were able to do this, one ought not to do it, as it would destroy the polis. Now the polis is made up not only of a number of human beings, but also of human beings differing in kind; a polis does not arise from persons who are similar (*ex homoiōn*). (1261a15–24)

Not only is actual sameness ontologically destructive, but so is perfect ideological homogenization: "That 'all say the same thing' is in one way fine (*kalon*) but impossible, while in another way it is not even productive of concord" (*homonoētikon*: 1261b31–32). The differences necessary to allow the existence of the polis pertain between citizens and noncitizens (who possess different sorts of *aretē*: 1259b18–1260b20), but there must also be inequalities among the citizens themselves: As we have seen, Aristotle can describe the polis as a multitude (*plēthos*) of *politai* and a composite entity, made up of "parts." The parts are both households and sociologically defined subgroups of the *politai*. The latter includes especially those who must work for their living (*penētes*) and the leisure class (*plousioi*), but also the wellborn and the baseborn, and the skilled and the incompetent.[27] In his discussion of Plato's *Laws* and the ideas proposed by Phaleas of Chalcedon (1264b26–1267b20), Aristotle denies that it

decision in *Board of Education v. Pico* (457 U.S. 853 [1984]), which endorsed the right of the state to "inculcate" in its citizens "the democratic ideology that infuses its institutions" (with the comments of Harris 1993). On education as cultural reproduction and the problem of coercion, see Gutmann 1987, 3–48.

[26] Cf. 1280b30–35: "The polis is . . . a *koinōnia* in living well of both *oikiai* and *genē* for the sake of a complete and autarkic life"; 1280b40–81a2: "The polis is a *koinōnia* of *genē* and *kōmai* for the sake of a complete and autarkic life."

[27] On the necessity of inequality to the polis, see 1280a7–25, 1282b14–83a23. Economic class, status, and order, and their place in Aristotle's understanding of the polis: Ober 1991a.

would be either possible or desirable to eliminate all differences in wealth (or income—cf. 1309a15–16) by equalizing property holdings.

The upshot is that each *politēs* necessarily played various and differentiated roles in the polis. As a master of an *oikos*, his interests were attached to those of women, children, and slaves (if he had them). His interests might also be connected, at least through relations of production and exchange, with free foreigners—metics, visitors to the polis, or men he met when he traveled outside the polis. As a member of an economic class, his interests were identified with those of one part of the citizen body and were likely to be in conflict with another. He might further identify his interests with other groups within the citizenship, such as the wellborn or the highly skilled, and this identity could potentially lead to conflict. Finally, he was a *politēs* tout court, and in this role he must identify his interests fully with those of his fellow *politai* and with the polis. But the polis' interest in autarky meant that even when acting in the public sphere, he could not ignore the existence of noncitizens, nor did he shed his sociological identity.

As he moved from the public sphere to the private, the citizen's role and behavior must necessarily change: most obviously he was a master within his *oikos* and a deliberating equal among his fellow citizens.[28] He played yet other roles when his polis was at war, when he engaged in economic relations with fellow citizens and foreigners, and when he dealt with members of different sociological subgroups as (e.g., in the case of an Athenian) *phratēr*, demesman, and Initiate.[29] If the citizens were unable to move with facility from sphere to sphere, unable in practice to differentiate between the behavior appropriate to each role and to mix spheres where appropriate, the polis would not survive: it would fail to reproduce itself culturally, would lose its autarky, or would degenerate into civil war.

In sum, Aristotle's polis is a pluralistic, differentiated society as well as a state.[30] It is a *plēthos* (or *plēthē*) of persons subdivided into diverse groups (*merē*,

[28] Of course in Athens, a man of twenty was a citizen, yet he might not yet be the master of an *oikos*. The complexities introduced by this disjunction between public and private standing are explored in Strauss 1993.

[29] If we look ahead to Athenian practice, there is in each case a significant grey area between public and private spheres: The soldier might be unable to serve the state as a hoplite without aid from a neighbor (Lys. 16.14, 31.15, 19); if captured by the enemy he might depend on private beneficence to bring him home (Lys. 19.59; Dem. 8.70–71). The trader in grain was legally required to ship his cargo to Athens ([Aristotle] *Ath. Pol.* 51.4; Dem. 34.37, 35.50–51; Lycurgus 1.27). Membership in a phratry (an association with links to cult, neighborhood, and perhaps kinship) could be brought forward to prove citizenship in the state (Dem. 57.54; cf. Hedrick [1991], who emphasizes the political as opposed to the tribal origins of the phratry). The mix of public and private interaction in the demes is too complex to sketch here, but see Whitehead 1986, esp. 223–52; Osborne 1985a. The Initiate might sit on a jury of fellow Initiates empaneled by the state to try sacrilege (Andocides 1).

[30] On the concept of differentiation, see Luhmann 1982; with discussion in Ober 1991a, 117,

moria). These groups inhabit a common territory (1260b40–1261a1), but their interests are not identical, nor are their desires standardized. Their interests cannot be homogenized because perfect communalization and perfect material equality are unattainable. A safe and stable polis cannot be achieved by equalizing the distribution of goods, or by eliminating sources of conflict through ideological means.[31] Aristotle's problem at this point (which I take to be the central problem of the *Politics* and of the historical Greek polis) was how to "preserve" (*sōzein*) the polis in the face of the competing interests of society's composite parts.

For Aristotle, predicating a natural hierarchy on naturalized slavery and naturally subordinate women (which linked the interests of slaves and women with the interests of the citizens through a utilitarian calculus) solved one part of the puzzle of how to preserve the polis. Yet the polis was founded on *politeia*: to change the *politeia* was to change the polis (1276b10). Because *politeia* was identified with *politeuma*, stability—saving the polis—meant avoiding any change in the criteria for becoming a *politēs*. It also meant functionally integrating, through a just distribution of social goods, the identities and practices of various naturalized social groups—the residents of the geo-polis clustered into parts. The system that determined who was a *politēs* and how social goods were distributed was the *politeia*. Thus the polis was preserved through the integrative and distributive powers of the *politeia*.

I have suggested above that Aristotle's discussion of polis, *politeia*, and *politeuma* leads to a definition of *politeia* as including the "ideological" system of norms, beliefs, and practices on the basis of which social goods were distributed. My argument that *politeia* must include ideology is strengthened by Aristotle's claim that the polis is not to be preserved through equalization of material goods but rather through just and consensual inequality, that is, through the willing agreement to continue the current form of *politeia* by the various "parts" of the polis: "If a *politeia* is going to be preserved, all the parts of the polis must wish it to exist and to continue on the same basis" (1270b21–22).[32]

132–33. On the issue of differentiation, my understanding of the polis is closer to that of M. Weber than to that of E. Durkheim; for the distinction, see Murray 1990a.

[31] Cf. 1297a7–13, where Aristotle explicitly rejects deception of the demos (one is tempted to say that he rejects false consciousness) as a route to good order. On conflict in Aristotle's polis, see Yack 1985.

[32] Compare 1281b21–30, 1294b34–41, 1296b14–17, 1309b16–18, 1267a39–40: a part of the polis that "shares in nothing" (*oudenos metechon*) will be hostile (*allotrion*) to the *politeia*; 1274a17–18: Solon made the Athenian demos *kurios* regarding elections and audits, lest it become a slave (*doulos*) and thereby hostile to the regime (*polemios*). This last is an example of the hostility and instability that results from the enslavement of those who are not "natural" slaves (see 1255b14–15). Ideological stability is prior to preserving a specific set of institutional relationships between governmental entities, which is why *Ath. Pol.* can see the *dēmokratia* of 462 as essentially continuous with that of his own time (despite interruptions in 411 and 404).

Although conceivably disaffection of any part of the polis could endanger the *politeia*, Aristotle is primarily concerned about the threat from the military and "militarizable" classes: disgruntled groups of free males.[33] He did not regard either justly treated (1330a32) "natural" slaves or women as serious threats.[34] This makes sense in light of his theory of polis formation: women and slaves were integrated into the *koinōnia* of the *oikos* through a purely natural (nonvolitional) process (1252a26–34). The next two steps (village- and polis-building) required (free male) heads of *oikoi* and then the "kingly" heads of *kōmai* to leave behind the realm of absolute mastery (1252b15–22, 27–30; cf. 1285b31–33) and enter into a political life that entailed "being ruled" as well as ruling. Compromising pristine authority was in one sense natural because it allowed the polis to achieve its natural *telos* of autarky and the *politai* to "live well." But it was also a voluntary compact (an exchange of sovereign authority for the chance of happiness), and so (unlike the fully natural *oikos*) liable to break down under the pressure of circumstances. Breakdown of the compact meant civil war and the destruction of the polis. Aristotle's concern with preserving the polis through management of existing relations between free males points to the residual quasi-contractarian element in his natural scheme.[35]

Aristotle's focus on disgruntled free males as a potentially dangerous category explains why the "uncorrupted" regime that he rather confusingly calls "polity" (*politeia*) was concerned to keep those sharing in the *politeia* more numerous than those not sharing (1297b4–6). It may also help explain why he regarded democracy as the best of the debased regimes (e.g., 1289b4–8): in a democracy, other than metics, there was no militarizable body of free men stranded outside the citizen body, and within that body the numerically superior ordinary citizens were the dominant element (*politeuma*; cf. 1302a8–13, 1302b25–27). Yet majority rule could not ensure stability (1294b34–41); in a democracy, as in other regimes, the dominant element was responsible for enunciating a *politeia* that would win the willing consent of all other parts.

---

[33] Potential destabilization of *politeia* by disaffected *politai* and other free males: 1277b33–78b5, esp. 1278a37–40: the free male who does not share in the prerogatives (*timai*) of citizenship is equivalent to (*hōsper*) a metic, and in some poleis this is concealed for the sake of deceiving the (excluded) inhabitants.

[34] Nevertheless, women could be described as a *plēthos*, comparable to the *plēthos* of males (1269b15–17). Since women possessed the power of deliberation (1260a12–13), this *plēthos* could presumably organize itself for common action. Such considerations provoked much unease in other literary genres, notably Aristophanic comedy and Euripidean tragedy; see below.

[35] A voluntary compromise of personal sovereignty is also entailed in the "best *politeia*," whose citizen will be capable and desirous (*dunamenos kai proairoumenos*) of ruling and being ruled by turns: 1284a1–3; cf. 1277a12–25. The nondeterministic role of nature in social relations is further underlined by the assumption that all deviant regimes (which are the commonest forms of *politeia*) are to be regarded as unnatural (*para phusin*: 1287b39–41). *Dēmokratia* is one of these, yet it is "not easy" for any regime other than democracy to arise now that poleis are large: 1286b20–22.

Individual members of the *koinōnia* must believe that their interests as subgroup members were likely to be protected by the continuation of the current regime.

The *politeia* thus had to do a lot of work in the *koinōnia* that was the polis. It was the ideology that maintained the authoritative status of the current *politeuma*. It was the cultural means by which the *politai* created and reproduced over generations their distinctive identity within the whole society, and the legal means whereby they formulated rules for ordering the *koinōnia* as a whole. The *politeia* must define the extent and legitimate occupants of the public sphere and coordinate the various private spheres. It must provide the individual with norms for conducting his private relations with members of other *oikoi* and other subsocieties, and for moving from the private sphere to the public. It must ensure that his behavior (when multiplied by similar actions of many individuals) did not destabilize the authority of the exisiting *politeuma*. It must distribute social goods equitably and protect the interests of all parts of the *polis*. Only if it did all these things could the *politeia* preserve its own integrity and that of the society.

In sum: the *politeia* by which the society was organized, while devised (in large part) by a part of the citizenry, must win and retain the voluntary consent of all citizens and (at least indirectly) those noncitizens connected to them. And this means it must generally be regarded by the members of society as a just system. A just *politeia* provided for stability through principles governing the distribution of material goods, political rights, and status privileges, such that each of the parts regarded it as worthwhile to support the current sociopolitical order. Thus, if the polis is a society, the *politeia* represents the terms of the social contract.[36] It is, indeed, also the basis of procedural law. But the politico-polis (community of citizens) is a subset of the polis-as-society, and neither polis nor *politeia* will be preserved intact if the *politeia* qua social contract is regarded as substantively unjust by any social group capable of bringing destabilizing force to bear. State institutions provided an important part of the social context, but any analytic hierarchy in which prescriptive state laws (how a lawmaking authority at a given time thought an institution was supposed to work) are elevated above actual social practice (how it was in fact used at a given time) can result in a serious misunderstanding of the polis. Aristotle makes this exact point when he states that a polis may be oligarchic or democratic according to its *nomoi*, but in disposition and actual practice it may be the opposite (1292b11–21). Returning to Aristotle's zoological analogy: viewing the polis as a society provides the substantive tissue and sinew without which the polis-as-state would be no more than a heap of unarticulated procedural bones.[37]

---

[36] Cf. 1276b29: *koinōnia d'estin hē politeia* ("The *koinōnia* is the *politeia*").

[37] For the tendency of Athenian law to focus on procedural rather than substantive matters, see, for example, Todd and Millett 1990. The flesh and bones metaphor was previously employed,

John Rawls

The understanding of the polis as a society developed above is indebted not only to Aristotle's *Politics*, but also to the moral philosophy of John Rawls. In *A Theory of Justice*, Rawls defines "a society" as

> a more or less self-sufficient association of persons who in their relations to one another recognize certain rules of conduct as binding and who for the most part act in accordance with them . . . these rules specify a system of cooperation designed to advance the good of those taking part in it. . . . [However,] a society . . . is typically marked by a conflict as well as by an identity of interests. . . . There is a conflict of interests since persons are not indifferent as to how the greater benefits produced by their collaboration are distributed. . . . A set of principles is required for choosing among the various social arrangements which determine this division of advantages and for underwriting an agreement on the proper distributive shares. These principles are the principles of social justice: they provide a way of assigning rights and duties in the basic institutions of society and they define the appropriate distribution of the benefits and burdens of social cooperation.[38]

Rawls goes on to suggest (4–5) that a (utopian) "well-ordered society" is regulated by a public and universally shared conception of justice, and that this conception of justice in turn limits the pursuit of other ends (i.e., regulates desire) and so constitutes the society's "fundamental charter." Like Aristotle, Rawls sees political equality as intrinsically desirable, but rejects complete equalization of access to most social goods (things that any rational person would want more rather than less of) as neither feasible nor desirable.[39] Rawls substitutes for equalization the "difference principle" by which inequality is to be allowed, but regulated by selecting social institutions on the basis of their maximization of payoffs to the "least advantaged" member(s) of society. Thus, Rawls' well-ordered society would permit distinctions in wealth and income, but its institutions would ensure that as the rich got richer, so did the poor.[40]

Rawls attempts to generate the fundamental, substantive principles of social

---

in reference to the relative importance of political factions and the "Constitution," by Connor (1971, 4–5). Connor's approach is attacked by Hansen (1989b). My own concern is more with substantive social practices than with political factions, but I believe that Connor's strictures on the limits of narrowly constitutional history (i.e., the evolution of procedural rules) remain valid.

[38] Rawls 1971, 4, referring specifically to the "macro-society" rather than to various subgroups within society: cf. Rawls 1971, 8, 61; Wolff 1977, 68, 77–80, 196, 202–3. Parenthetical numbers in the text of this section refer to the page numbers of Rawls 1971.

[39] Rawls (1971, 61) states his general conception of justice as follows: "All social values . . . are to be distributed equally unless an unequal distribution . . . is to everyone's advantage." Primary social goods are rights and liberties, opportunities and powers, income and wealth: Rawls 1971, 62, 92. Cf. Wolff 1977, 75.

[40] Difference principle: Rawls 1971, 75–83; Wolff 1977, 63–65.

justice appropriate to a well-ordered society by a complex thought experiment: He employs a conception of "justice as fairness"—a version of social contract theory (derived primarily from Locke and Kant)—to mediate what he sees as fatal flaws in utilitarian and intuitionist traditions of moral philosophy. Briefly, Rawls posits a group of rationally self-interested persons in an "original position" of equality. They must unanimously agree on the fundamental social rules under which they (and their descendants) will govern themselves forever. The catch is that they must debate possible rules under a "veil of ignorance"— that is to say, though each player has a basic understanding of economics, psychology, and politics, he does not know who he is: he is ignorant of his economic and social status, his powers and abilities, even his desires (other than his desire for justice). Finally, Rawls assumes that under the conditions of uncertainty that he has established, the players will employ the rather conservative "maximin" principle of decision making—that is, each player will attempt to reduce his risk of falling below a minimum standard (he will seek to maximize his minimum) rather than choose to gamble by risking his minimum in hope of a potentially higher payoff.[41]

The final results of this thought experiment (the hypothetical agreement that arises from the negotiations within the original position) are two "principles of justice":

> I. Each person is to have an equal right to the most extensive total system of equal basic liberties compatible with a similar system of liberty for all.
> II. Social and economic inequalities are to be arranged so they are both (a) to the greatest benefit of the least advantaged . . . (b) attached to offices and positions open to all under conditions of fair equality of opportunity.[42] (302)

The working of these two principles is further defined by two "priority rules" that state, in essence, that liberty is prior to all other goods (ergo principle [I] cannot be compromised to increase any other good) and that the principle of justice enunciated in principle [II] is prior to (and so cannot be compromised in favor of) efficiency of production or the overall welfare of the society. Thus, Rawls' well-ordered society is characterized by equal liberties (right to vote and hold office; freedom of speech, assembly, conscience, and thought; freedom of the person and to hold property; freedom from arbitrary arrest and seizure: 61) and unequal, but fair, distributions of material goods and other powers.

Can Rawls' theory of the just society really help us to understand the polis as a society? *A Theory of Justice*, while very influential, has been attacked as a

---

[41] Rawls' sources of inspiration: Rawls 1971, vii–viii, 11, 15, 22–45; Wolff 1977, 11–15. The original position: Rawls 1971, 17–22; the veil of ignorance: Rawls 1971, 12, 136–42. Maximin: Rawls 1971, 152–57; Wolff 1977, 50–51, 82–83.

[42] Rawls 1971, 302–3; cf. 60–90.

universal, objective description of social justice on a variety of grounds, including that (1) the veil of ignorance robs the players in the original position of the resources with which to make humanly meaningful decisions; that (2) the maximin rule is an excessively conservative decision-making principle; and that (3) the liberality of the two principles of justice is the result of liberal assumptions Rawls has built into the original position rather than a logical outcome of negotiations within it.[43] Moreover, we must keep in mind that Rawls did not concern himself with classical antiquity or the polis. Finally, his moral philosophy is far from identical to that of Aristotle. Most centrally, at least for our purposes, Rawls' theory avoids teleological naturalism in favor of a robust, individual-centered social contract. Rawls' lexically ordered principles forbid fixed hierarchies based on naturalized categories of persons. The first priority rule thus disallows the institution of slavery, regardless of any advantages accruing to slaves and masters (cf. 62–63). But the two philosophers' goals are not antithetical: both are interested in substantive rather than merely procedural justice, in ends rather than simply means, and in a society that is the best possible, not simply in one that is functionally workable. Rawls' conception of "justice as fairness" is much more extensive than Aristotle's "common interest" (*to koinēi sumpheron*: 1282b16–18), but both men tend to see justice as congruent with goodness. Both imagine the well-ordered society as a balance of political equalities and social inequalities; both are interested in stable (ideally permanent) regimes. In sum, I believe that there is sufficient common ground between Aristotle and Rawls on the subject of the just society to make measuring an actual society against the gap between their positions into a useful exercise.[44]

ATHENS

Athens in the fourth century B.C. was a society characterized by fundamental differences between citizens and noncitizens, and inequalities between sociologically defined groups within the citizenry; by both conflict and identity of interests between and within the diverse groups; and by a set of rules, norms, and practices—enunciated by the demos (mass of ordinary citizens qua dominant political element) and perpetuated by popular ideology—which required the consent of potentially disruptive subgroups (notably the Athenian elites).

[43] See, for example, discussion in Wolff 1977; Barber 1988, 54–90; Pogge 1989. Rawls has defended and refined his theory in a series of articles, e.g., Rawls 1987.

[44] Rawls on substantive versus formal or procedural justice: 1971, 54–60. Problem of inequality: 7, 96. Stable, permanent regime: 6, 12–13. His theory in accord with the "traditional" theory of justice, which is based on Aristotle: 10–11, cf. 424–33. See also Wolff 1977, 208–9; Nussbaum 1990; Wallach 1992, with bibliography. Contrast MacIntyre (1981), who would subordinate the moral rules typified in Rawlsian liberal tradition to the larger context of moral virtue that he finds in Aristotle.

Since Athens was a relatively stable society in the fourth century, we may ask (following Aristotle and Rawls) whether the various parts of the Athenian polis consented to the *politieia* enunciated by the demos because they recognized it as substantively just, or whether their consent was coerced or based on deception.[45]

The rest of this chapter focuses on a few of the ways the polis of Athens resolved or avoided destabilizing problems that have beset other societies (especially conflicts between households and between rich and poor citizens). It concludes by asking whether Athens' social stability was secured justly.[46] This exercise seems to me worthwhile in that it allows us to explore the "fit" between two important theories of society and a concrete historical example. It helps to define the extent to which Aristotle took Athens as a model and suggests responses to some of Rawls' critics.[47] Measuring classical Athens against carefully articulated conceptions of the well-ordered society should also make it easier to compare Athens to other human societies: In what ways was Athens historically distinctive? Can Athens be assimilated to the model of either "Mediterranean society" or Western society generally? Was the Athenian *politeia* more or less just than other known societies?

If, like Aristotle, we begin with the *oikos*, we may ask how the Athenian *politeia* affected the private realm and mediated between civil society and the state.[48] What rules governed an Athenian's behavior as he moved from *oikos* to *ekklēsia* or *dikastērion*, from the role of *despotēs* within his *oikos* to deliberating *politēs*? Were these roles integrated or differentiated? Did the Athenian citizen enter the public realm as a representative of his *oikos*, or as an individual? Did he carry forward the interests of the noncitizens with whom he was associated?

The first question confronting us is whether in practice a distinctly private sphere can be distinguished from the Athenian public sphere.[49] Although scholarly opinion has ranged between the poles of complete integration of the private within the public realm and more or less full distinction, recent work on the Athenian family (and its constituent members) seems to point toward a

[45] Stability of Athens in the fourth century (and the necessity of explaining it): Ober 1989b, esp. 17–20.

[46] Here I deliberately avoid the question of whether, in an ideological society, voluntary consent is possible. See Ober 1993 and 1994, and Chapter 10 above.

[47] For another approach to "historicist" political theory, see Wallach 1992. The sort of analysis I am proposing is inevitably based on limited evidence, but would have been much more difficult two decades ago, before the flowering of studies of democratic Athens as a state (for which see the bibliography in Hansen 1991) and as a society (for which see the studies cited below).

[48] Cf. Hansen 1989c, 19: "Family life . . . belonged in the private and not in the public sphere . . . the *polis* did not regulate all matters but only a limited range of social activities, mostly those connected with the state."

[49] Cf. Hansen 1989c, 18: "In many aspects of life the Athenians practiced a separation between a public and a private sphere . . . the dichotomy of the public and the private is apparent in all aspects of life."

middle ground: the *politēs* did not forget his role as *oikos*-member when he entered the public realm; certain accepted techniques of self-representation within public institutions allowed, encouraged, or even required him to make that membership explicit.[50] Yet the demos did try to keep public and private spheres sufficiently distinct as to prevent private interests from unduly influencing public decision making. The differentiation of the citizen's public and private roles was an important factor in the overall structure of Athenian society. On the other hand, the limited and conditional nature of that differentiation ensured that public decision making performed a significant role in the functional integration of the constituent subsocieties of the Athenian polis.[51]

The Athenian approach to the education of future citizens illustrates the interplay of public and private realms.[52] Decisions about the amount and kind of "formal" education that a given child received were left to the discretion of his *oikos*; there was no public school system, no standard curriculum. The state showed no interest in ensuring that Athens was a literate society or even that citizens could read public announcements.[53] Nor, until the reform of the *ephēbeia* in the mid-330s, did the Athenian state involve itself in formally educating future citizens in social values.[54] The contrast with Aristotle's best possible polis seems stark: The incomplete book 8 of the *Politics* is a detailed discussion of the educational system that would ensure that children developed the *aretē* that would reproduce, over generations, the polis and its *politeia*. Upon closer scrutiny, the contrast becomes less clear-cut. The Athenians were actually no less interested than Aristotle in sociocultural and political reproduction. They tended to believe, however, that the experience of life in the democratic polis, including participating in informal public discussion of the decisions made in Assembly and lawcourts, would in itself provide a normative education (*koinē paideia*: Aeschines 1.187) in social values. Rather than entering into the complexities of arranging by democratic means to create and maintain a necessarily coercive public institution, the Athenians supposed that the democratic *politeia* would imbue future citizens with its values through exemplary

[50] E.g., *dokimasia* (and especially the *dokimasia rhētorōn*: Aeschines 1); oaths taken in the *dikastēria* that entail death and destruction for one's *oikos* in the case of foreswearing (Aesch. 2.87); the display of family members as character witnesses at trials (Humphreys 1985c); legal actions concerning rights to citizenship (Dem. 57); attacks on one's opponents' family members in political trials and defense based on family members' liturgical service (Ober 1989b, 226–33).

[51] The bibliography on the relationship between *oikos* and polis is large and growing rapidly; see, recently, Humphreys 1983b; Foxhall 1989; Jameson 1990; Winkler 1990, 45–70; Halperin 1990, 88–112; D. Cohen 1992; Strauss 1993.

[52] Cf. Hansen 1989c, 19–20: "Education [et al.] were not political issues but mostly left to private enterprise . . . not much discussed in the *ekklesia* and citizens were allowed to do as they pleased."

[53] See, e.g., Harris 1989, 65–115; Thomas 1989.

[54] In the mid-330s B.C. the *ephēbeia*, formerly a system of military training, added a component of moral education: Ober 1985a, 90–95; Humphreys 1985b with literature cited.

decisions by its deliberative and judicial institutions and thereby gain their voluntary assent to its central principles.[55] Meanwhile, the system of choosing public officials by lot simply took for granted that those Athenians who chose to enter the lottery would be well enough educated to fulfill the duties of office. There was no "civil service examination"; access to whatever advantages office-holding might have offered remained open to all.[56]

How permeable was the boundary between the worlds of the citizen and of the *oikos* when it came to public deliberation?[57] Noncitizens lacked the privilege of free public speech (*isēgoria*), and thus had no formal right to participate in public debate. Yet Aristotle could have found in Athens the empirical proof of his conviction that women possessed deliberative ability (*to bouleutikon*). Most Athenian women did not live truly secluded lives. Anecdotal evidence shows that some women went regularly to the *agora* and that the Athenian citizen discussed public matters with female (as well as juvenile male) members of his *oikos*.[58] Although normal Assembly procedure assumed that citizen speakers would be addressing citizen audiences, noncitizens (e.g., ambassadors) could address the Assembly if invited to do so by an appropriate decree (Aesch. 2.58). Spectatorship was not unknown in the Assembly and was common in the *dikastēria*.[59] Women gave legally binding depositions under oath before arbitrators in public places; the practice of employing public state-appointed arbitrators (beginning in ca. 400 B.C.) for private disputes is itself evidence for the overlapping of public and private spheres.[60] By the latter part of the fourth

[55] Complexities of democratic control of education, and of designing an education in democratic values: Gutmann 1987. Athenian belief in the normative value of public political practice: Ober 1989b, 159–63.

[56] On the question of whether or not magistrates received regular state pay in the fourth century and the nature of their other perquisites, see Hansen 1979b, 1980; Gabrielsen 1981. There is no way of determining the extent of voluntary abstention by the illiterate and no evidence to suggest that questioning at *dokimasiai* focused on basic competence.

[57] Cf. Hansen 1989c, 20: "The Greek *polis* was a community of citizens to the exclusion of foreigners and slaves . . . the Athenian citizens isolated themselves from metics and slaves to debate political issues in the assembly, in the council and in the popular courts."

[58] Women in the *agora*: Dem. 57.33–34; cf. *Pol.* 1300a6–7, 1323a5–6. Husbands discuss court cases and Assembly business with their wives, daughters, sons, and mothers: Dem. 59.110–11; Lycurgus 1.141; Aesch. 1.186–87; cf. Aristophanes *Ecclesiazusae* 551ff. (a scene that assumes for its comic force that such conversations were normal). Activities of women outside the home at Athens: D. Cohen 1989, with catalog of passages.

[59] Spectators: Aristophanes *Ecclesiazusae* 241–44: Praxagora learned rhetoric by overhearing Assembly debates when her family was billeted in the city during the Peloponnesian War; spectatorship may have been more difficult after the construction of Pnyx II in the late fifth/early fourth century. References in the orators and archaeological remains make it clear that at least some Athenian courtrooms also allowed spectatorship; Aeschines (1.117) goes so far as to claim that the spectators judged the *dikastai*; cf. Thompson and Wycherley 1972, 59 and n. 170 with references cited.

[60] Date: MacDowell 1971 (although cf. Humphreys 1983a, 239–42). Previously, dispute arbi-

century, metics and even slaves were participating (as principals and unco-
erced witnesses) in certain trials before the people's courts.[61] Finally, complex
networks of gossip and rumor played a major role in public decision making
and flowed easily across social borders. Gossip permeated Athenian society,
linking the private life of its target with his public performance, and (at least
potentially) allowed all residents of the geo-polis to participate in the enforcement of social norms. Because Athenian norms tended to equate a politician's
private behavior with his public value, gossip and rumor had profound effects
on political practice.[62]

On the other hand, differentiation of public and private roles had significant
effects on Athenian social behavior and distinguishes Athens from other Mediterranean societies. As Paul Millett has argued, when compared to the society of
ancient Rome, Athens is remarkable for its lack of emphasis on patron-client
relationships. Although it is certainly possible to find evidence for specific instances of "patronistic" behavior, Athens does not manifest the characteristics of
a society fundamentally defined by clientage. Lesser *oikoi* were not formally tied
to "great houses," and relations of power were not institutionalized into a
public/private power pyramid.[63] Though there were indeed a few very wealthy
families in Athens, these families were unable to control Athenian society
through the matrix of reciprocal and interfamilial, but unequal and cross-
generational, obligations that typifies the society based on patronage.[64] This
conclusion has profound consequences for our understanding of Athenian society. Although the lower-class Athenian (and his family) might work for and/or
be in debt to members of the upper classes, the Athenian citizen did not enter the

---

tration had been an entirely private phenomenon, and hence the line between a private realm of
arbitration and a public realm of lawcourts may have been clearer; cf. Humphreys 1985c, 313–
16. Women's depositions under oath: Dem. 29.26, 33, 56; 39.3–4; 40.11; 59.45–48. Arbitration
in temples: Dem. 33.18, 36.15–16, 40.11; Isaeus 2.31; cf. Gernet 1954, 210 n. 2. In the Heliaia:
Dem. 47.12. In the Stoa Poikile: Dem. 45.17. Public arbitration in general: Gernet 1939; Harrell
1936. This issue is discussed in detail in Hunter 1994, 55–67.

[61] Metics: E. Cohen 1973; metics and slaves: E. Cohen 1991.

[62] Gossip: Ober 1989b, 148–51; Hunter 1990 (with catalog of references); Humphreys 1989.

[63] Millett 1989. This is one reason that prosopographical approaches to Athenian political
history are generally unsatisfactory: they are implicitly predicated on a misleading parallel with
the social structure of republican Rome (derived primarily from R. Syme) and, at a second remove, upon the elitist model of political behavior that Syme explicitly adopted; cf. Chapter 3. See
Syme 1939, vii: "The composition of the oligarchy of government . . . emerges as the dominant
theme of political history"; 7: "In all ages, whatever the form and name of government, be it
monarchy, republic, or democracy, an oligarchy lurks behind the façade"; cf. Linderski 1990.
Syme's latter comment is a virtual paraphrase of Robert Michels' "Iron Law of Oligarchy"—first
published in 1911 (German edition) and 1915 (English and Italian); see Michels [1915] 1962.
Ober 1989b was intended in part as a challenge to elitist political theory in general and Michels'
"Iron Law" in particular.

[64] Patronage as reciprocal but unequal obligations that can endure between family groups over
generations: Saller 1982; Wallace-Hadrill 1989.

public sphere as his employer / creditor's client. His vote was not owned or directly controlled by another, and thus Athenian decision making was dominated by interests, desires, and perceptions of the many rather than of the few. The democratic political system was implicated in, and in turn strengthened, a set of social norms that discouraged clientage in private life.[65]

The differentiation of public and private roles meant that the common (at least in Mediterranean societies) and socially volatile notion of esteem as inviolability (i.e., "that object of pride which must be defended at all costs") seems to have found its primary locus in the individual citizen rather than in the *oikos*. Whereas in other Mediterranean societies, the "flashpoint" of potentially catastrophic dishonor tended to be the household (and especially female relatives qua sexual beings or objects),[66] in Athens it was, imprimis, the citizen's body and his standing. The prime target of the hubristic man was held to be the bodily integrity or rights of other citizens; arrogantly disrespectful behavior of this sort (*hubris*) called for public action.[67] This suggests, in turn, that the ordinary Athenian often represented himself in public as an individual citizen and a member of the citizen group. His irreducible need for esteem may more accurately be described as a cooperative desire to ensure the maintenance of the personal dignity properly accorded to each citizen than as a competitive desire to augment his family's honor. Consequently, he was likely to demand from those in his society equal recognition rather than (or at any rate, before) special distinction. And thus the Athenian *politeia* was fundamentally democratic (based on equal dignity) rather than hierarchical (based on differential honors).[68] This certainly did not preclude Athenians from lusting after honors; *philotimia* was a psychological state as well known to Athenian public speakers (and their audiences) as to philosophers. But in democratic Athens, desire for outstanding honor remained a psychological condition (albeit a common one within elite status groups) rather than a generalized, definitive social value.[69] The Athenian was an *eleutheros* (free from the threat of being

[65] I am not making an argument for priority (i.e., claiming that open social relations came first and thus democracy flourished, or vice versa). Rather, I suppose that a non-clientistic social culture and a democratic political culture were mutually empowering and so grew up together.

[66] Male honor and the family in Mediterranean society: D. Cohen 1992, with literature cited. For other societies: Mandelbaum 1988; Small 1991.

[67] Definition of *hubris* as willfully and gratuitously inflicting shame (*aischunē*) upon another: Arist. *Rhet.* 1378b23–26. *Hubris* as an assault on the individual in Athens: Murray 1990b; Fisher 1990. The alternative argument, that adultery and *hubris* fit Mediterranean norms of honor and shame associated with family and sexuality: D. Cohen 1990. Aristotle (*Rhet.* 1391a41–19) links *hubris* and adultery as misdeeds typical of the newly wealthy.

[68] For the two models of honor, distinction, hierarchy versus dignity, recognition, democracy, see Taylor 1994. On Athenian conceptions of the individual self, honor, and dignity, see also Gouldner 1969, 87–110. I explore the issue of honor and dignity in more detail in Chapter 7.

[69] *Philotimia*: Whitehead 1983; Ober 1989b, 332–33. Cf. Goode 1978. In decentering the concept of honor as aggressive masculinity I am going against the grain of some recent anthro-

subjected to unanswerable indignities) before he was a *philotimos*—the democratic insistence on the public recognition of individual dignity is one reason that *eleutheria* was regarded as the definitive value of a democracy (e.g., 1294a9–11). Public honor and distinction had (in most cases) to be earned, rather than demanded on the basis of membership in a particular *oikos*.[70] And this meant that the Athenian demos, as the ultimate source of major public honors, could employ *philotimia* and its satisfaction as a form of social control over the elite. Likewise, *atimia* (and its verb forms) in Athens meant, imprimis, disenfranchisement (rather than personal or familial dishonor): it represented a withdrawal by the citizen group of its guarantee to safeguard someone's claim to equal dignity.

The issue of wealth inequality and the tension between economic classes will serve as a final illustration of public-private interchange. If the heads of wealthy and impoverished *oikoi* met as equal individuals in the public realm, did the Athenian *politeia* promote anything resembling Rawls' difference principle? Arguably, it did: As I (among others) have argued elsewhere, the system of public liturgies, along with certain legal procedures (notably *antidosis*) and the operation of the social norm of reciprocal gratitude (*charis*) within the people's courts, served a redistributive function within the polis. The richest Athenians were required and encouraged to subsidize materially (in direct and indirect ways) their poorest fellow citizens.[71] Moreover, the democratic procedures of the Assembly and courtroom prevented the private-realm wealth-power of the rich man (and of the rich as a class) from being generalized into an unassailable position of sociopolitical superiority. As Demosthenes emphasized time and again in *Against Meidias*, the collective legal power of the people could and should be used to humble any hubristic rich man who threatened the individual and collective dignity of the citizens. Indictments of wealthy litigants signaled to the wealth elite as a class that their control of material resources did not place them outside the norms of society or render them invulnerable to the wrath of the many.[72] He who violated the dignity of his

---

pologically oriented work on Athenian society, e.g., Halperin 1990; D. Cohen 1992. I tend to think that the aristocratic value of honor has been over-generalized to a universal Athenian (or Greek) value. What makes Athens distinct from other societies is not its hierarchical tendencies, but rather its egalitarian tendencies. Thus, even those who follow Foucault (1980a) in assuming a high degree of isomorphism of the political and the private should be looking for tendencies to equality and distributive justice at the private level, since these ideals dominate the Athenian public realm.

[70] The exception that proves the rule is honors done the descendants of the tyrant-slayers, Harmodius and Aristogeiton: Taylor 1991, 1–5. Athenian litigants did indeed mention great deeds of their ancestors in court, but tended to do so as part of an argument that they themselves are likely to act in the same way, rather than as part of a demand for distinction on the basis of membership ipso facto; cf. Ober 1989b, 226–30.

[71] Redistributive function of liturgies, taxes, and fines: Ober 1989b, 199–202; Osborne 1991.

[72] Cf. discussion in Ober 1989b, 209–11; above, Chapter 7.

fellow citizen would be punished by the collectivity. And thus the practice of Athenian law served social ends.[73] The principle of hierarchy was undermined in favor of democratic equality at the level of material distribution and everyday social behavior. As a result, power was discontinuous, rather than a naturalized, seamless web. If we are to believe the complaints of various critics of Athenian democracy, this discontinuity may even have affected the treatment and behavior of noncitizens.[74]

If we follow Aristotle in focusing on the *koinōnia* of citizens, fourth-century Athens provides quite a close fit to Rawls' well-ordered society. First, the fundamental principles of the *politeia*, reenacted in the democratic restoration of 403 B.C. (which one might almost think of as the Athenian "original position"), remained stable for some eighty years (cf. [Aristotle] *Ath. Pol.* 41.1). The details of how the rules worked remained revisable through the enactment of *nomoi* and *psēphismata*; but, as Aristotle (1289a13–15) recommended, (procedural) laws were enacted with a view to the (substantive) *politeia*, rather than vice versa. In accord with both Aristotle and Rawls, the Athenian *politeia* was founded on a balance between acknowledged social distinctions and political equalities. The Athenian emphasis on liberty as individual and collective dignity and on equal access to deliberative assemblies and public office (and its associated rewards) is a practical example of Rawls' first principle of justice and first priority rule; it also confirms Aristotle's (e.g., 1291b4–35, 1317a40–b17) comments about the priority of freedom and political equality in the democratic *politeia*. Moreover, the Athenian tolerance for economic inequality, counterbalanced by legal redistributive mechanisms that kept in check inequalities of power and (to some extent) of resources, seems to be a reasonable approximation of Rawls' second principle of justice. In this respect, Athens also conforms to Aristotle's requirement for dissimilarity within the polis.

Thus, if we stay within the citizenship, the Athenian social contract at least roughly recapitulates the principles developed within Rawls' thought experiment. Moreover, in emphasizing dignity before honor, the Athenians do seem to have employed what could be described as a maximin principle of limiting risk under conditions of uncertainty. The conditions of Athenian citizen-society are, of course, far from an empirical proof of the universality of Rawls' principles or the assumptions that underlie them. The Athenian preference for a maximin approach to decision making may, for example, find its roots in the realities of a premodern rural culture centered on subsistence agriculture rather

[73] See, for example, discussion by Humphreys (1983a, 1985a, 1985c); the essays collected in Cartledge, Millett and Todd 1990; Todd 1990; D. Cohen 1991, 1992.

[74] Complaints that democracy blurs distinctions between slaves, metics, women, and citizens, and renders discipline impossible: Aristotle *Pol.* 1313b32–38, 1319b27–30; Ps.-Xenophon 1.10–12; Plato *Rep.* 562b–563c; cf. Dem. 9.3; 21.47, 49. Varying views on Athenian treatment of slaves: Gouldner 1969, 33–34, 88–90; Garlan 1988, 145–53; Patterson 1991, 64–180.

than in human nature.[75] But in light of criticisms that have been leveled at Rawls' theory (and Rawls' own retreat from claims of universality), it is notable that the Athenian citizenry does seem to have come up with something like Rawlsian social justice without the problematic veil of ignorance and without a knowledge of modern liberal democratic principles, practices, or institutions.

When we move to the broader *koinōnia* of those resident within the geo-polis, the Athenian social order no longer conforms closely to Rawls' model of justice. Although Athenian society was stable and more or less autarkic in the fourth century,[76] the legally mandated and socially accepted positions of slaves, women, and metics violate Rawls' first principle. If we accept Rawls' liberal definition of justice, Athens cannot be judged a just society. Yet, without attempting an *apologia*, it may be worthwhile noting a few points in Athens' favor. Most obviously, no other known polis, and no other known complex ancient society, even approximates the Rawlsian ideal of social justice, at the level either of whole society or of citizen-society. Next, certain social practices and fourth-century changes in legal procedure might be read as the (tentative and conditional) extension of certain basic liberties to certain noncitizens.[77] The emphasis on citizen dignity over family honor, the lack of formal client-age, and discontinuities within the manifestation of power may have amelio-rated (again in tentative and conditional ways) the oppression of noncitizens. Finally, the Athenians (unlike Aristotle) never succeeded in representing unjust social relations to themselves as completely natural. No doubt most Athenians managed, most of the time, to ignore the contingent, problematic, and exploit-ative nature of their own social system. Yet the contradiction of a just society of citizens embedded in an unjust society at large created unease and ambiva-lence for which critics of the Athenian regime (e.g., Plato in the *Republic*, Aris-totle in *Politics*, books 7 and 8) attempted to find theoretical solutions. And those theoretical solutions seem, on the whole, rather less just than Athenian practice when viewed from a Rawlsian perspective. Moreover, that unease found a public forum in Athens: by sponsoring tragedy and comedy in the Theater of Dionysos, the Athenian state not only sanctioned but institu-tionalized the exploration of problems of social justice.[78] Nothing in Aristotle's

---

[75] Athenian citizens as peasants: Wood 1988; Todd 1990. The conservative risk-management strategies typical of peasant societies: Gallant 1991; cf. Sallares 1990.

[76] This does not, of course, mean that Athens did not require imports (although the necessity has often been over-rated: Garnsey 1988, 89–164), but rather that Athens was able to produce and defend goods adequate to secure the material needs of the population.

[77] See, for example, Foxhall 1989; Hunter 1989a, 1989b; Ober 1991c.

[78] Drama, and especially comedy, as (inter alia) political and social commentary: see the essays by S. Goldhill, J. Ober and B. Strauss, J. Henderson, and J. Redfield in Winkler and Zeitlin 1990; Rothwell 1990; Konstan 1990. Others have seen drama rather as a form of social control: e.g., Olson 1990. See Podlecki 1990 for a review of the vexed question of whether women attended the theater.

surviving text suggests that his best possible state would have encouraged this sort of introspection. Thus, if Rawlsian and Aristotelian visions of the just society can be regarded as distinct trajectories intersecting a common ground, the trajectory of fourth-century Athenian society intersects that same ground, and at a point somewhere between the two.

In conclusion, the Athenian state is not fully coextensive with Athenian society at large. It is misleading to claim complete homology or total isomorphism between the behavior of individual citizens, government institutions, the citizenry, and the society as a whole. Yet both Aristotelian and Athenian *politeiai* were deeply interested in the production and distribution of social goods; "state" (as defined above) does not exhaust the meanings of polis in the *Politics* or in Athens. If the politico-polis was not fully homologous to the polis as a society, neither was it separable from it. The citizenry remained an internally diverse subset of a larger society; the practices of the political sphere affected the larger society, and vice versa. The state remained socially embedded; social norms were created, maintained, and revised by the operations of state institutions. The polis was a *koinōnia* defined by tensions generated by the play of difference between and within the society of citizens, civil society, and society at large. Attempts to deal with these tensions provided the substance of Aristotle's *Politics* and Athenian politics.

A final word of caution: Describing the polis in the functionalist and contractarian terms I have employed in this chapter cannot offer a fully satisfactory explanation of the phenomenon of the polis. The approach I have adopted here takes society as self-sufficient and so ignores the consequences of international relations.[79] Moreover, it defers the important issue of the polis as a system for creating meaning; it leaves aside the positive content of citizenship as self-identification and empowerment.[80] In Aristotle's terms, it skirts the *telos* (living well) and focuses on somewhat pedestrian antecedent conditions. The picture of the polis presented here is thus only a sketch of certain features; it lacks the color and detail that make for real social existence. But I think that attempting to define the terms of the social contract underpinning the polis is worthwhile. For most modern readers, any assessment of the spiritual meanings the *politai* devised for themselves is likely to be based on a prior moral judgment of the polis as a society. After weighing Athenian society in the scales of social justice, we may still wish to celebrate the ideals of democratic, participatory citizenry; but we will have reminded ourselves of the deep and enduring injustices that characterized even the best of poleis.

[79] On which, see Raaflaub 1985, 1991; Ober 1991e.
[80] For thoughtful discussions, see Manville 1990; Meier 1984; Euben 1990.

BIBLIOGRAPHY

Adcock, F. E., and D. J. Mosley. 1975. *Diplomacy in Ancient Greece*. New York: St. Martin's Press.

Allen, J. W. 1941. *A History of Political Thought in the Sixteenth Century*. 2d ed. London: Methuen.

Anderson, Benedict. 1992. *Imagined Communities: Reflections on the Origins and Spread of Nationalism*. 2d ed. London: Verso.

Arendt, Hannah. 1959. *The Human Condition*. Garden City, N.Y.: Doubleday, Anchor.

———. 1963. *On Revolution*. New York: Viking Press.

———. 1968. *Between Past and Future: Eight Exercises in Political Thought*. 2d ed. New York: Viking.

Austin, J. L. 1975. *How to Do Things with Words*. Ed. J. O. Urmson and Marina Sbisà. 2d ed. Cambridge, Mass.: Harvard University Press.

Badian, E. 1993. *From Plataea to Potidaea: Studies in the History and Historiography of the Pentecontaetia*. Baltimore: The Johns Hopkins University Press.

Barber, Benjamin R. 1984. *Strong Democracy: Participatory Politics for a New Age*. Berkeley and Los Angeles: University of California Press.

———. 1988. *The Conquest of Politics*. Princeton: Princeton University Press.

Bell, Daniel. 1993. *Communitarianism and Its Critics*. Oxford: Clarendon.

Berlin, I. 1969. *Four Essays on Liberty*. London and New York: Oxford University Press.

Bers, Victor. 1985. "Dikastic Thorubos." In *Crux: Essays in Greek History Presented to G.E.M. de Ste. Croix (History of Political Theory 6.1–2)*, ed. Paul Cartledge and F. David Harvey, 1–15. London: Duckworth.

Bleicken, J. 1987. "Die Einheit der athenischen Demokratie in klassischen Zeit." *Hermes* 115:257–83.

Bloedow, E. F. 1981. "The Speeches of Archidamus and Sthenelaidas at Sparta." *Historia* 30:129–43.

Bobbio, Norberto. 1989. *Democracy and Dictatorship: The Nature and Limits of State Power*. Trans. P. Kennedy. Cambridge: Polity Press.

Boeckh, A. 1818. "Von den Zeitverhältnissen der Demosthenischen Rede gegen Meidias." *Abhandlungen der Berliner Akademie* 5:60–100 (*Gesammelte kleine Schriften*, vol. 5 [Leipzig, 1871], 153–204).

Boegehold, Alan. 1963. "Toward a Study of Athenian Voting Procedure." *Hesperia* 32:366–74.

Bowles, Samuel, and Herbert Gintis. 1986. *Democracy and Capitalism: Property, Community, and the Contradictions of Modern Social Thought*. New York: Basic Books.

Brunt, P. A. 1965. "Spartan Policy and Strategy in the Archidamian War." *Phoenix* 19:255–80.

Bugh, Glenn R. 1988. *The Horsemen of Athens*. Princeton: Princeton University Press.

Burn, A. R. 1960. *The Lyric Age of Greece*. London: Edward Arnold.

Bury, J. B., and R. Meiggs. 1975. *History of Greece to the Death of Alexander the Great*. 4th ed. London and New York: Macmillan.

Busolt, G. 1893–1904. *Griechische Geschichte bis zur Schlacht bei Chaeroneia.* 3 vols. in 4. Gotha: F. A. Perthes.

Carter, L. B. 1986. *The Quiet Athenian.* Oxford: Clarendon; New York: Oxford University Press.

Cartledge, Paul. 1977. "Hoplites and Heroes: Sparta's Contribution to the Technique of Ancient Warfare." *Journal of Hellenic Studies* 97:11–23.

———. 1991. "Richard Talbert's Revision of the Spartan-Helot Struggle: A Reply." *Historia* 40:379–85.

———. Forthcoming. "La nascita degli opliti e l'organizzazione militare." In *I Greci,* ed. Salvatore Settis et al., vol. 2, ch. 23. Turin: Einaudi.

Cartledge, Paul, Paul Millett, and Stephen Todd, eds. 1990. *Nomos: Essays in Athenian Law, Politics, and Society.* Cambridge: Cambridge University Press.

Cawkwell, G. L. 1975. "Thucydides' Judgment of Periclean Strategy." *Yale Classical Studies* 24:53–70.

Chambers, Mortimer. 1957. "Thucydides and Pericles." *Harvard Studies in Classical Philology* 62:79–92.

———, ed. and comm. 1990. *Aristoteles, Staat der Athener.* Aristotles Werke in deutscher Übersetzung, vol. 10.1. Berlin: Akademie-Verlag.

Christ, Matthew. 1990. "Liturgy Avoidance and Antidosis in Classical Athens." *Transactions of the American Philological Association* 120:147–69

Codrescu, Andrei. 1990. *The Disappearance of the Outside: A Manifesto for Escape.* Reading, Mass.: Addison Wesley.

Cohen, David. 1989. "Seclusion, Separation, and the Status of Women." *Greece and Rome* 36:1–15.

———. 1990. "The Social Context of Adultery at Athens." In Cartledge, Millett, and Todd 1990, 147–65.

———. 1991. "New Legal History?" Review article. *Rechtshistorisches Journal* 10:7–40.

———. 1992. *Law, Sexuality, and Society: The Enforcement of Morals in Classical Athens.* Cambridge: Cambridge University Press.

———. 1995. *Law, Violence, and Community in Classical Athens.* Cambridge: Cambridge University Press.

Cohen, Edward E. 1973. *Ancient Athenian Maritime Courts.* Princeton: Princeton University Press.

———. 1991. "Banking as 'Family Business': Legal Adaptations Affecting Wives and Slaves." In *Symposion 1990,* ed. M. Gagarin and D. Cohen, 239–63. Cologne and Vienna: Böhlau.

Cohen, G. A. 1978. *Karl Marx's Theory of History: A Defense.* Princeton: Princeton University Press.

Collins, S. L. 1989. *From Divine Cosmos to Sovereign State : An Intellectual History of the Idea of Order in Renaissance England.* New York: Oxford University Press.

Connor, W. R. 1971. *The New Politicians of Fifth-Century Athens.* Princeton: Princeton University Press.

———. 1974. "The Athenian Council: Method and Focus in Some Recent Literature." *Classical Journal* 70:32–40.

———. 1984. *Thucydides.* Princeton: Princeton University Press.

———. 1988. "Early Greek Land Warfare as Symbolic Expression." *Past and Present* 119:3–27.

Culham, Phyllis, and Lowell Edmunds, eds. 1989. *Classics: A Discipline and Profession in Crisis?* Lanham, Md.: University Press of America.

Dahl, Robert. 1957. "The Concept of Power." *Behavioral Science* 2:201–15.

———. 1989. *Democracy and Its Critics.* New Haven, Conn.: Yale University Press.

Davies, J. K. 1978. *Democracy and Classical Greece.* London: Fontana.

———. 1981. *Wealth and the Power of Wealth in Classical Athens.* New York: Arno Press.

Delbrück, Hans. 1975–85. *History of the Art of War in the Framework of Political History.* Trans. W. J. Renfroe. Westport, Conn.: Greenwood.

Derrida, Jacques. 1988. *Limited Inc.* Ed. Gerald Graff. Evanston, Ill.: Northwestern University Press.

Desan, Suzanne. 1989. "Crowds, Community, and Ritual in the Work of E. P. Thompson and Natalie Davis." In Hunt 1989, 47–71.

Develin, Robert. 1989. *Athenian Officials, 684–321 B.C.* Cambridge: Cambridge University Press.

Dewart, Leslie. 1969. *The Foundations of Belief.* New York: Herder and Herder.

Dover, K. J. 1988. "Anecdotes, Gossip and Scandal." In *The Greeks and Their Legacy: Collected Papers 2. Prose Literature, History, Society, Transmission, Influence,* 45–52. Oxford: Basil Blackwell.

Doyle, Arthur Conan. 1967. *The Annotated Sherlock Holmes.* Ed. William S. Baring-Gould. 2 vols. New York: C. N. Potter.

Doyle, William. 1980. *Origins of the French Revolution.* New York: Oxford University Press.

Ducrey, Pierre. 1968. *Le Traitement des prisonniers de guerre dans la Grèce antique.* Paris: Boccard.

———. 1985. *Guerre et guerriers dans la Grèce antique.* Paris: Payot.

Eadie, John W., and Josiah Ober, eds. 1985. *The Craft of the Ancient Historian: Essays in Honor of Chester G. Starr.* Lanham, Md.: University Press of America.

Eagleton, Terry. 1991. *Ideology: An Introduction.* London: Verso.

Easterling, P. E., and Bernard M. W. Knox, eds. 1985. *Cambridge History of Classical Literature.* Vol. 1. *Greek Literature.* Cambridge: Cambridge University Press.

Eder, Walter, ed. 1995. *Die athenische Demokratie im 4. Jh. v. Chr: Vollendung oder Verfall einer Verfassungsform?* Stuttgart: F. Steiner.

Ehrenberg, Victor. 1950. "Origins of Democracy." *Historia* 1:515–48.

———. 1973. *From Solon to Socrates.* 2d ed. London: Methuen.

Erbse, Hartmut. 1965. "Über die Midiana des Demosthenes." *Hermes* 84:135–41.

Euben, Peter. 1990. *The Tragedy of Political Theory: The Road Not Taken.* Princeton: Princeton University Press.

Euben, Peter, John Wallach, and Josiah Ober, eds. 1994. *Athenian Political Thought and the Reconstruction of American Democracy.* Ithaca, N.Y.: Cornell University Press.

Farnell, Lewis R. 1896–1909. *The Cults of the Greek States.* 5 vols. Oxford: Clarendon.

Farrar, Cynthia. 1988. *The Origins of Democratic Thinking: The Invention of Politics in Classical Athens.* Cambridge: Cambridge University Press.

———. 1992. "Ancient Greek Political Theory as a Response to Democracy." In *Democracy, The Unfinished Journey: 508 B.C. to A.D. 1993,* ed. John Dunn, 17–39. Oxford: Oxford University Press.

Femia, Joseph V. 1981. *Gramsci's Political Thought: Hegemony, Consciousness, and the Revolutionary Process.* Oxford: Oxford University Press.

Finley, M. I. 1962. "Athenian Demagogues." *Past and Present* 21:3–24.

———. 1983. *Politics in the Ancient World*. Cambridge: Cambridge University Press.

———. 1985a. *Ancient History: Evidence and Models*. London: Chatto and Windus.

———. 1985b. *Democracy Ancient and Modern*. 2d ed. New Brunswick, N.J.: Rutgers University Press.

Fish, Stanley. 1980. *Is There a Text in This Class? The Authority of Interpretative Communities*. Cambridge, Mass.: Harvard University Press.

Fisher, N.R.E. 1976. "*Hybris* and Dishonour I." *Greece and Rome* 23:177–93.

———. 1979. "*Hybris* and Dishonour II." *Greece and Rome* 26:32–47.

———. 1990. "Law of *hubris* in Athens." In Cartledge, Millett, and Todd 1990, 123–38.

———. 1992. *Hybris*. Warminster: Aris and Philips.

Fornara, Charles W., and Loren J. Samons II. 1991. *Athens from Cleisthenes to Pericles*. Berkeley: University of California Press.

Forrest, W. G. 1966. *The Emergence of Greek Democracy: The Character of Greek Politics, 800–400 B.C.* London: Weidenfeld and Nicolson.

Foucault, M. 1979. *Discipline and Punish: The Birth of the Prison*. Trans. Alan Sheridan. New York: Random House, Vintage.

———. 1980a. *The History of Sexuality*. Vol. 1, *An Introduction*. Trans. Robert Hurley. New York: Random House, Vintage.

———. 1980b. *Power / Knowledge: Selected Writings and Other Interviews, 1972–1977*. Ed. Colin Gordon. Trans. Colin Gordon, Leo Marshal, John Mepham, and Kate Soper. New York: Pantheon.

———. 1981. "Is It Useless to Revolt?" *Philosophy and Social Criticism* 8:5–9.

———. 1986. *The History of Sexuality*. Vol. 2, *The Use of Pleasure*. Trans. Robert Hurley. New York: Vintage Books.

———. 1991. "Questions of Method." In *The Foucault Effect: Studies in Governmentality*, ed. Graham Burchell, Colin Gordon, and Peter Miller, 73–87. Chicago: University of Chicago Press.

Foxhall, L. 1989. "Household, Gender, and Property in Classical Athens." *Classical Quarterly*, n.s. 39:22–44.

Frost, F. J. 1984. "The Athenian Military Before Cleisthenes." *Historia* 33:283–94.

Gabrielsen, Vincent. 1981. *Remuneration of State Officials in Fourth-Century B.C. Athens*. Odense University Classical Studies, vol. 11. Odense.

Gallant, Thomas. 1991. *Risk and Survival in Ancient Greece: Reconstructing the Rural Domestic Economy*. Stanford: Stanford University Press.

Garlan, Yvon. 1974. *Recherches de poliorcétique grecque: BEFAR 223*. Paris: École française d'Athènes.

———. 1975. *War in the Ancient World*. Trans. Janet Lloyd. New York: W. W. Norton.

———. 1988. *Slavery in Ancient Greece*. Trans. Janet Lloyd. 2d ed. Ithaca, N.Y.: Cornell University Press.

Garner, Richard. 1987. *Law and Society in Classical Athens*. New York: St. Martin's Press.

Garnsey, Peter. 1988. *Famine and Food Supply in the Graeco-Roman World: Responses to Risk and Crisis*. Cambridge: Cambridge University Press.

Gernet, Louis. 1939. "L'Institution des arbitres publics à Athènes." *Revue des études grecque* 52:103–19.

———. 1954. *Démosthène: Plaidoyers civils, I*. Paris: Les Belles Lettres.

Godechot, J. 1970. *The Taking of the Bastille, July 14, 1789*. Trans. J. Stewart. London: Faber and Faber.

Gomme, A. W. 1933. "A Forgotten Factor of Greek Naval Strategy." *Journal of Hellenic Studies* 53:16–24.

————. 1951. "The Working of the Athenian Democracy." *History* 36:12–28. [Reprinted in *More Essays in Greek History and Literature* (Oxford: B. Blackwell, 1962).]

Gomme, A. W., A. Andrewes, and K. J. Dover. 1945–81. *A Historical Commentary on Thucydides*. 5 vols. Oxford: Clarendon.

Goode, William J. 1978. *The Celebration of Heroes: Prestige as a Social Control System*. Berkeley: University of California Press.

Goodman, M. D., and A. J. Holladay. 1986. "Religious Scruples in Ancient Warfare." *Classical Quarterly* 36:151–71.

Gordon, Colin. 1991. "Governmental Rationality: An Introduction." In *The Foucault Effect: Studies in Governmentality*, ed. Graham Burchell, Colin Gordon, and Peter Miller, 1–51. Chicago: University of Chicago Press.

Gouldner, Alvin W. 1969. *The Hellenic World: A Sociological Analysis*. New York: Harper and Row, Harper Torchbooks.

Griffiths, Alan. 1989. "Was Kleomenes Mad?" In *Classical Sparta: Techniques Behind Her Success*, ed. A. Powell, 51–78. London: Routledge.

Grotius, Hugo. 1957. *Prolegomena to the Law of War and Peace*. Trans. Francis W. Kelsey. With an introduction by Edward Dumbauld. The Library of Liberal Arts. Indianapolis: Bobbs-Merrill.

Grundy, G. B. 1948. *Thucydides and the History of His Age*. 2 vols. 2d ed. Oxford: Blackwell.

Gunn, Giles B. 1992. *Thinking Across the American Grain: Ideology, Intellect, and the New Pragmatism*. Chicago: University of Chicago Press.

Gutmann, Amy. 1987. *Democratic Education*. Princeton: Princeton University Press.

Halliwell, Stephen. 1994. "Philosophy and Rhetoric." In *Persuasion: Greek Rhetoric in Action*, ed. I. Worthington, 222–43. London: Routledge.

Halperin, David M. 1990. *One Hundred Years of Homosexuality and Other Essays on Greek Love*. New York: Routledge.

Hammond, N.G.L. 1959. *A History of Greece to 322 B.C.* Oxford: Clarendon.

Hansen, M. H. 1978. "*Demos, Ecclesia* and *Dicasterion* in Classical Athens." *Greek, Roman, and Byzantine Studies* 19:127–46.

————. 1979a. "The Duration of a Meeting of the Athenian *Ecclesia*." *Classical Philology* 74:43–49.

————. 1979b. "*Misthos* for Magistrates in Classical Athens." *Symbolae Osloenses* 54:5–22.

————. 1980. "Perquisites for Magistrates in Fourth-Century Athens." *Classica et Mediaevalia* 32:105–25.

————. 1981. "Initiative and Decision: The Separation of Powers in Fourth-Century Athens." *Greek, Roman, and Byzantine Studies* 22:345–70.

————. 1985. *Demography and Democracy: The Number of Athenian Citizens in the Fourth Century B.C.* Herning, Denmark: Systime.

————. 1986. "The Origin of the Term *demokratia*." *Liverpool Classical Monthly* 11 (March): 35–36.

————. 1987. *The Athenian Assembly in the Age of Demosthenes*. Oxford: Basil Blackwell.

———. 1989a. *The Athenian Ecclesia II: A Collection of Articles, 1983–1989*. Copenhagen: Museum Tusculanum Press.

———. 1989b. "On the Importance of Institutions in an Analysis of Athenian Democracy." *Classica et Mediaevalia* 40:108–13. [= Hansen 1989a, 263–69.]

———. 1989c. *Was Athens a Democracy?* Historisk-filosofiske Meddelelser 59. Copenhagen: The Royal Danish Academy of Sciences and Letters.

———. 1990a. Review of Ober 1989b. *Classical Review* 40:348–56.

———. 1990b. "The Size of the Council of the Areopagos and Its Social Composition in the Fourth Century B.C." *Classica et Mediaevalia* 41:55–61.

———. 1991. *The Athenian Democracy in the Age of Demosthenes: Structure, Principles and Ideology*. Oxford: Blackwell.

Hanson, Victor D. 1983. *Warfare and Agriculture in Classical Greece*. Biblioteca di Studi Antichi 40. Pisa: Giardini.

———. 1989. *The Western Way of War: Infantry Battle in Classical Greece*. New York: Alfred Knopf.

———, ed. 1991. *Hoplites: The Classical Greek Battle Experience*. London: Routledge.

———. 1992. "Thucydides and the Desertion of Attic Slaves During the Decelean War." *Classical Antiquity* 11:210–28.

———. 1995. *The Other Greeks: The Family Farm and the Agrarian Roots of Western Civilization*. New York: Free Press.

———. 1996. "Hoplites into Democrats: The Ideology of Athenian Infantry." In Ober and Hedrick 1996, 289–312.

Harrell, Hansen C. 1936. *Public Arbitration in Athenian Law*. University of Missouri Studies, vol. 1, no. 1. Columbia: University of Missouri.

Harris, E. M. 1989. "Demosthenes' Speech Against Meidias." *Harvard Studies in Classical Philology* 92:117–36.

———. 1990. "The Constitution of the Five Thousand." *Harvard Studies in Classical Philology* 93:243–80.

Harris, William F. 1993. *The Interpretable Constitution*. Baltimore: The Johns Hopkins University Press.

Harris, William V. 1989. *Ancient Literacy*. Cambridge, Mass.: Harvard University Press.

Harrison, A.R.W. 1968–71. *The Law of Athens*. Oxford: Clarendon.

Harrison, E. B. 1981. "Motifs of the City-Siege on the Shield of Athena Parthenos." *American Journal of Archaeology* 85:245–363.

Hart, H. L. 1961. *The Concept of Law*. Oxford: Oxford University Press.

Harvey, F. D. 1965–66. "Two Kinds of Equality." *Classica et Mediaevalia* 26–27:101–46, 99–100.

Havelock, Eric A. 1957. *The Liberal Temper in Greek Politics*. New Haven, Conn.: Yale University Press.

Headlam, J. W. 1933. *Election by Lot at Athens*. 2d ed. Revised by D. C. MacGregor. Cambridge: Cambridge University Press.

Hedrick, Charles W., Jr. 1991. "Phratry Shrines of Attica and Athens." *Hesperia* 60:241–68.

———. 1993. "The Meaning of Material Culture: Herodotus, Thucydides, and Their Sources." In *Nomodeiktes: Greek Studies in Honor of Martin Ostwald*, ed. R. M. Rosen and J. Farrell, 17–37. Ann Arbor: University of Michigan Press.

Herman, Gabriel. 1993. "Tribal and Civic Codes of Behaviour in Lysias I." *Classical Quarterly*, n.s. 43:406–19.

————. 1994. "How Violent Was Athenian Society?" In *Ritual, Finance, Politics: Athenian Democratic Accounts Presented to David Lewis*, ed. R. Osborne and S. Hornblower, 99–117. Oxford: Clarendon.

————. 1995. "Honour, Revenge and the State in Fourth-Century Athens." In Eder 1995, 43–60.

Hignett, C. 1952. *A History of the Athenian Constitution to the End of the Fifth Century B.C.* Oxford: Clarendon.

Hobbes, T. [1651] 1950. *Leviathan.* New York: E. P. Dutton.

Holladay, A. J. 1978. "Athenian Strategy in the Archidamian War." *Historia* 27:399–427.

————. 1982. "'Hoplites and Heresies.'" *Journal of Hellenic Studies* 102:94–104.

Holmes, Stephen T. 1979. "Aristippus In and Out of Athens." *American Political Science Review* 73:113–28.

Hoy, David Couzens. 1988. "Foucault: Modern or Postmodern." In *After Foucault: Humanistic Knowledges and Postmodern Challenges*, ed. Jean Arac, 12–41. New Brunswick, N.J.: Rutgers University Press.

Humphreys, S. C. 1983a. "The Evolution of Legal Process in Ancient Athens." In *Tria Corda, Scritti in Onore di Arnaldo Momigliano*, ed. E. Gabba, 229–56. Biblioteca di Athenaeum, vol. 1. Como: Edizioni New Press.

————. 1983b. *The Family, Women and Death.* London: Routledge.

————. 1985a. "Law as Discourse." *History and Anthropology* 1:241–64.

————. 1985b. "Lycurgus of Butadae: An Athenian Aristocrat." In Eadie and Ober 1985, 199–252.

————. 1985c. "Social Relations on Stage: Witnesses in Classical Athens." *History and Anthropology* 1:313–69.

————. 1989. "Family Quarrels." *Journal of Hellenic Studies* 109:182–85.

Hunt, Lynn, ed. 1989. *The New Cultural History.* Berkeley and Los Angeles: University of California Press.

Hunter, Virginia. 1989a. "The Athenian Widow and Her Kin." *Journal of Family History* 14:291–311.

————. 1989b. "Women's Authority in Classical Athens: The Example of Kleoboule and Her Son (Dem. 27–29)." *Echos du monde classique / Classical Views* 8:39–48.

————. 1990. "Gossip and the Politics of Reputation in Classical Athens." *Phoenix* 44:299–325.

————. 1994. *Policing Athens: Social Control in the Attic Lawsuits, 420–320 B.C.* Princeton: Princeton University Press.

Jackson, A. H. 1991. "Hoplites and the Gods: The Dedication of Captured Arms and Armour." In Hanson 1991, 228–49.

Jameson, Michael H. 1977–78. "Agriculture and Slavery in Classical Athens." *Classical Journal* 73:122–45.

————. 1990. "Private Space and the Greek City." In *The Greek City from Homer to Alexander*, ed. Oswyn Murray and Simon Price, 171–95. Oxford: Oxford University Press.

————. 1992. "Agricultural Labor in Ancient Greece." In Wells 1992, 135–46.

Jones, A.H.M. 1957. *Athenian Democracy.* Oxford: B. Blackwell.

Jones, Nicholas F. 1987. *Public Organization in Ancient Greece.* Philadelphia: American Philosophical Society.

Kagan, Donald. 1969. *The Outbreak of the Peloponnesian War*. Ithaca, N.Y.: Cornell University Press.

——. 1974. *The Archidamian War*. Ithaca, N.Y.: Cornell University Press.

——. 1987. *The Fall of the Athenian Empire*. Ithaca, N.Y.: Cornell University Press.

Kallet-Marx, Lisa. 1994. "Institutions, Ideology and Political Consciousness in Ancient Greece: Some Recent Books on Athenian Democracy." *Journal of the History of Ideas* 55, 2:307–35.

Karavites, Peter. 1982. *Capitulations and Greek Interstate Relations. Hypomnemata* 71. Göttingen: Vandenhoeck and Ruprecht.

——. 1992. *Promise-Giving and Treaty-Making: Homer and the Near East. Mnemosyne* 119. Leiden: E. J. Brill.

Kateb, George. 1983. *Hannah Arendt: Politics, Conscience, Evil*. Totowa, N.J.: Rowman and Allanheld.

Kelly, T. 1982. "Thucydides and Spartan Strategy in the Archidamian War." *American Historical Review* 87:25–54.

Kennedy, George A., trans. and ed. 1991. *On Rhetoric: A Theory of Civic Discourse*. New York: Oxford University Press.

Kirk, Geoffrey S. 1968. "War and the Warrior in the Homeric Poems." In *Problèmes de la guerre en Grèce ancienne*, ed. Jean-Pierre Vernant, 93–117. The Hague: Mouton.

Knight, D. W. 1970. "Thucydides and the War Strategy of Pericles." *Mnemosyne*, 4th ser., 23:150–61.

Konstan, David. 1990. "A City in the Air: Aristophanes' *Birds*." *Arethusa* 23:183–207.

Krentz, Peter. 1985a. "Casualties in Hoplite Battles." *Greek, Roman, and Byzantine Studies* 26:13–20.

——. 1985b. "The Nature of Hoplite Battle." *Classical Antiquity* 4:50–61.

Kuhn, Thomas S. 1970. *The Structure of Scientific Revolutions*. 2d ed. Chicago: University of Chicago Press.

Labarbe, Jules. 1957. *La Loi navale de Thémistocle*. Paris: Les Belles Lettres.

Laix, Roger Alain de. 1973. *Probouleusis at Athens: A Study of Political Decision-Making*. University of California Publications in History 83. Berkeley and Los Angeles: University of California Press.

Langdon, M., and V. Watrous. 1977. "The Farm of Timesios: Rock-Cut Inscriptions in South Attica." *Hesperia* 46:162–77.

Large, David, ed. 1992. *Contending with Hitler: Varieties of German Resistance in the Third Reich*. Cambridge: Cambridge University Press.

Lasch, Christopher. 1995. *The Revolt of the Elites and the Betrayal of Democracy*. New York: Norton.

Lévêque, Pierre, and Pierre Vidal-Naquet. 1996. *Cleisthenes the Athenian: An Essay on the Representation of Space and Time in Greek Political Thought from the End of the Sixth Century to the Death of Plato*. Trans. David Ames Curtis. Atlantic Highlands, N.J.: Humanities Press International.

Lewis, D. M. 1963. "Cleisthenes and Attica." *Historia* 12:22–40.

Linderski, J. 1990. "Mommsen and Syme: Law and Power in the Principate of Augustus." In *Between Republic and Empire: Interpretations of Augustus and His Principate*, ed. Kurt A. Raaflaub and Mark Toher, 42–53. Berkeley and Los Angeles: University of California Press.

Lintott, A. 1982. *Violence, Civil Strife, and Revolution in the Classical City, 750–330 B.C.* London: Croom Helm.

Locke, J. [1689] 1970. *Two Treatises of Government.* Cambridge: Cambridge University Press.

Lohmann, Hans. 1992. "Agriculture and Country Life in Classical Attica." In Wells 1992, 29–60.

———. 1993. *Atene: Forschungen zu Siedlungs- und Wirtschaftsstruktur des klassischen Attika.* Cologne: Bohlau Verlag.

Lonis, R. 1969. *Les Usages de la guerre entre grecs et barbares.* Annales littéraires de l'Université de Besançon 104. Paris: Les Belles Lettres.

Loraux, Nicole. 1986. *The Invention of Athens: The Funeral Oration in the Classical City.* Trans. Alan Sheridan. Cambridge, Mass.: Cambridge University Press.

Lord, Carnes, ed. and trans. 1984. *Aristotle: The Politics.* Chicago: University of Chicago Press.

Luhmann, Niklas. 1982. *The Differentiation of Society.* Trans. Stephen Holmes and Charles Larmore. European Perspectives. New York: Columbia University Press.

McCargar, David J. 1974. "Isagoras, Son of Teisandros, and Isagoras, Eponymous Archon of 508/7: A Case of Mistaken Identity." *Phoenix* 28:275–81.

McClelland, J. S. 1989. *The Crowd and the Mob: From Plato to Canetti.* London: Unwin Hyman.

MacDowell, Douglas M. 1971. "The Chronology of Athenian Speeches and Legal Innovations in 401–398 B.C." *Revue internationale des droits de l'antiquité* 18:267–73.

———. 1975. *The Law in Classical Athens.* Ithaca, N.Y.: Cornell University Press.

———, ed. and trans. 1990. *Demosthenes: Against Meidias (Oration 21).* Oxford: Clarendon.

MacIntyre, Alasdair. 1981. *After Virtue: A Study in Moral Theory.* Notre Dame, Ind.: University of Notre Dame Press.

Mandelbaum, D. G. 1988. *Women's Seclusion and Men's Honor.* Tucson: University of Arizona Press.

Manville, P. B. 1990. *The Origins of Citizenship in Ancient Athens.* Princeton: Princeton University Press.

Markle, Minor M. 1985. "Jury Pay and Assembly Pay at Athens." In *Crux: Essays in Greek History Presented to G.E.M. de Ste. Croix (History of Political Theory* 6.1–2), ed. Paul Cartledge and F. David Harvey, 265–97. London: Duckworth.

Marsden, E. W. 1969. *Greek and Roman Artillery: Historical Development.* Oxford: Clarendon.

———. 1971. *Greek and Roman Artillery: Technical Treatises.* Oxford: Clarendon.

Meier, C. 1970. *Enstehung des Begriffs Demokratie; Vier Prolegomena zu einer historischen Theorie.* 2d ed. Frankfurt am Main: Suhrkamp Verlag.

———. 1984. *Introduction à l'anthropologie politique de l'antiquité classique.* Trans. P. Blanchaud. Paris: Presses Universitaires de France.

———. 1990. *The Greek Discovery of Politics.* Trans. David McLintock. Cambridge, Mass.: Harvard University Press.

Meiggs, Russell. 1972. *The Athenian Empire.* Oxford: Oxford University Press.

Michels, Robert. [1915] 1962. *Political Parties: A Sociological Study of the Oligarchical Tendencies of Modern Democracy.* Trans. Eden and Cedar Paul. Intro. by Seymour Martin Lipset. New York: Free Press.

Miller, David, ed. 1991. *The Blackwell Encyclopaedia of Polticial Thought.* Oxford: Blackwell.

Miller, Fred D., Jr. 1995. *Nature, Justice, and Rights in Aristotle's "Politics."* Oxford: Clarendon.

Millett, Paul. 1989. "Patronage and Its Avoidance in Classical Athens." In Wallace-Hadrill 1989, 15–47.

Montesquieu, Charles de Secondat, Baron de. [1748] 1949. *The Spirit of the Laws.* Trans. Thomas Nugent. 2 vols. New York: Hafner.

Morris, Ian. 1993. "The Power of Topoi." *Topoi* 3:271–83.

———. 1996. "The Strong Principle of Equality and the Archaic Origins of Greek Democracy." In Ober and Hedrick 1996, 19–48.

———. Forthcoming. *Darkness and Heroes: Manhood, Equality, and Democracy in Iron Age Greece.* Oxford: Blackwell.

Morris, Ian, and Kurt A. Raaflaub, eds. 1996. *Democracy 2500: Questions and Challenges.* Atlanta: American Philological Association.

Mossé, Claude. 1962. *La Fin de la démocratie athénienne: Aspects sociaux et politiques du déclin de la cité grecque au IVe siècle avant J.C.* Paris: Presses Universitaires de France.

———. 1973. *Athens in Decline, 404–86 B.C.* Trans. J. Stewart. London: Routledge and Kegan Paul.

———. 1995. *Politique et société en Grèce ancienne: Le Modèle athénien.* Paris: Aubier.

Moxon, I. 1978. "Thucydides' Account of Spartan Strategy and Foreign Policy in the Archidamian War." *Rivista storica dell'Antichita* 8:7–26.

Munn, Mark. 1987. "Agesilaos' Boiotian Campaigns and the Theban Stockade of 378–377 B.C." *Classical Antiquity* 6:106–38.

Murray, Oswyn. 1980. *Early Greece.* London: Fontana.

———. 1990a. "Cities of Reason." In Murray and Price 1990, 1–25.

———. 1990b. "The Solonian Law of *hubris*." In Cartledge, Millett, and Todd 1990, 139–45.

Murray, Oswyn, and Simon Price, eds. 1990. *The Greek City from Homer to Alexander.* Oxford: Oxford University Press.

Nixon, Lucia, and Simon Price. 1990. "The Size and Resources of Greek Cities." In Murray and Price 1990, 137–70.

Novick, Peter. 1988. *That Noble Dream: The "Objectivity Question" and the American Historical Profession.* Cambridge: Cambridge University Press.

Nussbaum, M. 1990. "Aristotelian Social Democracy." In *Liberalism and the Good*, ed. R. Bruce Douglas, 203–52. New York: Routledge.

Nye, Robert A. 1977. *The Anti-Democratic Sources of Elite Theory: Pareto, Mosca, Michels.* London and Beverly Hills: Sage.

Ober, Josiah. 1985a. *Fortress Attica: Defense of the Athenian Land Frontier, 404–322 B.C. Mnemosyne*, suppl. 84. Leiden: E.J. Brill.

———. 1985b. "Review of Hanson, *Warfare and Agriculture in Classical Greece.*" *Helios* 12:91–101.

———. 1987. "Early Artillery Towers: Messenia, Boiotia, Attica, Megarid." *American Journal of Archaeology* 91:569–604.

———. 1989a. "The Defense of the Athenian Land Frontier, 404–322 B.C.: A Reply." *Phoenix* 43:294–301.

————. 1989b. *Mass and Elite in Democratic Athens: Rhetoric, Ideology, and the Power of the People.* Princeton: Princeton University Press.

————. 1991a. "Aristotle's Political Sociology: Class, Status, and Order in the *Politics.*" In *Essays on the Foundations of Aristotelian Political Science,* ed. Carnes Lord and David K. O'Connor, 112–35. Berkeley and Los Angeles: University of California Press.

————. 1991b. "The Athenians and Their Democracy." *Echos du monde classique/ Classical Views,* n.s. 10:81–96. [Chapter 9 here.]

————. 1991c. "Comments on Edward E. Cohen, 'Banking as Family Business.'" In *Symposion 1990,* ed. M. Gagarin and D. Cohen, 265–71. Cologne and Vienna: Böhlau.

————. 1991d. "Hoplites and Obstacles." In Hanson 1991, 173–96.

————. 1991e. "National Ideology and Strategic Defense of the Population, from Athens to Star Wars." In *Hegemonic Rivalry: From Thucydides to the Nuclear Age,* ed. Richard Ned Lebow and Barry S. Strauss, 251–67. Boulder, Colo.: Westview.

————. 1993. "Thucydides' Criticism of Democratic Knowledge." In *Nomodeiktes: Greek Studies in Honor of Martin Ostwald,* ed. R. M. Rosen and J. Farrell, 81–98. Ann Arbor: University of Michigan Press.

————. 1994. "Democratic Ideology and Counter-Hegemonic Discourse: The Case of Thucydides." In *Athenian Identity and Civic Ideology,* ed. A. Boegehold and A. Scafuro, 102–26. Baltimore: The Johns Hopkins University Press.

————. 1996. "Revolution Matters: Democracy as Demotic Action, Response to Kurt Raaflaub." In Morris and Raaflaub 1996.

Ober, Josiah, and Charles Hedrick, eds. 1993. *The Birth of Democracy: An Exhibition Celebrating the 2500th Anniversary of Democracy.* Princeton: American School of Classical Studies at Athens.

————. 1996. *Dēmokratia: A Conversation on Democracies, Ancient and Modern.* Princeton: Princeton University Press.

Ober, Josiah, and Barry Strauss. 1990. "Drama, Political Rhetoric, and the Discourse of Athenian Democracy." In Winkler and Zeitlin 1990, 237–70.

Olson, Douglas S. 1990. "Economics and Ideology in Aristophanes' *Wealth.*" *Harvard Studies in Classical Philology* 93:223–42.

Orwell, George. 1949. *Nineteen Eighty-Four.* New York: Harcourt.

Osborne, Robin. 1985a. *Demos: The Discovery of Classical Attika.* Cambridge: Cambridge University Press.

————. 1985b. "Law in Action in Classical Athens." *Journal of Hellenic Studies* 105: 40–58.

————. 1991. "Pride and Prejudice, Sense and Subsistence: Exchange and Society in the Greek City." In *City and Country in the Ancient World,* ed. John Rich and Andrew Wallace-Hadrill, 119–45. London and New York: Routledge.

Ostwald, Martin. 1969. *Nomos and the Beginnings of the Athenian Democracy.* Oxford: Clarendon.

————. 1986. *From Popular Sovereignty to the Sovereignty of Law: Law, Society, and Politics in Fifth-Century Athens.* Berkeley and Los Angeles: University of California Press.

Patterson, Cynthia. 1992. Review of Ober 1989b. *American Journal of Philology* 113: 110–15.

Patterson, Orlando. 1991. *Freedom in the Making of Western Culture.* New York: Basic Books.

Petrey, Sandy. 1988. *Realism and Revolution: Balzac, Stendahl, Zola and the Performances of History*. Ithaca, N.Y.: Cornell University Press.

———. 1990. *Speech Acts and Literary Theory*. New York: Routledge.

Podlecki, A. J. 1990. "Could Women Attend the Theatre in Ancient Athens? A Collection of Testimonia." *Ancient World* 21:27–43.

Pogge, Thomas. 1989. *Realizing Rawls*. Ithaca, N.Y.: Cornell University Press.

Pope, M. 1988. "Thucydides and Democracy." *Historia* 37:276–96.

Pritchett, W. K. 1971–92. *Studies in Ancient Greek Topography*. 8 vols. Berkeley: University of California Press, and Amsterdam: J. C. Gieben.

———. 1974–91. *The Greek State at War*. 5 vols. Berkeley: University of California Press.

Putnam, Robert. 1993. *Making Democracy Work: Civic Traditions in Modern Italy*. Princeton: Princeton University Press.

Raaflaub, Kurt A. 1983. "Democracy, Oligarchy, and the Concept of the 'Free Citizen' in Late Fifth-Century Athens." *Political Theory* 11:517–44.

———. 1985. *Die Entdeckung der Freiheit: Zur historischen Semantik und Gesellschaftsgeschichte eines politischen Grundbegriffes der Griechen*. In *Vestigia: Beiträge zur alten Geschichte*, vol. 37. Munich: C. H. Beck.

———. 1991. "City-State, Territory, and Empire in Classical Antiquity." In *City-States in Classical Antiquity and Medieval Italy*, ed. Anthony Molho, Kurt Raaflaub, and Julia Emlen, 565–87. Stuttgart: Franz Steiner Verlag.

———. 1995. "Kleisthenes, Ephialtes und die Begründung der Demokratie." In *Demokratia: Der Weg der Griechen zur Demokratie*, ed. Konrad H. Kinzl. *Wege der Forschung*. Darmstadt: Wissenschaftliche Buchgesellschaft.

———. 1996a. "Equality and Inequalities in the Athenian Democracy." In Ober and Hedrick 1996.

———. 1996b. "Power in the Hands of the People: Foundations of Athenian Democracy." In Morris and Raaflaub 1996.

———. 1996c. "The Thetes and Democracy: Response to J. Ober." In Morris and Raaflaub 1996.

Raubitschek, A. 1962. "Demokratia." *Hesperia* 31:238.

Rawls, John. 1971. *A Theory of Justice*. Cambridge, Mass.: Harvard University Press.

———. 1987. "The Basic Liberties and Their Priority." In *Liberty, Equality, and the Law: Selected Tanner Lectures on Moral Philosophy*. The Tanner Lectures on Human Values 3, ed. S. M. McMurrin. Salt Lake City: University of Utah Press.

———. 1993. *Political Liberalism*. New York: Columbia University Press.

Rhodes, P. J. 1972. "The Five Thousand in the Athenian Revolution of 411 B.C." *Journal of Hellenic Studies* 92:115–27.

———. 1981. *A Commentary on the Aristotelian "Athenaion Politeia."* Oxford: Clarendon.

Rijksbaron, Albert. 1984. *The Syntax and Semantics of the Verb in Classical Greek*. Amsterdam: J. C. Gieben.

Roberts, Jennifer Tolbert. 1982. *Accountability in Athenian Government*. Madison: University of Wisconsin Press.

———. 1989. "Athenians on the Sceptered Isle." *Classical Journal* 84:193–205.

———. 1994. *Athens on Trial: The Antidemocratic Tradition in Western Thought*. Princeton: Princeton University Press.

de Romilly, Jacqueline. 1962. "Les Intentions d'Archidamos et le livre II de Thucydide." *Revue des études anciennes* 64:287–97.

———. 1968. "Guerre et paix entre cités." In Vernant 1968, 207–20.

Rorty, Richard. 1982. *Consequences of Pragmatism: Essays, 1972–80.* Minneapolis: University of Minnesota Press.

Rothwell, Kenneth J. 1990. *Politics and Persuasion in Aristophanes' Ecclesiazusae. Mnemosyne*, suppl. 111. Leiden: E. J. Brill.

Ruschenbusch, E. 1985. "Die Zahl der Griechischen Staaten und Arealgrösse und Burgerzahl der 'Normalpolis.'" *Zeitschrift für Papyrologie und Epigraphik* 59:253–63.

Said, Edward W. 1975. *Beginnings: Intention and Method.* New York: Basic.

———. 1986. "Foucault and the Imagination of Power." In *Foucault: A Critical Reader*, ed. David Couzens Hoy, 149–55. Oxford: Basil Blackwell.

———. 1988. "Michel Foucault, 1926–1984." In *After Foucault: Humanistic Knowledges and Postmodern Challenges*, ed. Jean Arac, 1–112. New Brunswick, N.J.: Rutgers University Press.

Ste. Croix, G.E.M. de. 1956. "The Constitution of the 5000." *Historia* 5:1–23.

———. 1972. *The Origins of the Peloponnesian War.* Ithaca, N.Y.: Cornell University Press.

Sallares, Robert. 1991. *Ecology of the Ancient Greek World.* London: Duckworth.

Saller, Richard P. 1982. *Personal Patronage Under the Early Empire.* Cambridge: Cambridge University Press.

Saxenhouse, Arlene. 1991. "Aristotle: Defective Males, Hierarchy, and the Limits of Politics." In *Feminist Interpretations and Political Theory*, ed. Mary Lyndon Shanley and Carole Pateman, 32–52. University Park: Pennsylvania State University Press.

Seager, R. "Elitism and Democracy in Classical Athens." In *The Rich, the Well Born, and the Powerful*, ed. F. C. Jaher, 7–26. Urbana: University of Illinois Press.

Sealey, Raphael. 1973. "The Origins of *Demokratia*." *California Studies in Classical Antiquity* 6:253–95.

———. 1976. *A History of the Greek City States, ca. 700–300 B.C.* Berkeley and Los Angeles: University of California Press.

———. 1987. *The Athenian Republic: Democracy or the Rule of Law?* University Park: Pennsylvania State University Press.

Searle, John R. 1969. *Speech Acts: An Essay in the Philosophy of Language.* Cambridge: Cambridge University Press.

———. 1977. "Reiterating the Differences: A Reply to Derrida." *Glyph* 2:198–208.

Sen, Amartya. 1990. "Individual Freedom as a Social Commitment." *New York Review of Books* 37, 10 (June 14): 49–54.

Shaw, Brent. 1991. "The Paradoxes of People Power." *Helios* 18:194–214.

Sinclair, R. K. 1988. *Democracy and Participation in Athens.* Cambridge: Cambridge University Press.

Skinner, Quentin, et al. 1988. *Meaning and Context: Quentin Skinner and His Critics.* Ed. James Tully. Princeton: Princeton University Press.

Small, David. 1991. "Initial Study of the Structure of Women's Seclusion in the Archaeological Past." In *The Archaeology of Gender*, ed. D. Walde, 336–42. Calgary: Calgary University Press.

Spence, I. G. 1990. "Perikles and the Defense of Attika During the Peloponnesian War." *Journal of Hellenic Studies* 110:91–109.

―――. 1993. *The Cavalry of Classical Greece: A Social and Military History with Particular Reference to Athens.* Oxford: Clarendon.

Stanton, G. R. 1990. *Athenian Politics c. 800–500 B.C.: A Sourcebook.* London and New York: Routledge.

Starr, Chester G. 1979. "Thucydides on Sea Power." *Mnemosyne,* 4th ser., 31:343–50.

―――. 1983. *The Flawed Mirror.* Lawrence, Kans.: Coronado.

Stockton, D. 1990. *The Classical Athenian Democracy.* Oxford and New York: Oxford University Press.

Strauss, B. S. 1986. *Athens After the Peloponnesian War.* Ithaca, N.Y.: Cornell University Press.

―――. 1989. "Athens and Sparta." In *Seapower and Strategy,* ed. C. S. Gray and R. W. Barnett, 77–99. Annapolis, Md.: Naval Institute Press.

―――. 1991. "On Aristotle's Critique of Athenian Democracy." In *Essays on the Foundations of Aristotelian Political Science,* ed. Carnes Lord and David K. O'Connor, 212–33. Berkeley and Los Angeles: University of California Press.

―――. 1993. *Fathers and Sons in Athens: Ideology and Society in the Era of the Peloponnesian War.* Princeton: Princeton University Press.

―――. 1996. "The Athenian Trireme, School of Democracy." In Ober and Hedrick 1996, 313–25.

Swanson, Judith A. 1992. *The Public and the Private in Aristotle's Political Philosophy.* Ithaca, N.Y.: Cornell University Press.

Syme, Ronald. 1939. *The Roman Revolution.* Oxford: Oxford University Press.

Talbert, Richard J. A. 1989. "The Role of the Helots in the Class Struggle at Sparta." *Historia* 38:22–40.

Taylor, Charles. 1986. "Foucault on Freedom and Truth." In *Foucault: A Critical Reader,* ed. David Couzens Hoy, 69–102. Oxford: Basil Blackwell.

―――. 1989. *Sources of the Self: The Making of the Modern Identity.* Cambridge, Mass.: Harvard University Press.

―――. 1994. "The Politics of Recognition." In Charles Taylor et al., *Multiculturalism: Examining the Politics of Recognition,* ed. Amy Gutmann, 25–73. Princeton: Princeton University Press.

Taylor, Michael W. 1991. *The Tyrant Slayers: The Heroic Image in Fifth Century B.C. Athenian Art and Politics.* 2d ed. Salem, N.H.: Ayer Company Publishers.

Thomas, Rosalind. 1989. *Oral Tradition and Written Record in Classical Athens.* Cambridge: Cambridge University Press.

Thompson, Homer A., and R. E. Wycherley. 1972. *The Agora of Athens: The History, Shape and Uses of an Ancient City Center.* The Athenian Agora, vol. 14. Princeton: American School of Classical Studies.

Tlaba, Gabriel Masooane. 1987. *Politics and Freedom: Human Will and Action in the Thought of Hannah Arendt.* Lanham, Md.: University Press of America.

Todd, S. C. 1990. "*Lady Chatterley's Lover* and the Attic Orators: The Social Composition of the Athenian Jury." *Journal of Hellenic Studies* 110:146–73.

Todd, Stephen, and Paul Millett. 1990. "Law, Society and Athens." In Cartledge, Millett, and Todd 1990, 1–18.

Tulis, J. K. 1987. *The Rhetorical Presidency.* Princeton: Princeton University Press.

Vernant, Jean-Pierre, ed. 1968. *Problèmes de la guerre en Grèce ancienne.* The Hague: Mouton.

————. 1982. *The Origins of Greek Thought*. Ithaca, N.Y.: Cornell University Press.

Vickers, B. F. 1988. *In Defense of Rhetoric*. Oxford: Clarendon.

Vidal-Naquet, Pierre. 1986. *The Black Hunter*. Trans. Andrew Szegedy-Maszak. Baltimore: The Johns Hopkins University Press.

Wade-Gery, H. T. 1933. "Studies in the Structure of Athenian Society: II. The Laws of Kleisthenes." *Classical Quarterly* 27:17–29.

Wallace, Robert W. 1989. *The Areopagos Council, to 307 B.C.* Baltimore and London: The Johns Hopkins University Press.

Wallace-Hadrill, Andrew, ed. 1989. *Patronage in Ancient Society*. New York and London: Routledge.

Wallach, John. 1992. "Contemporary Aristotelianism." *Political Theory* 20:613–41.

Wees, Hans van. 1988. "Kings in Combat: Battles and Heroes in the *Iliad*." *Classical Quarterly* 38:1–24.

————. 1992. *Status Warriors: War, Violence and Society in Homer and History*. Amsterdam: Gieben.

————. 1994. "The Homeric Way of War: The *Iliad* and the Hoplite Phalanx." *Greece and Rome* 41:1–18, 131–55.

Wells, Berit, ed. 1992. *Agriculture in Ancient Greece*. Stockholm: P. Astroms.

Welskopf, E. C. 1965. "Elitevorstellung und Elitebildung in der hellenischen Polis." *Klio* 43/44:49–64.

West, Cornel. 1989. *The American Evasion of Philosophy: A Genealogy of Pragmatism*. Madison: University of Wisconsin Press.

Westbrook, Robert B. 1991. *John Dewey and American Democracy*. Ithaca, N.Y.: Cornell University Press.

Westlake, H. D. 1945. "Seaborne Raids in Periclean Strategy." *Classical Quarterly* 39:75–84.

de Wet, B. X. 1969. "The So-Called Defensive Policy of Pericles." *Acta Classica* 12:103–19.

Wheeler, Everett L. 1987. "Ephorus and the Prohibition of Missiles." *Transactions of the American Philological Association* 117:157–82.

White, Hayden. 1973. *Metahistory: Six Critiques*. Middletown, Conn.: Wesleyan University Press.

Whitehead, David. 1981. "The Archaic Athenian Zeugitai." *Classical Quarterly* 31:282–86.

————. 1983. "Competitive Outlay and Community Profit: *Philotimia* in Democratic Athens." *Classica et Mediaevalia* 34:55–74.

————. 1986. *The Demes of Attica, 508/7–ca. 250 B.C.* Princeton: Princeton University Press.

————. 1993. "Cardinal Virtues: The Language of Public Approbation in Democratic Athens." *Classica et Mediaevalia* 44:37–75.

Wick, T. E. 1979. "Megara, Athens, and the West in the Archidamian War: A Study in Thucydides." *Historia* 28:1–14.

Wickens, J. 1983. "Demias' Grave at Timesios' Farm." *Hesperia* 52:96–99.

Wickham Legg, L. G., ed. 1905. *Select Documents Illustrative of the French Revolution*. Oxford: Clarendon.

Will, E. 1975. "Le Territoire, la ville, et la poliorcétique grecque." *Revue historique* 253:297–318.

Wilson, Peter. 1991. "Demosthenes 21 (*Against Meidias*): Democratic Abuse." *Proceedings of the Cambridge Philological Society*, n.s. 37:164–95.

Winkler, John J. 1990. *The Constraints of Desire: The Anthropology of Sex and Gender in Ancient Greece*. New York: Routledge.

Winkler, John J., and Froma I. Zeitlin, eds. 1990. *Nothing to Do with Dionysos? Athenian Drama in Its Social Context*. Princeton: Princeton University Press.

Wolf, Eric. 1971. "On Peasant Rebellions." In *Peasants and Peasant Societies*, ed. T. Shanin, 264–74. Harmondsworth: Penguin.

Wolff, Robert Paul. 1977. *Understanding Rawls: A Reconstruction and Critique of "A Theory of Justice."* Princeton: Princeton University Press.

Wolin, Sheldon S. 1988. "On the Theory and Practice of Power." In *After Foucault: Humanistic Knowledges and Postmodern Challenges*, ed. Jean Arac, 179–203. New Brunswick, N.J.: Rutgers University Press.

———. 1994. "Norm and Form: The Constitutionalizing of Democracy." In Euben, Wallach, and Ober 1994, 29–58.

———. 1996. "Transgression, Equality, and Voice." In Ober and Hedrick 1996, 63–90.

Wood, Ellen Meiksins. 1988. *Peasant-Citizen and Slave: The Foundations of Athenian Democracy*. London: Verso.

———. 1996. "Demos vs. 'We, the People': Freedom and Democracy Ancient and Modern." In Ober and Hedrick 1996, 121–37.

Wood, Gordon S. 1992. *The Radicalism of the American Revolution*. New York: Knopf.

Worley, Leslie J. 1994. *Hippeis: The Cavalry of Ancient Greece*. Boulder, Colo.: Westview.

Wycherley, R. E. 1978. *The Stones of Athens*. Princeton: Princeton University Press.

Yack, Bernard. 1985. "Community and Conflict in Aristotle's Political Philosophy." *Review of Politics* 47:92–112.

Yunis, Harvey. 1991. Review of Ober 1989b. *Classical Philology* 86:67–74.

———. 1996. *Taming Democracy: Models of Political Rhetoric in Classical Athens*. Ithaca, N.Y.: Cornell University Press.

Zimmern, Alfred. 1961. *The Greek Commonwealth*. 5th ed., rev. Oxford: Oxford University Press.

INDEX

action: and discourse, 105–6; and speech, 33, 151–54. *See also* practice
Adcock, F. E., 56n
Aeschines, 93–94, 115–16
agriculture: and social class, 124, 135–39; and warfare, 58
Alcmaeonids, and the Athenian Revolution, 37 and n, 42
Allen, D., 97n
Allen, J. W., 121n
Althusser, L., 26
Anderson, B., 117
Andrewes, A., 130n
antidosis, 28, 184
archai, definition of, 164–66
archonship (Archaic) 37 and n
Arendt, H., 144–45
Areopagus, 38 and n, 50n
aristocracy. *See* elites
Aristophanes: as critic of democracy, 157; on the Athenian Revolution, 45–46
Aristotle, 20, 29; as critic of democracy, 155–56, 157–58; on equality and inequality, 91; on the nature of the polis, 161–63, 164–75, 185–87
[Aristotle], on the Athenian Revolution, 40, 45
Assembly, 10–11, 151; composition of, 23, 77, 113; and the courts, 116–19; and intra-elite competition, 27–28; and non-citizens, 181–82; and Pericles, 74–76, 77, 83; powers of, 116–17; procedures of, 108, 115–16; two-way communication in, 112, 116. See also *ekklēsia*; institutions; laws
Assembly (Archaic) 38–39
Athens, as model for modern democracy, 19–20, 179
atimia, 87, 94, 162, 184; and hubris, 99–100
Attica, Spartan ravaging of, 74–78, 81
Austin, J. L., 8 and n, 33, 47, 141, 150–54, 165
autarky, of the polis, 88, 168, 172, 174. *See also* self-sufficiency
authority: and the Athenian Revolution,

48–50; of conceptual models, 111–12; of the demos, 4, 52. *See also* power
autochthony, 148; and equality, 27

Badian, E., 72
Barber, B. R., 125n, 146n
Barnes, J., 169
Bastille, 48n
Berlin, I., 125n, 134n
Bers, V., 24n
Bleicken, J., 129n
Bloedow, E. F., 75n
Blundell, M. W., 158n
Bobbio, N., 164n
Bodin, J., 121n
Boeckh, A., 94n
boulē, 23, 132. *See also* Council; institutions
boulē (Archaic): and the Athenian Revolution, 35, 39–40, 44–46, 49–50; nature of, 48
Bowles, S., 114n, 121n
Brunt, P. A., 76n, 83n
Bugh, G., 59n, 60n, 73
Burn, A. R., 34n
Bury, J. B., 35n
Busolt, G., 81n

Cambridge School, 146
Cartledge, P., 55, 60n, 61n, 140
catapults. *See* technology
cavalry, 73; and the defense of Attica, 79–82
Cawkwell, G. L., 75n, 76n, 84n
Chambers, M., 40n, 45n, 48
citizenship, 166–71; and the Athenian Revolution, 38; and education, 26; and exclusion, 54, 138, 148, 162, 181–82; as political institution, 113–14; and slavery, 124; of thetes, 54
class, and military tactics, 59–60. *See also* demos; elites; hoplites; ideology; masses; middle class
Cleisthenes: as interpreter, 52; exile of, 35 and n; leadership of, 32–52; "realist" and "idealist" views of, 41; self-interest of, 41. *See also* "Great Man" history
Cleomenes I, 36, 39, 40, 43, 44, 46, 48

About the Author

Josiah Ober is the David Magie Professor of Ancient History in the Classics Department of Princeton University. He is the author of *Mass and Elite in Democratic Athens: Rhetoric, Ideology, and the Power of the People* (Princeton).